## Public Policy and Politics

Series Editors: Colin Fudge a                          ........v.c.vn

Important shifts in the nature of public policy-making are taking place, particularly at the local level. Increasing financial pressures on local government, the struggle to maintain public services, the emergence of new areas of concern, such as employment and economic development, and increasing partisanship in local politics, are all creating new strains but at the same time opening up new possibilities.

The series is designed to provide up-to-date, comprehensive and authoritative analyses of public policy and politics in practice. Public policy involves the expression of explicit or implicit intentions by government which result in specific consequences for different groups within society. It is used by power-holders to control, regulate, influence or change our lives and therefore has to be located within a political context. Two key themes are stressed throughout the series. First, the books link discussion of the substance of policy to the politics of the policy-making process. Second, each volume aims to bridge theory and practice. The books capture the dynamics of public policy-making but, equally important, aim to increase understanding of practice by locating these discussions within differing theoretical perspectives. Given the complexity of the processes and the issues involved, there is a strong emphasis on interdisciplinary approaches.

The series is focused on public policy and politics in contemporary Britain. It embraces not only local and central government activity, but also central–local relations, public-sector/private-sector relations and the role of non-governmental agencies. Comparisons with other advanced societies will form an integral part of appropriate volumes. Each book presents and evaluates practice by drawing on relevant theories and applying them to both the *substance* of policy (for example, housing, employment, local government finance) and to the *processes* of policy development and implementation (for example, planning, management, organisational and political bargaining).

Every effort has been made to make the books in the series as readable and usable as possible. Our hope is that it will be of value to all those interested in public policy and politics – whether as students, practitioners or academics. We shall be satisfied if the series helps in a modest way to improve understanding and debate about public policy and politics in Britain in the 1980s and 1990s.

# Public Policy and Politics

## Series Editors: Colin Fudge and Robin Hambleton

PUBLISHED

Kate Ascher, *The Politics of Privatisation*

Gideon Ben-Tovim, John Gabriel, Ian Law and Kathleen Stredder, *The Local Politics of Race*

Christopher C. Hood, *The Tools of Government*

Peter Malpass and Alan Murie, *Housing Policy and Practice*

K. Newton and T. J. Karran, *The Politics of Local Expenditure*

Gerry Stoker, *The Politics of Local Government*

Ken Young and Charlie Mason (eds), *Urban Economic Development*

FORTHCOMING

Tony Eddison and Eugene Ring, *Management and Human Behaviour*

Robin Hambleton, *An Introduction to Local Policy-Making*

Ian Henry, *The Politics of Leisure Policy*

Martin Laffin, *Managing under Pressure: Industrial Relations in Local Government*

Stewart Lansley and Christian Wolmar, *Councils in Conflict: The Rise and Fall of 'Local Socialism'*

---

### Series Standing Order

If you would like to receive future titles in this series as they are published, you can make use of our standing order facility. To place a standing order please contact your bookseller or, in case of difficulty, write to us at the address below with your name and address and the name of the series. Please state with which title you wish to begin your standing order. (If you live outside the United Kingdom we may not have the rights for your area, in which case we will forward your order to the publisher concerned.)

Customer Services Department, Macmillan Distribution Ltd
Houndmills, Basingstoke, Hampshire, RG21 2XS, England.

# The Politics of Local Government

Gerry Stoker

MACMILLAN
EDUCATION

First published 1988

Published by
MACMILLAN EDUCATION LTD
Houndmills, Basingstoke, Hampshire RG21 2XS
and London
Companies and representatives
throughout the world

Typeset by Wessex Typesetters
(Division of The Eastern Press Ltd)
Frome, Somerset

Printed in Great Britain by
Richard Clay Ltd,
Bungay, Suffolk


British Library Cataloguing in Publication Data
Stoker, Gerry, *1955–*
The politics of local government.—
(Public policy and politics).
1. Great Britain. Local government. Political
aspects
I. Title   II. Series
352.041
ISBN 0–333–44269–5 (hardcover)
ISBN 0–333–44270–9 (paperback)

*For Deborah, Bethany and Robert*

# Contents

# List of Tables and Figures

**Tables**

**Figures**

# Acknowledgements

When writing a book an author draws on the support of a considerable range of people. I would like to thank my former colleagues at Leicester Polytechnic – Kris Beuret, Tim Brindley, Clive Gray and David Wilson – who helped me teach and think about local politics. My knowledge of local government has been substantially increased through contact with colleagues at the Institute of Local Government Studies. John Gibson gave me some useful advice on local government finance and statistics. Special thanks go to John Benington, Andrew Coulson, Chris Game, Steve Leach, Ken Spencer, John Stewart and Kieron Walsh all of whom made valuable comments on various draft chapters. George Jones at the LSE read most of the book in its penultimate draft and his reactions were very helpful, challenging and encouraging. Robin Hambleton provided valuable support. Rod Rhodes gave me some useful comments on a draft of Chapter 3 and the opportunity to see the manuscript of his book on sub-central government. A final academic colleague I wish to mention is Stephen Young of Manchester University. His intellectual rigour and scholarship have been an inspiration.

Many other people have contributed to the production of this book. Steven Kennedy of Macmillan has provided constant help and encouragement. Keith Povey helped to substantially improve the product. Elaine Gallagher bore the brunt of the typing with considerable fortitude, helped by Dot Woolley and Fay Buck. At a vital stage Caroline Raine the Institute's Administrator found me access to extra typing resources.

This book also draws on the insights of the many local authority councillors and officers with whom I have had contact. Their willingness to discuss and debate the nature and operation of local government makes writing a book like this possible.

This book has also drawn on the support of friends and my

family. A very big thank you goes to Deborah, Bethany and Robert for their many interruptions, cuddles and attempts at showing interest in something they felt was too time-consuming and fundamentally boring.

Finally in a book of this kind, surveying a wide field of study, omissions and inaccuracies are inevitable. I accept full responsibility for any errors and the views expressed in the book.

GERRY STOKER

The author and publishers wish to thank the following who have kindly given permission for the use of copyright material:

N. Flynn and K. Walsh for a table from *Competitive Tendering*, INLOGOV, 1987; the Controller of Her Majesty's Stationery Office for tables from *Widdicombe Research Vols I and II*, 1986; Institute of Local Government Studies for a table from *Reports on the Future Role and Organisation of Local Government*, edited by Howard Davis, 1986; School for Advanced Urban Studies for a table from *Local State: Theory and Practice*, WP20, edited by Martin Boddy and Colin Fudge, 1981.

# Guide to Reading the Book

Local government has during the last decade found itself buffeted and challenged by a range of forces including public expenditure constraints, economic restructuring, increased politicisation and changed public perceptions. Local government has become a focus for some wider conflicts between Left and Right as well as an arena for political competition between business, trade union, environmental, community action, women's and ethnic minority groups. From being a quiet back-water of routine administration and parochial politics, local government has been pushed into the limelight. In the light of these developments of aim of this book is to examine the changed world of local government politics.

This book has been designed to be read as a whole or by dipping into particular chapters or sections. Its underlying concern with the politics of local government is pursued in a variety of ways.

Part I of the book considers the institutions of local government as part of the political system of modern Britain. The discussion challenges the narrow focus that often accompanies the study of local government by placing local politics in a broader context and by directing attention not only at elected local government but also at the increasing role undertaken by a range of non-elected local governmental and quasi-governmental agencies.

Chapter 1 argues that to understand local government we must place it in the context of particular historical circumstances and consider its relationship with a range of social and economic interests. Chapter 2 examines elected local authorities as political institutions and considers their organisation, the nature of councillors and the operation of party systems and electoral accountability. For those familiar with the basic features of local authorities this might be an appropriate chapter to skip. Chapter 3 examines the world of non-elected local government. It is concerned with the growing importance of a variety of non-elected agencies operating at a local level. These agencies have been created by central government, local authorities and partnerships of public and private sector sponsors. The chapter considers which interests control and benefit from the actions of different types of non-elected organisation.

Part II examines the everyday politics of local government. Its focus is on policy processes within local authorities and decision-making influences from the wider political environment. Chapter 4 examines the internal politics of local authorities, starting from a concern with the relationship between officers and councillors and moving on to examine party group and departmental influences on policy making and implementation. Chapter 5 considers the world of local interest group politics and the nature of the relationships that different interests establish with local authorities. A picture of considerable diversity within the world of local government is assembled but a trend towards a greater 'openness' in local politics is identified. Chapter 6 examines the non-local governmental influences on local authorities. A complex set of inter-organisational relations are identified and the increasingly strained nature of central–local relations during the 1980s is examined.

Part III focuses on a number of contentious and critical issues which have confronted local authorities in the last decade. The concern is with some of the major political conflicts affecting local government. Chapter 7 examines the struggle over local spending. Chapter 8 looks at the issue of privatisation. Chapter 9 considers the rise of local socialism.

Part IV examines competing visions of what the role of local government is and should be in our society. Chapter 10 identifies various theories of local government and politics and critically assesses the interpretations that they provide. Chapter 11 considers the future of local government in the light of the Conservatives' programme of reforms. The reform package, its underlying themes and its implications for local government are examined. The chapter concludes with an outline of an alternative vision of what the future of local government should be.

This book is about local government in Britain and does not deal with the position in Northern Ireland. The main reason for not considering Northern Ireland is that the system of local government in the province is substantially different from that operating in the 'mainstream' British context. For an excellent discussion of local government in Northern Ireland see the special issue of *Local Government Studies*, vol. 12, no. 5 (1986) edited by Michael Connolly.

# I  INTRODUCING LOCAL GOVERNMENT

# 1 Local Government in Context

## The origins of modern local government

The rise of local government is closely tied to the process of industrialisation which gathered momentum in Britain from the middle of the eighteenth century. The movement of population from rural to urban areas was accompanied by severe problems of overcrowding, law and order, and ill-health. The immediate response to this was the creation of a series of *ad hoc*, single-purpose bodies which included poor law boards, turnpike trusts and boards of improvement commissioners. The powers of the improvement commissioners varied but often included responsibility for paving, cleansing, the lighting of streets and the provision of watchmen. These *ad hoc* responses were viewed by many as inadequate in administrative terms. Moreover, the *ad hoc* bodies operated alongside a system of local government institutions effectively controlled by Tory squires and traditional landowning interests. The prosperous entrepreneurs that increasingly dominated the expanding towns and cities resented their lack of control over the full range of civic affairs. In response to these pressures the 1835 act created elected municipal councils and gave to them a range of powers and property.

The creation of these municipal boroughs or corporations in many towns and cities is widely viewed as the beginning of our modern system of local government. The municipal boroughs shared key characteristics of modern local authorities in that they were responsible for a range of functions and directly elected. The functions of these municipal boroughs were, of course, very different to those of modern local authorities and the franchise was limited to male rate-payers of more than three years residence.

3

Crucially, however, the principle of local self-government had been established.

The middle years of the nineteenth century witnessed a continued concern with the consequences of industrialisation and urbanisation. Various legislative measures gave additional or new responsibility for public health, highways, housing, poor relief and education to the institutions of local government. The municipal boroughs took some of the powers, as did the long-established and unelected county and parish agencies in rural areas. There was also a substantial proliferation of *ad hoc* bodies. The result was a very complex local government system with a range of agencies, all, perhaps, able to raise a rate and with overlapping boundaries.

The extension of the franchise to agricultural workers was followed in 1888 by the creation of all-purpose and directly elected county councils. For towns and cities with populations greater than 50 000 the 1888 Act also established elected county borough councils, independent of the county councils and based on the existing municipal boroughs. London was given its own directly elected county council. In 1894 and 1899 further reforms established a range of directly elected multi-purpose authorities below the county councils. In urban areas the prime responsibility for local government remained with the all-purpose county boroughs. These various reforms established the basic structure of local authorities that lasted until well past the Second World War.

The structure of local government may have been relatively stable in the early decades of the twentieth century but there was considerable change and development in the functions undertaken by local authorities. The concern with public health, highways and lighting, and law and order remained. Some responsibilities were transferred from existing *ad hoc* bodies. For example, in 1902 school boards were abolished and in their place local authorities took on the provision of education and set up separate committees to oversee the service. As new responsibilities were taken on by the state, so many of these were placed in the hands of local authorities. These included town planning responsibilities, the building of low-cost housing and the provision of a range of welfare services. In addition local authorities took on the development of public utilities such as gas, electricity, water and, in the case of Hull, a telephone system. Local authorities also had some responsibility for poor relief and were instrumental in the management and provision of hospital and other health services. Between 1900 and 1938 total local authority expenditure increased nearly four-fold in real terms (Dunleavy, 1984, Table 3.2).

The inheritance of the modern system of local government has a richness and diversity which we cannot hope to capture here (see Keith-Lucas and Richards, 1978; Alexander, 1985; Widdicombe, 1986d, pp. 81–105). The linchpins of the modern system remain directly elected, multi-purpose local authorities. Their organisation and responsibilities differ substantially from the institutions of the pre-Second World War period but they are still major spenders of public money and providers of public services. However, rather like the original elected local authorities, today's local councils operate alongside a range of non-elected, single-purpose agencies, such as health authorities. In this book most of our discussion is directed towards the politics of local authorities but we also focus attention on the increasingly substantial role taken by non-elected agencies of local government.

Local government is an important part of the system of government in Britain. In 1986–7 local authorities spent approximately £40 billion and employed nearly three million people. This accounted for about a quarter of all public expenditure and a tenth of the gross domestic product. The cliché about local government 'looking after us from the cradle to the grave' is almost inadequate to capture the range of modern local government activity. Manchester City Council's *A–Z Guide* contains information about its services under more than 700 separate headings, starting with advice about abandoned motor vehicles and ending with a reference to zebra crossings. Local authorities have a role in education, housing, welfare, land-use planning, leisure, transport, public health, refuse disposal, street lighting, traffic management, the arts, consumer protection, police and fire services, tourism, emergency action and disaster relief, economic development and many other areas. They, along with other governmental organisations operating at a local level, are key agents of the welfare state.

The scale and scope of modern local government means that it is essential to place its study in the context of the society in which it operates. Dearlove (1979, p. 12) comments that the 'necessity for this cannot be doubted when we are faced with something of such massive significance as local government. . . . We have to see how it fits into the historical trend of our times; and have to assess its significance for different groups and interests in society'. These twin tasks provide the focus for the discussion in this chapter. First a brief account of the post-war development of local government is outlined in the context of changes in the social and economic environment. The aim is not to provide a detailed history but rather to relate the shifting pattern of local government activity to dominant trends and developments within society. The second half of the chapter attempts to establish the importance of local government activity by examining the way it is experienced by different groups and interests. We draw attention to the way the public as consumers establish a diverse and complex set of relations with local government. We also examine the position of local government employees and the way that local authorities affect and influence private industrial and commercial interests within their areas.

**The post-war development of local government**

The post-Second World War history of local government has been described in terms of decline (Robson, 1966; Loughlin *et al.*, 1985; Bryne, 1986, pp. 17–23). Considerable play is made of the loss of local control over several important functions and the increasing domination by the centre of finance and expenditure. The brief historical review, provided below, challenges this interpretation as too one-sided. Local government has lost some functions but it has also gained further responsibilities, and the attempts of central government to control local spending have not been wholly successful. This argument is pursued in an analysis which divides the post-war history of local government into three periods: 1945–55, 1955–75 and 1975 to the mid-1980s. The aim is to capture important shifts in the economic and political climate and corresponding changes in the organisation and operation of local government.

*Launching the Welfare State: 1945–55*

The welfare legislation of the 1940s, along with the commitments of the post-war Labour Government in the areas of housing and employment, built on the reforming legislation of the previous century to produce the Welfare State in a recognisably modern form (Taylor-Gooby, 1984; Thane, 1982). The task of developing services was largely taken by elected local authorities. Newton and Karran (1985, pp. 60–1) note a dozen important pieces of legislation 'which had the effect of increasing local spending by virtue of creating new local responsibilities'. This period, however, also saw the creation of one of the major quasi-governmental agencies, the National Health Service, and the removal of some public utilities from local government, in particular gas and electricity services were nationalised. Nevertheless elected local government was to be a prime vehicle in the drive to create the Welfare State.

Despite its new responsibilities the institutional apparatus of local government remained largely unchanged. Major towns and cities were the responsibility of all-purpose authorities. There were 81 county boroughs in England and Wales and equivalent authorities with all local government powers in the four major cities of Scotland: Glasgow, Edinburgh, Dundee and Aberdeen. Outside these major centres 61 county authorities shared local government powers with 1356 county districts, composed of non-county boroughs, urban districts and rural districts in England and Wales. In Scotland, county authorities shared responsibility with 26 large boroughs and 171 small boroughs, as well as a range of small district authorities. Local government in London was shared between 28 metropolitan boroughs and the London County Council.

The system was widely regarded as inadequate and obsolete. A few academics and some official reports called for radical reform to create a local government system capable of dealing with new demands and changing population patterns (Robson, 1948; Barlow, 1940). Indeed, Aneurun Bevan, the minister in the post-war Labour Government responsible for local authorities, drew up plans to replace the existing structure by about 240 'new all-purpose authorities' (Foot, 1975, pp. 263–4). This scheme came to nothing and no new proposals emerged from the Conservative administration which followed. There was some 'institutional tinkering' based on the work of the Boundary Commission of 1945–8. Various *ad hoc* arrangements to jointly administer some services were made between authorities. But there was no real desire on the part of either the local authorities or the concerned central departments to engage in fundamental reform. The 'principle of adjustment rather than restructuring' dominated. Thus 'there was an accurate perception of the problems of the local government system together with an unshakable reluctance to adopt radical solutions to them' (Alexander, 1982a, p. 13).

The ideological environment was dictated by the building of the 'welfare consensus'. As Taylor-Gooby (1984, p. 18) notes the 'consensus did not descend ready-made from heaven. It had to be constructed and maintained, and neither process was without conflict'. The attitude of many Conservative politicians to welfare reforms was ambivalent and not all acquiesced to Keynesian management of the economy. However, according to Taylor-Gooby (1984, p. 19) 'the departure of Churchill in 1955 and the accession of Macmillan in 1957, marked the acceptance by the mainstream of the Party that there was no road back'.

The local ideological climate was in most areas apolitical in character (Bulpitt, 1983). Party colonisation of local politics was incomplete, with only about half of all councils under political control. When parties did control local authorities, this 'control could be purely nominal with little or no impact over and beyond the election' (Rhodes, 1985, p. 43). Only in some major towns and cities did party politics exercise considerable influence over policy-making.

The years 1945–55, then, saw the launching of the Welfare State to which the growth of local government was tied. Underlying these developments was the substantial economic growth during the period. The domestic product grew by about 20 per cent in real terms and there were other signs of growing affluence with rising numbers of homeowners, car users and so on. Macmillan's famous statement, made in 1957, 'most of our people have never had it so good', was more than politician's rhetoric.

*Expansion and modernisation: 1955–75*

Economic growth continued, slowly but steadily, in the remainder of the 1950s. The 1960s showed growth again. It was only by the mid-1970s that severe economic problems became manifest.

Between 1955 and 1975 Gross Domestic Product increased by approximately two-thirds in real terms. This period also saw a sustained expansion in local government.

Newton and Karran (1985, pp. 59–64) show how the scope of local activities broadened in response to pressures for a range of new public services. They identify nearly 50 pieces of legislation, enacted during the period, which had the effect of giving local authorities new responsibilities. In the field of planning and environmental control alone local authorities acquired new powers for pollution control, the reclamation and conservation of land, the preservation of wild creatures and flowers, the provision of camping and picnic sites, the removal of dangerous industrial tips, the control of dangerous litter and poisonous waste, and the regulation of listed buildings.

There was also a substantial improvement in service quality. The period 1955–75 saw bigger, airier and lighter schools, better trained teachers, and more carefully planned books and syllabuses. Larger, more elaborate leisure centres were provided, as well as better staffed and stocked libraries. Better roads, pedestrian lights and public buildings were developed. This list indicates only the tip of the iceberg in the improvements introduced during this period.

The expanding role of local government is reflected in increased public expenditure. Table 1.1 shows local authority current expenditure in 1975 was nearly three times larger in real terms than that in 1955. The level of capital spending also more than doubled during the same period. Spending increased on other welfare state activities with, for example, health service expenditure undergoing an expansion equivalent to that of local authorities. The expansion of local spending went along with a general rise in public expenditure. In 1955 local authority expenditure constituted 28 per cent of public expenditure and by 1975 this proportion had increased to only just over 30 per cent. Local authorities were, however, consuming an increased proportion of the nation's resources. Local expenditure constituted 9.1 per cent of the Gross Domestic Product in 1955 and this had risen to 14.9 per cent in 1975. It reached its peak in 1976 when local authorities spent £15.40 for every £100 available to the nation.

Increased public expenditure was reflected in a growing number of local authority employees. Table 1.2 shows that between 1952

**TABLE 1.1    Local authority expenditure, 1955–75 (constant 1975 prices)**

| Year | Current expenditure (£ million) | Capital expenditure (£ million) |
|------|--------------------------------|--------------------------------|
| 1955 | 4676    | 2027 |
| 1960 | 5903    | 1821 |
| 1965 | 7852    | 3331 |
| 1970 | 11 699  | 3858 |
| 1975 | 13 598  | 4569 |

Notes:  (1) All figures are for Great Britain.
        (2) Current (or revenue) spending covers the day-to-day running of local
            authorities including salaries and wages and the purchase of materials.
            Capital spending pays for investments in long-term physical assets
            such as buildings, land and machinery.
Source:  Calculated from figures provided in Foster *et al.* (1980) Appendix 1.4 Al
         pp. 102–31.

and 1972 there was a fifty per cent increase in the number of full-time employees and an over two hundred per cent increase in the number of part-time local authority workers.

The expansion of local government, particularly from the mid-1960s, drew on grants provided by central government. As Table 1.3 shows the share of current spending financed by central government increased substantially between 1966/7 and 1975/6. The proportion from miscellaneous sources, primarily fees and charges for local authority services, remained constant. The contribution from rates – a local tax levied on industrial, commercial and domestic property – declined. The growing reliance of local authorities on central government support became on element in a wider debate about local government reform.

Modernisation joins expansion as a dominant theme in the development of local government during this period. Reorganisation in London, 1963–5, led the way with an enlarged Greater London Council and 32 boroughs (plus the Inner London Education Authority and the City of London Corporation) replacing a total of 87 authorities. The reform of London's local government helped to break down resistance to radical restructuring. There followed a series of reports and investigations examining the organisation and management of local authorities (Maud, 1967; Mallaby, 1967; Redcliffe-Maud, 1969; Wheatley, 1969; Bains, 1972; Paterson, 1973). The debate was conducted in terms of

**TABLE 1.2   Local authority employment, 1952–72 (thousands)**

|  | Male | | Female | | Male & Female | |
|---|---|---|---|---|---|---|
|  | Full-time | Part-time | Full-time | Part-time | Full-time | Part-time |
| 1952 | 798 | 44 | 395 | 211 | 1193 | 255 |
| 1972 | 1089 | 125 | 667 | 703 | 1756 | 828 |
| Percentage increase 1952–72 | 36.5 | 184.1 | 68.9 | 233.2 | 47.2 | 224.7 |

Notes:   These figures relate to UK local authority employment.
Source:  Calculated from figures provided in Newton and Karran (1984), Table 2.1, p. 28.

**TABLE 1.3   Local authority income sources, 1953–76 (current expenditure)**

| Percentage of income made by: | Rates | Central government grants | Miscellaneous |
|---|---|---|---|
| England & Wales | | | |
| 1953/4 | 33.4 | 35.4 | 31.4 |
| England | | | |
| 1958/9 | 32.7 | 36.1 | 31.2 |
| 1966/7 | 34.2 | 36.5 | 29.3 |
| 1975/6 | 23.9 | 46.8 | 29.3 |

Source:  Adapted from Travers (1986) Table App. 7, p. 211.

structure, efficiency, planning and the rational allocation of functions. However, what emerged was heavily influenced by party political considerations and other vested interests (Wood, 1976; Alexander 1982a; Page and Midwinter, 1979).

In the reform of 1972–4 the multi-tiered nature of the previous system remained and was to some extent reinforced. In England and Wales local government powers were shared between 53 counties (6 metropolitan and 47 non-metropolitan) and 369 districts (36 metropolitan and 333 non-metropolitan). In Scotland most of local government became the responsibility of 9 regions and 53 districts. In short all-purpose authorities no longer operated.

The details of these systems are considered further in Chapter

2. For the present it can be noted that reorganisation resulted in a considerable reduction in the overall number of authorities, from around 1500 to about 500. Modernised local government covered larger areas and local authorities were, in general, bigger and had new and streamlined management structures. By 1975 these organisations were responsible for a substantial range of services and resources. Local government, in the words of one commentator, 'had become big business' (Benington, 1975).

Other changes, however, led to loss of functions from local authorities with responsibility for water and sewerage being taken out of local authority control in England and Wales and most of the remaining local health functions being handed over to health authorities.

The ideological climate of the period was heavily infused with a commitment to efficiency, planning and technological progress. It was not only local government that had to be modernised; it was the rest of Britain. The administration of central government was reformed; so too was that of the health and other public services. The spirit of restructuring was also applied in the management of the economy, with experiments in planning, intervention and organisational reform.

These years of expansion gave considerable scope for professional influence and growth. Planners, teachers and social workers seemed to grow in confidence and stature. Directors of Education, headteachers and other educational professionals carried forward school reorganisations, new systems of teaching and launched a range of experimental initiatives. Planners and engineers facilitated and encouraged the large-scale redevelopment of their towns and cities. The development of new housing estates, roads, shopping centres and other facilities was promoted and guided by local authority professionals. Professionals in many cases dominated local authority policy and decision-making.

Behind the scenes, however, there were growing signs of discord. Social reformers pointed to gaps and limitations in the range and impact of welfare services, despite all the increased expenditure (Taylor-Gooby, 1984). Political and community activists began to call for the greater involvement of ordinary citizens in the decisions that affected their lives, such as house demolition or road building (Hain, 1975; O'Malley, 1977). The early 1970s was also a period of intense activity by the women's movement, often centred on welfare issues (Wilson, 1977). The Heath Government flirted with but soon abandoned the ideas of the 'new right', which criticised state intervention and argued for a greater reliance on the market (Young, 1974). Finally, the early 1970s saw large-scale industrial action over wages as a response to the Heath Government's industrial relations legislation and incomes policy. Local authority and welfare state workers were for the first time prominent in taking strike action.

Local politics was less calm than in the immediate post-war period. There was the conflict and turmoil stimulated by reorganisation. Party politics was increasingly dominant in local elections and reorganisation is widely held to have confirmed this process.

There was also evidence of a growing politicisation of decision-making in London (Kramer and Young, 1978) and outside (Newton, 1976). Local politics was beginning to come to life.

The period 1955–75 has been described as local government's 'years of greatest affluence' (Newton and Karran, 1985, p. 52). As we have seen it was a time when local government expanded and its structure and management were modernised. Between 1973 and 1975, however, the world capitalist economy experienced a slump unparalleled since before the war. This recession had major consequences for local government after 1975.

*From constraint to instability: 1975 to the mid-1980s*

The contemporary history of local government is closely tied in with the economic panic caused by the 1973–5 slump. World trade declined by 14 per cent and in Britain the effect was heightened by the underlying weakness of the economy. Unemployment began to rise, inflation was in double figures and the strain on resources to fund state programmes was considerable. Public expenditure cuts were by no means the inevitable solution but they were the response that emerged.

Labour's Anthony Crosland told local authorities that 'the party was over'. Matters were brought to a head in 1976 when the country borrowed from the International Monetary Fund. A condition of the loan was a halt to the growth of public spending.

Labour's programme of 'cuts' was targeted mainly at the capital spending of local authorities. As authorities had already begun to cut capital projects because of the dire effects of steeply increasing interest rates on their finances, the extra central government pressure led to a rapid fall in capital spending (see Table 1.4). Cash limits on current spending were also introduced. The cuts were painful and reversed a long-established trend of growth but they were achieved by a mix of discussion, compromise and conflict within the established machinery of government.

A rather different picture emerges post-1979. The Thatcher Government argued vigorously for cuts in public expenditure, a reflection of their rejection of Keynesian economic management and their commitment to monetarism. Local government was selected as a particular target. 'Within weeks of taking office local government was strongly criticised by ministers who claimed that it was wasteful, profligate, irresponsible, unaccountable, luxurious and out of control' (Newton and Karran, 1985, p. 116). The Thatcher Governments pursued a strategy of confrontation and

**TABLE 1.4   Local authority expenditure, 1976–87 (constant 1984/5 prices)**

| Year | Current expenditure (£ million) | Capital expenditure (£ million) |
|------|---------------------------------|---------------------------------|
| 1976/7 | 25596 | 7898 |
| 1977/8 | 25360 | 6191 |
| 1978/9 | 26291 | 5981 |
| 1979/80 | 27058 | 6588 |
| 1980/1 | 26951 | 5764 |
| 1981/2 | 26978 | 4843 |
| 1982/3 | 27598 | 5479 |
| 1983/4 | 29476 | 5508 |
| 1984/5 | 29877 | 5349 |
| 1985/6 | 29339 | 4598 |
| 1986/7 (estimate) | 30236 | 3952 |

Notes:   (1) Current expenditure figures are for Great Britain. The figures are for total current expenditure. Calculations of constant price figures, with 1984/5 as base year, were made using the repricing index provided in *Association of County Councils* (1986), Table J, p. 310.
(2) Capital spending figures are for gross expenditure by English local authorities and cover spending funded by loans plus that funded by the sale of assets.
(3) The sharp jump in current expenditure in 1983/4 reflects the transfer of responsibility for housing benefit expenditure from central government to local authorities, and the slight drop in 1985/6 probably reflects various creative accounting measures taken by local authorities rather than any effective reduction in spending.

Sources: Current expenditure figures taken from H. M. Treasury (1982 and 1987) and capital expenditure figures provided by the Association of Metropolitan Authorities.

constantly changed the machinery of government in their attempts to control the expenditure and finances of local authorities.

A key weapon for the Conservatives was to reduce the contribution of central government grants towards local authority expenditure. Table 1.5 shows the declining proportion of local authority income for current expenditure obtained through central grants, and the increased proportions made up by rates and miscellaneous sources including changes for services. On the capital side an increasing proportion of local spending was financed by asset sales, particularly from 1979 onwards.

Paradoxically, despite the aggressive nature of the Conservative's attack on local government, progress in reducing expenditure up to the mid-1980s was modest.

Local capital spending remained at historically low levels but current expenditure continued to increase in real terms (see Table 1.4 and Figure 1.1). Total current expenditure was about 12 per cent higher in 1986/7 than in 1979/80. However this figure is misleading because it is affected by the shift in responsibility for housing benefit from central government to local authorities in the early 1980s. If allowance is made for this transfer it still emerges that current spending grew by at least, 5–6 per cent in real terms between 1979/80 and 1986/7. The dramatic growth in local authority employment up to the mid-1970s was checked. The number of full-time employees in English local government fell by about five per cent between 1979 and 1982 but has since remained relatively stable. Part-time employment also fell during the early 1980s but by 1985 was back at about the same level as 1979 (see Table 1.6). This limited progress reflects the fact, as we shall see in Chapter 7, that central government's onslaught was met with resistance by many local authorities.

The battle over local spending took place against the backcloth of continuing changes in Britain's economy. In particular the

**TABLE 1.5   Local authority income sources, 1976–85 (current expenditure)**

| Percentage of income made up by: | Rates | Central government grants | Miscellaneous |
|---|---|---|---|
| 1975/6 | 23.9 | 46.8 | 29.3 |
| 1978/9 | 23.2 | 44.0 | 32.8 |
| 1984/5 | 27.0 | 39.2 | 33.8 |

Note:   These figures relate to England only.
Source: Travers (1986) Table App. 7, p. 211.

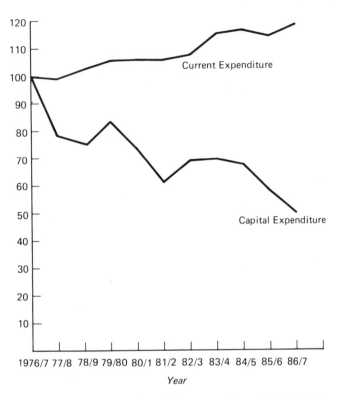

**FIGURE 1.1    Trends in local authority expenditure, 1976–87 (index
               1976/7 = 100)**

growth and expansion experienced by much of the South East
contrasted sharply with the further decline and de-industrialisation
which hit much of the rest of England, Scotland and Wales. Local
authorities in Britain's M4 Growth Corridor – in a line stretching
from Heathrow Airport through Reading to Swindon and Bristol –
saw the rise of new 'hi-tech' and electronics industries (Boddy *et
al.*, 1986). In contrast authorities in areas such as the West
Midlands watched as the manufacturing base of their towns and
cities collapsed (Spencer *et al.*, 1986). The different problems
posed in areas of growth and decline led to diverse responses by
local authorities as they attempted to grapple with rapid economic
change (Brindley *et al.*, 1988).

**TABLE 1.6  Local authority employment, 1975–85 (thousands)**

| Year | Full-time | Part-time |
|------|-----------|-----------|
| 1975 | 1608 | 862 |
| 1976 | 1625 | 851 |
| 1977 | 1606 | 853 |
| 1978 | 1600 | 869 |
| 1979 | 1626 | 886 |
| 1980 | 1609 | 865 |
| 1981 | 1578 | 843 |
| 1982 | 1552 | 840 |
| 1983 | 1558 | 852 |
| 1984 | 1551 | 858 |
| 1985 | 1545 | 873 |

Notes:   (1) Separate figures for male and female employment have not been available since 1974.
　　　　 (2) These figures are for England only.
Sources: Department of the Environment (1981; 1983; 1986).

Other material changes have provided local authorities with new challenges. They include changes in social structure, in the role of women or the significance of ethnic minorities, and the rise in the number of elderly people. Gyford in his evidence to the Widdicombe Committee (1986e, p. 110) argues more generally that there has been 'a move away from a society with a large degree of consensus on interests and values, towards a more diverse and fragmented society within which there are asserted a plurality of sectional interests and values'. The emergence of sectionalism has led to a growth of groups conscious of their own particular identities and rights as gay people, tenants, parents, patients, claimants and disabled people.

The ideological climate showed marked changes, such as the emergence of a more assertive and active public. People became less willing to accept authoritarian styles of leadership. There was a loss of confidence in the professional experts amongst the public and indeed amongst some of the experts themselves. 'Increasingly the professional claims of planners, architects, road engineers, social workers and teachers began to be called into question by a sceptical public informed by a combination of more widespread educational opportunity, investigate journalism in the media and –

sometimes the most crucial – their own lay experience of professional solutions' (Widdicombe 1986e, p. 108).

Some writers (Golding and Middleton, 1983) suggest that there was a collapse of public support for the welfare state. But Taylor-Gooby (1985) convincingly argues, by way of survey evidence, that general public support for the 'welfare consensus' had by no means disappeared. Indeed, the sustained commitment of public opinion to maintaining and improving many aspects of welfare service delivery helped to explain the degree of support and success achieved by local authorities in resisting expenditure cuts.

It is clear, however, that there was an important shift in the ideology of the central state élite, the politicians and officials responsible for managing central government decision-making. We have already noted their concern with public expenditure reductions. Another dimension to the changed ideological pattern was privatisation, the shifting of state assets and responsibilities to the private sector (see Chapter 8 for a full discussion). A greater concern with and a more authoritarian and less liberal approach towards a range of law and order, moral and civil liberties issues was also an element of 'Thatcherism' (Hall, 1979). Finally, a desire to push women back into traditional family roles would also seem to have been part of the shift in the assumptions of central state élite (Rose and Rose, 1982).

The reaction of the local political community to these developments was varied. Some local authorities were enthusiastic supporters of privatisation and the welfare backlash. Others developed defensive and pragmatic strategies, seeking to protect existing services. Some sought to challenge directly both central government's financial controls and its policies by developing alternative forms of local government provision and operation. The strategies of this last group are considered in more detail in Chapter 9.

In general, it is plain that the local political scene became more highly charged. The concern of party groups to organise and implement manifesto policies grew. This was accompanied by an increasing gap between the ideological positions and policy preferences of Conservative and Labour party groups, divergencies which were sometimes also reflected within the groups (Widdicombe, 1986b; Leach, 1986). Local government became one of the hottest topics in British politics.

The climate of conflict and instability is illustrated by the Conservatives' abolition of the Greater London Council (GLC) and the six metropolitan counties. It was a manifesto commitment in 1983 premised to a large extent on a 'gut reaction' against the political style of the GLC's left-wing Labour leader, Ken Livingstone, which emerged onto the agenda in an effort to disguise the failure of the first Thatcher Government to abolish the rates (O'Leary, 1987; Forrester *et al.*, 1984). No serious cost-benefit analysis of the reform was allowed. The Government wanted to make a dramatic gesture, to show that it could take action against those who opposed it.

With the abolition of the GLC and the six Metropolitan Councils in April 1986 the future structure of local government was placed back on the political agenda. New directions in service delivery and new policy concerns – such as local economic policy, race relations and the treatment of women – fuelled debate about the future role of local government. The increased use of a range of quasi-governmental bodies to carry out local government functions, such as Urban Development Corporations or private trusts, also helped to create a climate of uncertainty and instability in the mid-1980s.

## The impact of local government

The discussion of local government's post-war history makes plain the scale and scope of its activities. We have seen how a range of social, economic and political factors have conditioned the development of local government. In this section we examine the impact of local government in terms of the public with which it interacts, its employees and workforce and its relationship with business interests.

### The public

Local government is experienced differently by different groups in society. At a commonsense level it is clear, for instance, that an unemployed council tenant is likely to have a very different understanding of, and relation with, a range of local authority service delivers than a well-paid owner-occupier.

Survey evidence (Widdicombe, 1986d) indicates that higher status groups generally have more knowledge about the structure and organisation of local government. Over two-thirds of the AB (professional and managerial) socio-economic group can be described as well- or quite well-informed, compared to only a third of socio-economic group E (unskilled manual workers). This high status group is also more satisfied with the way local authorities provide services. Less than a fifth felt their local council ran things 'not at all well', whereas as nearly a third of socio-economic group E described their local authority in these terms. Finally, it would appear that when professional/managerial people are unhappy about a council decision they are more likely to challenge that policy through a range of effective channels.

The higher status groups in society make disproportionate use of local services relative to their need. Contrary to the widespread belief that public expenditure benefits primarily the less well-off there is a considerable evidence that many welfare services are distributed in a manner which favours higher social groups (Le Grand, 1982; George and Wilding, 1984, Ch. 3). The evidence is subject to a number of methodological problems (Burch and Wood, 1983, pp. 204–6) and it relates primarily to health, education, housing and transport services. Nevertheless, Newton and Karran (1985, p. 65) comment:

> Certainly the wealthier sections of society appear to make particularly heavy claims on local services such as roads, education, environmental control and consumer protection, and may well do so for such things as parks, libraries and museums and art galleries.

Thus far we have sought to establish that local government is experienced differently by different groups in society. We chose to look at the impact of local services in terms of social class or occupational categories. But there are other, equally valid 'accounting units'. A number of studies have shown the disadvantaged access of women to local government services such as public transport, education and housing, as well as inadequate levels of provision in child-care support and other services (Ungerson, 1985;

GLC, 1985). Other research has highlighted the disadvantaged position of ethnic minorities with respect to local service delivery and politics (Ouseley, 1984; Ben-Tovim *et al.*, 1986). For the present we turn our attention to a discussion of 'consumption sectors'.

The impact of local government on British social structure is, in some respects, more profound than has so far been made clear. The very growth of state intervention has itself helped to create 'consumption sectors', groups of people with an interest in consuming a particular public service or good. As the Welfare State has grown so have 'new social cleavages related to the accessibility and use of certain collective services' (Castells, 1978, pp. 15–16) Castells imagined that these new social structures would encourage the development of cross-class alliances leading to a radical challenge to the capitalist state. Their effects, however, have not been so clear-cut.

It would seem that state intervention has created client groups with a vested interest in maintaining their service and improving their position. Service providers may seek to mobilise these groups to resist threatened reductions in expenditure or highlight gaps in service provision. Thus, for example, parents may protest over cuts in education expenditure. On the other hand, governments can win support from sectoral groups, as it would seem in the case the Thatcher Government's Right-to-Buy policy directed at council tenants.

There have been two major attempts to theorise about consumption sectors. First we will examine the work of Cawson and Saunders (1983) who identify a distinctive sphere of consumption sector politics based on the state's welfare provision. People's consumption location, they argue, provides a separate material basis for social and political cleavage. Their work concentrates on the development of a plurality of state consumer groups who battle with each other primarily at the local level. Bus users, parents of school children, council tenants and so on, compete with each other to avoid cuts or increases in their services. This fragmented and issue-specific politics is the opposite of that imagined by Castells.

Dunleavy's (1979; 1980) treatment of the concept is different. He emphasises the distinction between those who consume public sector services and those who obtain them through the market.

The key cleavages thus include those between home owners and council tenants, car owners and public transport users and parents of children in private as opposed to state education. He sees these cleavages as partially independent of class differences and as stemming from distinctive material interests (Dunleavy and Husbands, 1985). Dunleavy also emphasises the role of ideology, suggesting that the public/private social cleavage is reinforced by perceptions of relative costs and subsidies.

Consumption sector theory is still emergent and tentative (Flynn, 1986). Moreover, it is difficult to be certain about the strength of consumption sector effects, particularly in relation to voting behaviour. Some studies provide empirical confirmation of their impact (Dunleavy and Husbands, 1985; Duke and Edgell, 1984); but others argue strongly against it (Franklin and Page, 1984; Heath *et al.*, 1985).

In the broader context of local government politics, however, consumption sector theories have a considerable validity. It is plausible and reasonable to suggest that the growth of state intervention at the local level has helped to create new social cleavages. In looking at local politics it is possible to see the competition of consumer groups for public resources, as well as the conflict between those who are dependent on a public service and those who consume that service through the private market.

The impact of local government on the public, it has been argued, is diverse and profound. As service consumers people experience local government differently, while the growth of state intervention has itself restructured social relations leading to new sources of conflict and alliance. The impact of local authorities as employers has had equally major effects, as we shall see in the next section.

*Local authority employees*

Local authorities are, by any standards, major employers. Many councils are the largest single employers in their area and, in total, about one in ten of the working population were employed by elected local government in the mid-1980s. The health services share of the nation's workforce was about five per cent, that of the public corporations approximately seven per cent and total public sector employment around 30 per cent.

As noted earlier, 1955–75 were the years of greatest expansion, with numbers of local authority employees remaining relatively stable since then.

Table 1.2 demonstrates that the growth in full-time staff was overshadowed by an even greater rise in part-time staff. It also shows that the rate of employment growth was greater for women than for men. The expansion of the female workforce was part of a general trend leading to increasing numbers of women taking employment. In the Britain of the 1980s more women go back to work after having children than in any other European Community country. Local government provides a major source of employment for them.

The growth in local authority employment contributed to establishment to what has been described as the 'new middle-class' of top managers and salaried professionals (King and Raynor, 1981). The more senior local government officers, however, are much more likely to be men than women. A 1982 report found in all Britain's local authorities that only one chief executive and only one per cent of chief officers were women (quoted in Rahman, 1986, p. 15). By 1987 the number of female chief executives had increased to four. Women tend to be concentrated in the lower white collar grades, while men dominate the senior positions. Figure 1.2 illustrates the position in Leicester City Council in March 1986. Women held 70 per cent of the lowest grade (S123) white collar posts and only 7 per cent of highest paid (PO and above) posts.

The expansion in the Welfare State and local government has gone, hand in hand, with the rise of the major state-employed professional groupings. These professionals derive much of their status and power from the state. They define needs, allocate resources and give a legitimacy and coherence to state intervention and provision. They are a powerful group. Their influence over many aspects of the policy process is clear. So too is the potential for control they exercise over their individual clients (Wilding, 1982).

This new middle-class of managers and salaried professionals is only one element in local authority employment. The bulk of local

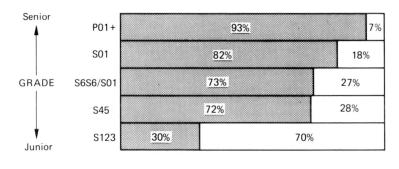

**FIGURE 1.2   Leicester City white-collar staff by grade and sex (March 1986)**

authorities employees work in a variety of lower status manual and non-manual jobs.

There are nearly three-quarters of a million administrative, technical and clerical 'white-collar' staff. They include typists, clerical assistants, clerks in schools, technicians, nursery nurses and welfare assistants. The majority are women. Local authorities also employ over a million manual workers on a full-time and part-time basis. They are the people who clean our streets and schools, the dinner ladies and home helps, the caretakers and council gardeners. Three-quarters of them are women, the majority working part-time. In addition, there are a substantial number of miscellaneous workers whose jobs are neither wholly clerical or wholly manual – cashiers in canteens, ticket sellers, traffic wardens and pest controllers.

Some of these local authorities employees have for a long time suffered from low pay. Rahman (1985, p. 5) notes that between the 1880s and 1920s road and sewage workers were in the bottom seventh of 38 industrial groupings in terms of pay. Their position improved relative to other manual workers during the years of the depression. Thereafter and throughout the post-war period the position of public sector manual workers has declined. In 1966 nearly 50 per cent of local authority manual workers earned less than £15 a week compared to only 16 per cent of the workforce as a whole. Karran (1984) suggests that during the period of greatest expansion local authorities altered their employment patterns, more or less deliberately, in favour of more lower paid women and part-time workers, so as to obtain the maximum amount of labour at lowest cost. The size of the local government's wages budget has not increased nearly as fast as the numbers on the payroll.

The Low Pay Unit's definition of low pay is two-thirds of median male earnings, which in 1985 was equivalent to an hourly rate of £3, a weekly rate of £115 and an annual salary of £5980. Using this definition, it emerges that 45 per cent of all full-time local authority manual workers in England and Wales earned low wages in 1985. The figures for women manuals only are even more stark: 80 per cent of full-time and 92 per cent of part-time female manuals were earning low wages (Rahman, 1985, p. 9).

The position of non-manual workers is better but not as sharply different as the traditional image of town hall white-collar staff, as comfortable and well-off, suggests. Using the Low Pay Unit's definition, one-third of all non-manual and miscellaneous local authority workers were low wage earners in 1985. Women employees were again in the worst position; with 38 per cent of full-time non-manuals, 68 per cent of full-time miscellaneous workers and 70 per cent of part-time females from both groups capable of being categorised as low paid. (Rahman, 1986, pp. 9–10).

Some may regard the Low Pay Unit's definition of low pay as unreasonable; yet it is comparable with a definition based on supplementary benefit levels and is slightly lower than the 'decency threshold' of the Council of Europe (Low Pay Unit, 1985, p. 6). The specific proportions of local authority employees receiving low wages may be subject to question; that substantial numbers have been and are low paid cannot be seriously doubted. The particularly disadvantaged position of women employees is also clear and there is evidence that ethnic minorities are concentrated in lowest grades of local authority service (Rahman, 1985 and

1986). Problems of low pay are also evident in the nursing and ancillary areas of the health service.

To summarise, local authorities provide employment for a substantial number and range of people. They are often the biggest single employer in their area. There is a pronounced difference between the types of jobs done by men and women. Men dominate the higher managerial grades. The majority of other white-collar staff are women working as typists, receptionists and administrators. Women constitute three-quarters of the manual workforce, most of them working part-time. They are typically concentrated in low status, low grade jobs. Professional and managerial employees form part of a relatively well-to-do 'new middle-class'. However, a substantial proportion of lower grade non-manuals and manuals earn low wages.

*Business interests*

Business interests experience the impact of local government in a variety of forms. Below we examine four of the ways in which local authorities affect the performance of economic and business activity in their areas.

The first is related to the local authority role as a major employer and a creator of demand. The importance of local authority spending for the local economy is illustrated by a 'jobs audit' undertaken for Sheffield City Council for 1984/5 (Sheffield City Council, 1985, Ch. 3). In addition to the 32 564 people directly employed by the local authority a further 9843 jobs were dependent on the spending of the City Council and its employees. Council contracts with local firms supported 2082 jobs. The spending from these jobs supported a further 600 local jobs. While the spending of the City Council's employees created an additional 7163 jobs in local service industries. The total jobs thus supported was 42 409, about 19 per cent of all jobs in Sheffield. If the impact of other public sector agencies in Sheffield is also considered the result is roughly to double the number of jobs in the city directly or indirectly dependent on public expenditure.

The jobs audit clearly shows the power of council spending to support jobs. From the viewpoint of business interests it also shows that local government and its employees are important consumers of privately produced goods and services.

A second role performed by local government is essential to private business interests, namely its provision and maintenance of much of the infrastructure necessary for the routine working of the economy. Local authorities are involved in building and maintaining roads and bridges. They provide police and fire services to protect ships, offices and factories. Local government is responsible for refuse disposal. It educates the population and prepares it for its working life; it runs public transport systems which get people to work. It supports some health services and houses a large proportion of the working population. It plans our cities and towns. In addition to these services local authorities, from mid-1970s, onwards, have increasingly developed a range of facilities directly to support and encourage local economic development. These include the provision of sites and premises, business advice and 'soft' loans (Boddy, 1982; Young and Mason, 1983).

Private sector business interests also experience local authorities as regulators. Local Government responsibilities in providing planning permission for land development, or change of use for buildings, are relevant here. As too are the environmental health and consumer protection services provided by local authorities. The extent to which any particular business is affected by these roles will vary according to its type and nature. Smaller businesses, perhaps, feel the impact of regulation to a greater extent than larger concerns.

It is sometimes suggested that local authorities adopt procedures which lead to delays and that business interests have become entangled in unnecessary 'red tape'. In the case of planning permission, at least, there is a grain of truth in such charges and there is evidence of local authorities using delay to stop unwanted developments. Amenity and community action groups, however, would not regard local authority controls over land-use as unnecessary. Indeed they would complain that property developers and house-builders who know the system have often proved themselves adept at obtaining planning permission against the wishes of the local community.

The role of local government that attracts the greatest degree of protest from the business community is its revenue raising. Non-domestic rates have attracted considerable criticism during the 1980s as an unfair burden on business. There was a similar period of business agitation against rates payments in the 1920s which resulted in the complete exemption of agriculture from rates and the 75 per cent de-rating of industry under the 1929 Local Government Act. It would seem that hard economic times go hand in hand with increased political activity against rates.

The critics of business rates develop three main arguments (Birdseye and Webb, 1984; May, 1984). First they argue that non-domestic rates bills have increased rapidly during the 1980s in a period of economic recession when business finds it most difficult to meet increased payments. Second an excessive rates burden, it is claimed, damages profitability and the viability of local economic activity. Finally it is suggested that the variation in rates level between areas has an arbitrary impact on the performance and competitiveness of firms in different localities.

Midwinter and Muir (1987, Ch. 3), however, suggest that these criticisms are 'misplaced, mistaken and misconceived' (p. 102). The period 1979–82 did see a rapid rise in rates, a response by local authorities to a loss of central government grant. However, between 1983 and 1986 the increase was only 13 per cent. Taking the 1980s as a whole it is difficult to justify the claim that rates have increased irresponsibly, particularly in comparison to other taxes. Moreover, rates form a very small element in the total production costs of industry. It has been estimated that rates are less than three per cent of industrial wage and salary costs. Overall 'rates are small beer in comparison to other costs faced by business and industry' (p. 77). Finally, studies of the impact of rates on local economic activity show little evidence of damage to the competitiveness of industry. Work undertaken for the Thatcher Government by a group of Cambridge University economists (Crawford *et al.*, 1985) showed no discernible connection between rate increases and changes in manufacturing employment. Measuring the effect of rates on business performance is fraught with methodological difficulties. Midwinter and Mair conclude 'we do not, and could not, claim that rates have no impact on the viability and employment capacity of some businesses. . . . What we can state is that any such effect is on a very small scale, is not systematic, and exists only in anecdotal evidence' (p. 103).

Local authorities provide a range of services to the private sector which if they did not provide then other agencies would have to. Plainly, businesses would like to pay less and be interfered with less. In some cases the antagonism felt towards local government is very strong. The 'jobs audit' report notes the 'psychology' of local business attitudes towards Sheffield City Council, 'which consisted of the feelings that times were hard in Sheffield, the rates were a burden, the council was not giving priority to the needs of local businesses, and that business activity must be better in other places with councils more sympathetic to business interests' (Sheffield City Council, 1985, p. 163). Yet local government cannot fairly be described as a parasite which is sapping the vitality of the private sector. 'On the contrary', as Newton and Karran (1985, p. 33) argue, 'it is an integral and essential part of the nation's industrial and commercial system'.

This first chapter has placed local government in context, in its development and its impact. Modern local government emerges as an important set of institutions with a range of major functions and roles. In the next two chapters we examine in more detail the structure and range of elected and non-elected local government.

# 2 Elected Local Government

This chapter introduces elected local government. The discussion is divided into four main parts which examine in turn elected local government's institutions, its political representatives, their party organisation and their electoral accountability. It closes with a brief comment on the role of parish and community councils.

## The organisation of elected local government

A similar structure of elected local government obtains throughout the non-metropolitan areas of England, the whole of Wales and mainland Scotland. In all of these areas there are two tiers of multi-purpose local authorities. The upper tier authorities are known as counties in England and Wales and as regions in Scotland. The lower tier authorities are known as districts. The principal functions of each type of local authority are listed in Table 2.1.

The allocation of responsibilities, however, is not quite as clear-cut as the table suggests. There are a number of overlapping functions. As a result, for example, there have been conflicts between upper and lower tier authorities in areas such as land-use planning (Leach and Moore, 1979).

The strategic planning considerations of a county may not sit happily with the local planning responsibilities of a district. The county might seek to develop and protect a 'regional' shopping centre within its area and argue for major new development to take place in that location. The individual districts, in contrast, may prefer to attract the best possible shopping facilities in their

**TABLE 2.1   The organisation of elected local government**

|  | Main functions |
|---|---|
| **WALES** | |
| 8 county councils | Strategic planning, transport, police, fire services, education and social services |
| 37 district councils | Housing, local planning, environmental health and leisure services |
| About 800 community and town councils | Consultation |
| **SCOTLAND** | |
| 9 regions | Strategic planning, transport, police, fire services, education, social services and water |
| 53 districts | Housing, local planning, environmental health and leisure services |
| Over 1200 community councils | Consultation |
| 3 island areas | All regional and district powers |
| **ENGLAND** | |
| *Non-metropolitan areas* | |
| 39 counties ⎫<br>296 districts ⎭ | Much the same split of responsibilities as authorities in Wales |
| About 9000 local (parish & town) councils | Consultation and Local amenities |
| *Metropolitan areas*<br>(West Midlands, South Yorkshire, West Yorkshire, Tyne and Wear, Greater Manchester and Merseyside)<br><br>*36 districts* | Education, social services, housing, local planning, environmental health, leisure services; and (via joint boards) transport, police, fire services and civil defence; and (via other joint arrangements) strategic planning, waste disposal, grants to voluntary organisations, trading standards, etc. |
| *London*<br>Inner London Education Authority<br>32 London boroughs<br>City of London Corporation | Education in inner London<br>Housing, social services, local planning, leisure, environmental health, education (outer London boroughs); and (via joint boards) fire services and civil defence; and (via other joint arrangements) strategic planning, waste disposal, grants to voluntary organisations, etc. |

Sources: Byrne (1986); Leach *et al.* (1987).

area. Considerable friction and tension has emerged in a number of cases as a result of such conflicts.

Indeed a degree of tension between upper and lower tier authorities has characterised the operation of local government since reorganisation in 1974 (Alexander, 1982b, Ch. 3). Overlapping responsibilities provide one cause of friction but other factors have contributed to tensions between tiers. Agency agreements whereby a county pays a district to undertake for it functions such as road maintenance or traffic management have in some cases led to difficulties with counties fearing a loss of control and districts resenting their position as 'employees' of the county. District counils often resent their loss of functions to counties. Leicester City Council, for example, still complains that education and social services became the responsibility of Leicestershire County Council in the 1974 reorganisation. This reflects not only a concern about status but also a feeling that the interests and priorities of the County are not necessarily the same as those of its major city. Leicester City, with its large ethnic minority population, has been critical of the County for failing sufficiently to adjust its education and welfare policies to meet the needs of such groups. Such differences in concern and commitment can exist even when the two tiers are under the control of the same party. A two-tier system operating in the context of competitive party politics is even more prone to inter-authority tensions.

The history of the Greater London Council illustrates the impact of political conflict well. Young and Kramer (1978) describe how the strategic policy-making of the GLC was thwarted by London boroughs who disagreed with its political objectives. In particular suburban Conservative boroughs continually challenged GLC leadership in the areas of housing, planning and transport. Their attacks helped to create the environment for the abolition of the GLC and the six Metropolitan Counties in 1986.

It is not easy to describe the local government system that was established after 1986 in London and the metropolitan areas of the country. Table 2.1 provides a rough guide but it does not convey the full complexity of post-1986 arrangements. It has been estimated that the new system involves London being administered by between 70 or 80 separate public bodies. A MORI opinion survey in metropolitan areas in 1987 revealed considerable and increased public confusion and uncertainty about the allocation of local government responsibilities under the revised system (Leach *et al.*, 1987). The London boroughs and the metropolitan districts are multi-purpose local authorities for their areas. But post-abolition, instead of sharing responsibility with county authorities, they operate in the context of complex system of joint-working arrangements and quasi-governmental agencies.

London is one of few major capital cities in the industrialised world without a local, directly-elected strategic authority to oversee it. After abolition the London boroughs took over responsibility from the GLC for many of its functions, yet in order to undertake these tasks various joint-working arrangements have had to be established. Thus strategic planning is pursued through a joint Planning Advisory Commission under the guidance of central government. Joint Committees have been established to oversee the allocation of grants to voluntary organisations and on a more *ad hoc* basis in other policy areas. For waste disposal a London-wide Waste Regulation Authority has been established, along with four statutory waste disposal authorities (combining groups of four or more London boroughs), and three voluntary waste disposal authorities (which draw their membership from the remaining London boroughs with the exception of Bexley). One statutory joint board has been established to deal with fire services and civil defence. All of the various joint committees, boards and authorities have their operation overseen by councillors appointed by the London boroughs. They are not directly elected agencies.

With the reform of 1986 other responsibilities of the GLC were transferred to a range of quasi-government agencies. Land drainage and flood protection has gone to the Thames Water Authority; the Arts Council has taken on the South Bank complex; responsibility for listed buildings has been transferred to the Historic Buildings and Monuments Commission and other functions have been taken on by the Sports Council, the Thamesmead Trust and other bodies. In addition prior to abolition in 1984 a London Regional Transport Authority was established to take over transport responsibilities from the GLC. Finally a residuary body appointed by the Government has been established to dispose of the GLC's property, debts and assets. This is a substantial task in itself but in addition the residuary body has taken on responsibility for functions for which no adequate arrangements could be made. These included the Research and Intelligence Unit, traffic light control and street naming!

Under the reform package of 1986 the Inner London Education Authority, which has previously been controlled by nominees from the inner London Boroughs, was made subject to direct elections. Following the 1987 general election victory of the Conservatives further changes in the government of education in inner London are in the offing, with proposals which will mean that boroughs will have to run their own education services in the future. We shall return to this issue in Chapter 11.

In the metropolitan areas outside London a similar complex pattern dominates the operation of local government, although there has been less transfer of functions to quasi-governmental agencies. In each of the six metropolitan areas there are three joint boards for police, transport and fire and civil defence. In Greater Manchester and Merseyside there are joint boards dealing with waste disposal. Beyond this a variety of joint committees dealing with strategic planning, waste disposal, arts, recreation, voluntary organisations and economic development has been established. The pattern of such joint-working arrangements varies from area to area (Leach *et al.*, 1987). Again none of these 'joint' agencies are directly elected. Most are 'controlled' by councillors nominated from the constituent metropolitan districts. As in the case of London the Government has appointed a residuary body in each of the metropolitan areas with responsibility for the disposal of the abolished County Councils' assets and other miscellaneous functions for which no joint-working arrangements could be established.

The nature of these non-directly elected and appointed agencies and how they fit into a growing pattern of non-elected local government is examined in Chapter 3. Here we conclude that the system of local government established after 1986 in London and metropolitan areas is fragmented and confused contrary to Government's claims that their reforms would 'streamline' local administration.

### The characteristics of councillors

The traditional councillor stereotype is a white, middle-aged, white-collar male. Indeed, the 1976 survey of the Robinson Committee (1977) showed that 83 per cent were male, 74 per cent were aged 45 or over and 66 per cent were, or had been, in non-manual occupations. The overall picture produced by the Widdicombe researchers (1986c) is one of little change. In 1985 81 per cent of councillors were male, 74 per cent were aged 45 and over and 69 per cent were, or had been, in non-manual occupations. In addition it emerges that 85 per cent of councillors

were owner-occupiers, with only 10 per cent renting their home
from a local authority. This general view, however, disguises a
more diverse reality. In the English metropolitan areas and London
there has been a marked increase over the last ten years in the
numbers of councillors aged under 45, but a decrease in the
number of such councillors serving on shire district councils (see
Table 2.2). As many as 50 per cent of councillors serving on
London borough councils are under 45. Table 2.3 reveals that
Labour, and especially Liberal, councillors tend to be younger. It
also shows the under-representation of women is evenly spread,
with the Labour Party just getting the wooden spoon! In Welsh
counties only 5 per cent of all councillors are female.

Table 2.3 also shows that the employment and social characteristics of councillors varies by political party. Labour councillors are
four times more likely to be unemployed than are Conservatives.
Labour is the only major political party to have a substantial
proportion (35 per cent) of people working in manual occupations,
and the income level of Labour councillors is more modest than

**TABLE 2.2  Councillors by age and type of authority: 1976, 1985**

|  | 18–44 | | 45–59 | | 60 and over | |
|  | 1976 | 1985 | 1976 | 1985 | 1976 | 1985 |
|  | % | % | % | % | % | % |
|---|---|---|---|---|---|---|
| England |  |  |  |  |  |  |
| Metropolitan Counties | 20 | 36 | 42 | 36 | 39 | 28 |
| Shire Counties | 16 | 22 | 38 | 32 | 47 | 44 |
| London Boroughs | 39 | 50 | 37 | 30 | 22 | 19 |
| Metropolitan Districts | 26 | 36 | 44 | 37 | 27 | 25 |
| Shire Districts | 27 | 22 | 40 | 39 | 31 | 37 |
| Wales |  |  |  |  |  |  |
| Counties | 10 | 8 | 44 | 37 | 47 | 54 |
| Districts | 31 | 17 | 42 | 41 | 41 | 42 |
| Scotland |  |  |  |  |  |  |
| Regions and Islands | 13 | 20 | 51 | 41 | 35 | 38 |
| Districts | 23 | 32 | 40 | 42 | 36 | 26 |
| Base | * | (401) | * | (579) | * | (554) |

* Bases not given for 1976.
Source: Widdicombe (1986c) Table 2.4, p. 22.

that of other parties. In general, non-manual workers are over represented on councils when compared with the population as a whole. Indeed the two highest status socio-economic groups provide 41 per cent of all councillors and yet constitute only 14 per cent of the total population.

The Widdicombe research (1986c, Tables 3.1 and 3.7) challenges some of the popular misconceptions about council membership. In particular, it is clear that local authorities are not dominated by the unemployed or by those employed in the public sector. Only four per cent of all councillors are unemployed. They are more likely to be found in the Labour Party, as noted previously. The proportion of unemployed councillors in Scotland is nine per cent. Of those councillors in employment 36 per cent work in the public sector, a percentage similar to the population as a whole. Many of these public sector employed councillors work for one local authority and act as a representative on another. Half of these so-called 'twin-trackers' are teachers or lecturers.

Councillors spend a substantial amount of time on council business (74 hours a month on average). A large number of local authorities have one or more 'full-time' councillors, that is councillors for whom council work has become effectively a full-time job. This is particularly the case in larger, metropolitan and London-based councils but it is not confined to such authorities. Most full-time councillors live off the allowances and expenses that they are entitled to claim (Widdicombe, 1986b, pp. 65–7). The level of remuneration, however, is very modest.

There are differences in the type of councillor attracted to different authorities. Overall, councillors are socially unrepresentative of the population as a whole. Their claim to legitimacy rests on the fact that they are elected. In 1985, 83 per cent of councillors entered the local political arena on a party ticket.

## Party politics in local government

The developments of the post-war period have already been noted in Chapter 1, with a shift from an apolitical climate to intensive 'politicisation'. Indeed some commentators argue that local government has traditionally been political, and that the main break with tradition had been the growth in the influence of

**TABLE 2.3** Councillors by political party membership, age, gender, activity status, socio-economic group and income

| | Con. % | Lab. % | Lib. % | Ind. % | Other % | All councillors % |
|---|---|---|---|---|---|---|
| Age: 60+ | 37 | 32 | 22 | 52 | 30 | 36 |
| 45–59 | 42 | 33 | 30 | 36 | 33 | 37 |
| 18–44 | 19 | 33 | 49 | 11 | 33 | 26 |
| Gender: Male | 78 | 83 | 79 | 81 | 81 | 81 |
| Female | 21 | 17 | 21 | 19 | 19 | 19 |
| Activity Status: | | | | | | |
| Employed (full or part-time) | 64 | 59 | 74 | 47 | 67 | 60 |
| Unemployed | 2 | 8 | 3 | 1 | 2 | 4 |
| Retired | 24 | 22 | 13 | 40 | 30 | 25 |
| Permanently sick/disabled | – | 2 | – | 1 | – | 1 |
| Looking after a home | 9 | 6 | 9 | 9 | 7 | 8 |
| Other | – | 1 | – | – | – | 1 |
| Socio-economic Group: | | | | | | |
| Professional | 11 | 6 | 15 | 8 | 5 | 9 |
| Employers/managers | 42 | 20 | 28 | 37 | 26 | 32 |
| Intermediate non-manual | 14 | 22 | 23 | 11 | 30 | 18 |
| Junior non-manual | 8 | 11 | 15 | 6 | 2 | 10 |
| Skilled manual/own account non-professional | 10 | 25 | 8 | 14 | 14 | 16 |
| Semi-skilled manual | 1 | 8 | 4 | 5 | – | 4 |
| Unskilled manual | – | 2 | – | 1 | – | 1 |
| Armed Forces/NA | 12 | 8 | 8 | 16 | 5 | 11 |
| Income | | | | | | |
| 15 000+ | 25 | 7 | 18 | 14 | 33 | 16 |
| £10 000–£14 999 | 22 | 23 | 29 | 17 | 2 | 22 |
| £ 6 000–£ 9 999 | 23 | 28 | 23 | 27 | 25 | 26 |
| Up to £5 999 | 22 | 38 | 23 | 29 | 23 | 28 |
| None | 1 | 1 | 2 | 2 | – | 1 |
| Refused/NA | 8 | 4 | 3 | 10 | 12 | 7 |
| Base | (595) | (496) | (133) | (224) | (43) | (1557) |

Note: As the numbers of Scottish National Party, Social Democratic Party, Plaid Cymru and 'other' party members are too small for separate analysis, all have been grouped into one category of 'other political party'.

Source: Widdicombe (39 1986c), Table 4.5, p. 39.

professional officers in the quarter century after the Second World War. On this argument elected members are merely reasserting the traditional basis of local government (Widdicombe, 1986a, para. 4.5). Studies by Jones (1969) and Alexander (1985) would lend support to the argument that we are seeing a return to politics rather than its introduction into local government.

The present-day reassertion of politics emerges in the party control of local authorities. Table 2.4 provides a comprehensive picture of party control in all local authorities in Britain in 1985. It shows that the Labour Party and the Conservatives are the dominant parties in local government. The Alliance (the Liberal Party and the Social Democratic Party) have seen a growth in the number of their councillors during the 1980s, but this has translated into overall control of only a very few councils. Table 2.4 also indicates that the proportion of councils controlled by a majority political party or a coalition of parties was in 1985 over 80 per cent (even allowing for those 'hung' local authorities where Independents shared power). This contrasts with the position in 1965 when the Maud Committee (1967) found only 50 per cent of local authorities under party control. The Independent-dominated councils in 1985 constituted only 16 per cent of the total and were drawn from the more rural parts of Britain. An interesting feature is the rise of the hung council, where no party has overall control; about half of all upper tier authorities fell into this category in 1985. The increased numbers of hung councils reflects a variety of factors including the rise of the Alliance and the unpopularity of the Conservatives at a local level during the years of the Thatcher Governments.

Party influence is also reflected in the political organisation of local authorities. It is now almost universal practice for councillors of the same political party on an authority to organise themselves in a political group which meets to pre-determine the line to be taken on matters coming before the council. The frequency of group meetings varies between the main parties, with Labour groups normally meeting twice as frequently as the Conservatives. Group discipline and cohesion is also greater in the Labour Party. Nevertheless, group solidarity is the norm for all parties: 92 per cent of Conservative and 99 per cent of Labour groups in power always or usually vote together at council meetings – the respective

39

**TABLE 2.4  Political control by type of authority: July 1985**

| | Metropolitan counties districts % | GLC & London boroughs % | English & Welsh counties, Scottish regions & islands % | All ex-county boroughs in shire counties and Scottish regions % | All other Scottish & shire districts % | All Authorities % |
|---|---|---|---|---|---|---|
| Conservative majority | 14 | 45 | 19 | 27 | 40 | 35 |
| Labour majority | 69 | 40 | 20 | 53 | 23 | 30 |
| Alliance & other majority | 0 | 3 | 2 | 0 | 1 | 1 |
| Independent dominated | 0 | 0 | 10 | 0 | 24 | 16 |
| All hung coalition or minority administrations | 17 | 12 | 49 | 20 | 8 | 18 |
| Base | (42) | (33) | (59) | (51) | (335) | (520) |

Source:  Widdicombe (1986b), Table 2.4 (corrected).

figures for voting at committee meetings are 79 and 85 per cent
(Widdicombe 1986b, Tables 2.3 and 2.5).

There appears to have been a sharpening of political intensity
in British local government. Even where authorities are organised
on party lines it is possible for the parties to operate on a bi-
partisan basis, sharing some decision-making. Examples of this
practice during the earlier post-war period are provided in Bulpitt
(1967). However, there is now a general tendency towards one
party forming the administration and the other(s) providing the
opposition. In 94 per cent of all authorities organised on party
lines the majority party take all committee chairs, in 91 per cent
all committee vice-chairs and in 90 per cent all sub-committee
chairs (Widdicombe 1986b, Tables A.13, A.14, A.15).

There is also a greater determination to push through party
policies. This has emerged particularly in those big city authorities
where formal party politics has long been normal. The Widdicombe
survey of councillors (1986c, Table 7.17) reveals that 63 per cent
of councillors agree that 'the first concern of the elected member
is to implement the party manifesto', (87 per cent of Labour
councillors and 61 per cent of Conservatives). In many authorities
comprehensive and detailed manifestos are produced. The commitment of councillors has increased, with more frequent group
meetings and the establishment of numerous *ad hoc* working
parties possibly involving party activists who are not councillors.

Finally more antagonistic inter-party relations have emerged.
Widdicombe (1986b, p. 197) refers to 'frequent reports of an
increasing gap between the ideological positions and policy preferences of Conservative and Labour groups, divergences which
were sometimes also reflected within groups'.

Among Conservatives a broad division can be drawn between
'wet' and 'dry' camps. The former have a longer tradition in local
government. They are 'localists' and see their role primarily in
terms of defending and promoting their area and its particular
interests. As a consequence they often express resentment at
central intervention even if it comes from a national government
under their party's control. They are less likely to use the language
of party politics and more willing to trust and rely on their officers
to pursue policies in the best interests of the area. The 'dry' camp
in contrast is much more involved with the ideological concerns
and commitments of the 'New Right'. They may display a strong

and active commitment to council house sales, contracting out, 'value for money' studies by external consultants and cutting back on spending. They have less trust in the officer structure and less commitment to local government institutions. Local government they argue needs a 'good shake up' and would benefit from being run on more business-like lines.

Within the Labour party several groupings can be observed. The dominant tradition is of councillors who see local government as a key part of the Welfare State. For them local government is about building homes, schools and leisure centres and providing good housing, education, social and transport services to their constituents. Their role is based on a patron–client relationship. Their task is to ensure the best possible public provision for those who elected them. Their role is to set the guidelines and find the resources, and look after the individual concerns of their constituents. Within these constraints they look to the officer structure to develop provision, manage and run the local government machine.

Competing with this traditional approach Labour local authorities in many towns and cities have seen the rise of the 'Urban Left', a diverse group of councillors with a more critical and yet broader vision of the role of local government. For them providing services to people is not good enough. Their commitment is to involving a wider range of the public in the process of decision-making and implementation. In particular disadvantaged groups including the unemployed, women, ethnic minorities and other sectional interests are encouraged to become involved in local politics. Urban Left councillors are less willing to pass over their decision-making responsibilities to the officer structure even in the sphere implementation. New ways of working and demands are placed on officers. Decentralised forms of service, new units dealing with racial or women's issues may be created, cutting across professional responsibilities and departmental structures. Moreover although delivering good services is seen as vital the Urban Left see local government as having a wider role. For them local politics should also be about raising public concern about nuclear power and disarmament, ill-health, economic restructuring, equal opportunities and new forms of poverty. There are within the Urban Left a range of political priorities and differences. These will be explored further in Chapter 9.

Finally the political concerns of the main centre party within
local government can be considered. Within the Alliance the
Liberal Party overwhelmingly dominates in terms of numbers of
councillors. With the split-up of the Alliance the Social and
Liberal Democrats have, as a consequence, gained the lion's share
of council seats. The Liberal presence in local government has
been in many cases based on a commitment to a 'community
politics' which emphasises campaigning on local issues and regular
contact with the electors through 'Focus' leaflets and other means.
Pinkney (1984) argues that Liberals tend to favour open
government and decentralisation initiatives, support public spending and provision in some areas (recreation and social services)
but in others are in favour of privatisation or alternative forms
of provision, such as cooperative housing. Environmental and
conservation issues are also likely to be key Liberal concerns.
Their attitude to local government bureaucracy is often critical.
This is illustrated by the programme of reforms introduced in
Tower Hamlets after the Liberals took control in 1986. They have
broken the structure of their London Borough into seven areas
controlled by neighbourhood committees of ward councillors.
This, they argue, will make the bureaucracy not only more
accessible to the public but also more manageable for councillors.
Indeed a principal concern of Liberals is to return representative
democracy to a dominant position within local decision-making.
Ward councillors, responsible to their local electorate, need to
reassert control over the direction of policy and service delivery
for their 'patches'.

These rough portraits give some indication of the different forms
and direction of 'politicisation' in local government over the last
decade. Politics has returned to local government in the form of
party influence and activity. Party politics not only dominates
elections, much local political debate but also as we shall show in
Chapter 4 has a considerable impact on local policy-making.

**Local electoral accountability**

In this section we move on to consider how and to what extent
party politics contributes to the electoral accountability of local
government. The Widdicombe Committee (1986a, para. 4.17) note
that party politics is still 'often regarded as an alien presence'.

Public opinion appears to favour a non-party system, with 52 per cent believing it would be better compared to only 34 per cent favouring a party system (Widdicombe, 1986d, Table 6.5). Widdicombe, however, argues that party politics in local government is both inevitable and desirable. It provides an organisational basis through which citizens can achieve the government and the services they want without themselves needing to partake directly in the process of government. 'If the political party for whom they vote fails to deliver, that party can be held accountable through the ballot box at the next election (1986a, para. 4.12). This claim is subject to a number of challenges as will become clear in this section which discusses the accountability of elected local government. Electoral accountability through the competition of political parties for public support has been seen as the essential currency of representative democracy for much of the twentieth century. It finds its clearest expression in Schumpter's (1954) conception of democracy as electoral competition for office between two or more élites, requiring the incumbent élite to obtain the periodic approval of an otherwise little-involved mass electorate. The existence of an alternative government élite on this view ensures that effective electoral choice is available on a wide range of issues, and that the incumbent élite is constrained in formulating policy by the need to anticipate its electoral implications. The question is how adequate is the accountability achieved through party competition in local elections? A number of points have to be considered.

*Taxation and representation*

First the operation of local electoral democracy has been criticised on the grounds that many of those who vote have little or no responsibility for paying for local services. The Thatcher Government's Green Paper *Paying for Local Government* (HM Government, 1986), for example, claims that of the 35 million electors in England only 12 million are liable to pay full rates. It criticises 'the poor linkage between those who vote and those who pay' (para. 1.36) and argues that as a consequence voters that receive partial or full relief from rates payments are encouraged to vote for higher local authority spending since they have little responsibility for paying for these better services. These arguments underlie the proposed introduction of 'community charge' to replace rates.

The Government's case has been countered on three grounds (Stewart *et al.*, 1984). The Conservatives have stood the long established principle of 'no taxation without representation' on its head by arguing for 'no representation without taxation'. This formulation contradicts fundamental democratic values. It is really being suggested that only men of wealth and property should be allowed to vote? Second the Thatcher Government's calculations rest on the assumption that only heads of household pay rates. Rates clearly reduce total household income and as such concern, and in practice are paid by, all members of the household. Finally, the Widdicombe Committee (1986a, para. 2.78) argues on the basis of its unpublished data that 94 per cent of all electors believe themselves to be ratepayers. Plainly in the minds of electors at least the linkage between voting and paying is strong. 'Psychologically, local electorates are ratepayers, whether or not they actually pay them' (Widdicombe, 1986d, p. 133).

*Low turn-out*

A second criticism of local elections is that results are based on a very low turn-out. Certainly turn-out in elections has been low. Average turn-out in contested elections between 1973–8 in local authorities ranged from 39 per cent in Metropolitan Counties to 52 per cent in Welsh districts (Widdicombe, 1986d, p. 111). These figures are proportions based on those who are on the electoral register. Effective non-registration runs at between 8 and 11 per cent for the country as a whole, and as high as 19 per cent in Inner London (Todd and Butcher, 1982, pp. 10–11). The young, ethnic minorities and the geographically mobile are particularly prone to under-registration. This feature can have serious implications for local government if such groups are concentrated in particular areas. In the London Borough of Kensington and Chelsea, for example, about a quarter of those otherwise eligible to vote in a local election cannot do so because they are not on a register (Widdicombe, 1986d, p. 113).

In judging turn-out figures a point of comparison is needed. Turn-out in British Parliamentary elections post 1951 has averaged

76 per cent. British local election turn-out compares unfavourably with much of Europe – for example, France 70 per cent, Sweden 90 per cent – but compares less badly with English speaking countries – for exmaple, USA 25 per cent, New Zealand 53 per cent – (Widdicombe, 1986e, Table 5.8). Overall, this analysis does suggest that turn-out in British local elections is disappointing.

It has been argued, however, that low turn-out produces no serious distortion in the results of local elections. The research undertaken by Professor Miller for the Widdicombe Committee (1986d, pp. 140–5) indicates that in most respects local government voters are representative of the full electorate. The main area of concern relates to young people who appear much less likely to vote than other social categories. This disparity, combined with the tendency towards under-registration within this group, represents a bias in the local electoral system.

*National and local influences*

A third criticism is that local elections are determined by national as opposed to local issues. Dunleavy (1980, p. 136), for example, claims:

Of course, local parties go through the motions of mounting election campaigns, producing manifestos, canvassing electors, holding a few meetings, distributing leaflets and guessing the result. But the evidence now available suggests that these activities have only a very marginal impact on which party is elected in any particular locality. For local election results overwhelmingly reflect national swings of opinion for or against the incumbent government, as these are modified by the different social bases in different areas.

The main supporting evidence is provided by Newton's (1976 pp. 14–15) study of Birmingham's local elections 1945–65, which found that 'no more than 10 per cent of the variance in Birmingham election results may be attributable to local factors'. Newton goes on to argue: 'the conclusion must be that local factors have a relatively insignificant impact on local election results' (p. 16).

A number of writers have claimed that reorganisation in the

mid-1970s and the increased political intensity of local government which followed has led to a more major role for local factors in influencing election results. For example, Jones and Stewart (1983, pp. 16–18) describe as a fallacy the notion that local government elections are solely determined by the popularity of national government. They accept that national factors have a dominant effect but maintain that local factors have additional effects. They point to significant variations in local election results in 1982 which they claim can only be explained by local influences. The salutary lesson is that local elections can matter and that the actions of a local authority can affect the election. A number of other studies point to the impact of local issues (Waller, 1979; Bristow, 1982).

Moreover, in over 500 interviews conducted with officers and councillors, the Widdicombe researchers (1986b, pp. 44–7) found that many felt that recent electoral history in these areas had been affected by local factors:

> Rather than local events and considerations having very little impact on local election results, the emphasis of the impressions we received was that, in a small but not insignificant number of cases, they can have a decisive impact on individual ward-level elections, and occasionally, as a consequence, on the overall election outcome within an authority. Much more frequently, though, while perhaps the net result of a council-wide set of elections may not be changed by the presence of 'local considerations', these latter may still contribute quite significantly to that result (p. 44).

It would appear, at least in the minds of officers and councillors, that local factors are considered to be of some importance.

As the Widdicombe Committee (1986, para. 2.75) notes 'the extent to which local elections are determined by local rather than national issues is likely to remain a matter of debate'. The evidence submitted by Professor Miller to the Widdicombe Committee (1986d, pp. 158–72) suggests that 80 per cent of local voters vote exactly in accordance with their national party choice. The remainder it could be claimed are making a local choice. Of these some have no national preference; those that do may be prepared to vote for a non-party local candidate or even against their national party identification. These findings give support to both camps. Plainly, national party allegiances and attitudes to national politics play a major part in local election results. Nevertheless, there is a detectable element of local influence in local election choice. A fifth of all electors voting according to local preferences could have a decisive effect on many elections. One difficulty is defining what constitutes a 'national' as opposed to a 'local' influence. Indeed, a determined 'localist' could argue that national party allegiances are in part structured by the performance of parties in local government, a consideration which Professor Miller neglects.

To summarise, national factors dominate but local influences may be of increasing significance. The actions of a local authority are as a consequence subject to accountability through the ballot box but in a flawed and ambiguous manner. A local ruling party may be swept from power because of the performance of its colleagues at the national level, rather than on the basis of an assessment of its own performance. On the other hand, where local factors are influential they may decisively shape the result. Much more frequently, though, local considerations may be detected but not change the net result in council elections. Their impact in such cases will depend on the interpretation placed on events by the ruling party group and senior officers as to what, if any, policy change results. In short, there is an element of irrationality in the system in that incumbent parties may be removed irrespective of their responsiveness to local opinion or adjustments made to policy on the basis of guesses about the meaning of electoral 'signals'. Schumpter's (1954) model of accountability through electoral competition, therefore, has only a limited applicability at the local level.

*Continuous single-party control*

There is a further criticism which needs to be considered. Namely that the conditions of political competition required by the Schumpterian model do not apply over large areas of the country in which a single party consistently dominates or maintains control of the local authority. Dunleavy (1980, p. 137–8), for example, estimated that 25 out of 53 non-metropolitan county councils in England and Wales would remain in continuous Conservative control. In the 1985 elections, however, the total number of Conservative held county councils dropped to ten.

The rise of the Alliance and an increasing volatility in local elections has weakened the grip of single-party control in many authorities. Moreover, it could be argued that the continuous control of one party indicates popular satisfaction with its performance. Changing electoral preferences may also be reflected by changes in the composition and policies of the ruling party. We noted earlier in the chapter the rise of new factions within each of the main parties.

It remains the case that in many authorities, primarily those at a lower tier, the prospect of an alteration in control is remote. As a consequence some of these authorities are or have been inward-looking and oligarchic in practice, as a number of case studies have shown (Dumbleton, 1976; Dunleavy, 1977; Dearlove, 1973; Jacobs, 1976). Moreover, in so far as greater volatility in voting behaviour, stimulated often by non-local considerations, has led to the removal of incumbent ruling parties this serves as a random destabiliser rather than a direct check on the performance of the local authority by its local electorate.

*Beyond local electoral accountability*

The conclusion suggested by the above discussion is that the accountability of local authorities to their communities achieved through local elections is partially effective but flawed. The fact of continuous single-party control in many authorities, the limited extent to which voting reflects local considerations and the issue of low turn-out emerge as the most serious criticisms. The Widdicombe Committee's Schumpterian vision of a local democracy kept viable by the competition for local support among political parties is not wholly matched by reality.

This assessment does not necessarily mean that local authorities are not accountable to their populations, as other forms of accountability exist and are, to a degree, effective. These include the regular contact between councillors and officers and members of the public; and the role of groups in actively representing a range of sectional interests. These checks on local authorities will be considered further in Chapter 5.

## Parish and community councils

There is a third tier in British local government, that of the parish or community council. In urban areas they are sometimes called 'town councils' and are entitled to have a 'town mayor'. As Table 2.1 indicates there are a substantial number of these councils. Their impact on local politics, however, varies considerably.

Parish councils operate in England, mainly in freestanding towns, rural and suburban locations. They are largely absent from cities, although in 1986 Birmingham City Council unveiled plans to establish 84 parish councils within its area (Collingridge, 1986). These plans were subsequently rejected. Parish councils vary considerably in size (from a few acres to nearly 100 square miles) and in population (from a few hundred up to 40 000). They have the power to raise a rate which is collected for them by the district council. In addition parishes may also levy the 'free two pence' to spend on matters of concern to the local community. In 1985/6 an average of £50 000 per council was raised, although in practice there is a considerable difference in the amount of resources available to different councils. A case study in Berkshire (Short *et al.*, 1986, p. 170) reveals a range (in 1983) stretching from £2500 to over £600 000 per year.

The disposal of these sums of money takes a variety of forms. Some is directed towards streetlighting and footpaths. The maintenance (or indeed purchase of) parish halls or recreation grounds is also a well-established activity. Some parishes have begun to take action in other fields: such as preservation schemes, providing off-street car parking, employing neighbourhood street cleaners, supporting local voluntary schemes which provide care for the elderly and housebound, and undertaking youth schemes and play group work. Action against vandalism or local unemployment problems have also occupied the attention of some parish councils.

It is sometimes argued that more important than these executive functions is the consultative role of parish councils (Perrin, 1986). Parish councils are elected by public ballot. Berkshire parish councils' average turn-out was about 20 to 25 per cent, with 50 per cent of all seats uncontested (Short *et al.*, 1986, ch. 5). Party labels are often used, but there is a considerable emphasis on keeping party politics to a minimum. In the face of a hostile upper tier authority, Labour-controlled parish councils, usually in former urban district areas, have developed both a service delivery and advocacy role. In growth counties such as Berkshire and elsewhere in South-East England parish councils have emerged as major opponents of development pressure (Short *et al.*, 1986). The right of parish councils to be consulted on planning applications and their contacts with district and county planning officers and councillors can give them some leverage in influencing decisions on particular schemes and to a less extent general land release policies.

In Scotland and Wales community councils provide the grass roots element in elected local government. Unlike parish councils they have no power to raise a rate and have few executive functions, except perhaps for organising community festivals. Their key role is representing the views of their area to district, county and regional tiers of local government.

Evidence from Scotland suggests that community councils are more active and widely supported in the rural areas and small towns than in the cities (Keating and Midwinter, 1983, p. 114). This is despite the efforts of Glasgow District Council, for example, to foster community councils to give its deprived communities more political weight. A pattern of varying degrees of success emerged in the initial period following local government reorganisation in 1972–4 (Materson, 1980). A later assessment indicated that most community councils were places for information-giving by local authorities and other public agencies and only rarely had real involvement in decision-making (Rutherford *et al.*, 1984). In contrast, the Widdicombe (1986b, p. 146) researchers drawing on the evidence of interviews undertaken in Wales and Scotland comment:

We were particularly impressed by the value which councillors (particularly Independents) placed on such bodies as sounding boards for local opinion. Councillors regularly voiced this mechanism as the most important avenue for consultation with the public.

**Conclusions**

This chapter has reviewed the organisation and the changing

nature of political representation of elected local government. Some important changes have undoubtedly occurred since reorganisation in the mid-1970s. The structure has been further modified by the abolition of the GLC and the six Metropolitan Counties. The role of political parties in elections and in the organisation of local authority business has increased. The influence of local factors on election results may also have increased. Certainly there is increased volatility in local elections. The rise of the Alliance parties and the greater polarisation in the programmes and policies of the two main parties have also affected local government quite strongly.

We have noted the limited effectiveness of the electoral accountability of local authorities to their populations, low turn-out, the influence of national factors on voting and the existence in many areas of continuous single-party control raise serious doubts about a vision of local democracy kept viable by the competition for local support among political parties. Finally, this chapter discussed the operation of the statutory third tier to elected local government of parish or community councils. They are organisations which vary considerably in their effectiveness but which are capable in some instances of expressing with considerable force local opinion to the upper tiers of local government and beyond.

In this chapter we have concentrated on identifying the broad patterns and features of elected local government. It is worth emphasising that each elected local authority has its own particular features and political style (cf. Stanyer, 1976). Indeed diversity is a key characteristic of British local authorities. The sources of diversity are many. They include differences in the functional responsibilities and size of local authorities. They reflect the different challenges facing localities as a result of social and economic changes identified in Chapter 1. Running an authority such as Sheffield in the face of massive de-industrialisation is a vastly different experience to managing the 'hi-tech', growth economy of Berkshire. The social inequalities and mixed population structure of the London Borough of Haringey is another world again.

# 3 Non-Elected Local Government

Beyond elected local authorities there are a range of government or quasi-governmental agencies that carry responsibility for some element of local public policy and service provision. These agencies seek to develop policies which are specific to particular localities. They have a local dimension to their work which involves them in regular inter-action with local authority policy-makers. Unlike local authorities these agencies do not have an electoral base. Their governing or management committees are appointed rather than elected through a system of party competition. They also differ from multi-functional local authorities in that their concern is usually with one purpose or policy area. We consider these agencies as participants in a non-elected local government sector.

Non-elected local government organisations occupy the governmental space between, on the one hand, central government, its territorial ministries and departments, and on the other hand, elected local government. They are a mixed group of organisations. In this chapter we develop a six-fold classification: joint boards, inter-governmental forums, public/private partnership organisations, user organisations, local authority implementation agencies and locally orientated, central government 'arms-length' agencies.

In the last category we include central government sponsored agencies, such as district health authorities and urban development corporations, which have a major local dimension to their work. But we exclude agencies, such as the United Kingdom Atomic Energy Authority, whose interventions in local politics are less frequent and not designed, to any great extent, to meet the needs of a particular locality. Further, we exclude from non-elected local government those voluntary organisations that form part of the quasi-non-governmental world operating at the local level. Organisations such as the many housing associations that operate in Britain would fall outside our definition of non-elected local government on this basis. They receive funds from the public sector and are crucial to the housing renewal strategies of many local authorities but they are not formally part of the public sector. In Chapter 5 there is a discussion of the increasingly close working relationship between many voluntary organisations and elected local government.

In practice, the division is not always clearcut between central government 'arms-length' agencies that have a major local dimension to their work and those that do not. Distinguishing between governmental, quasi-governmental and quasi-non-governmental forms in the 'real' world is not necessarily easy as different types of organisation merge into one another. Yet the drawing of analytical boundaries is justified so long as it provides a platform on which to build knowledge. The aim of this chapter is to develop a better understanding of the organisations that populate the world of non-elected local government.

The chapter opens with an examination of the diverse range of rationales and objectives associated with the growth of non-elected local government. The middle sections of the chapter are devoted to a more detailed examination of the six categories of organisation that we have identified. The final section of the chapter considers some of the conflicts and tensions surrounding the different forms of non-elected local government. We begin to explore issues such as what influences and which interests direct this mixed group of organisations.

## The growth of non-elected local government

The operation of non-elected agencies within the local arena is not a new phenomenon. Prior to reorganisation in 1972–4 local authorities worked through a variety of joint committees and boards to achieve economies of scale in service provision (for example in bus operation); to undertake the joint management of a shared facility (for example, a crematorium); or to plan transport and land-use policies across a number of authorities (Flynn and

Leach, 1984). Central government too created a number of powerful single-purpose agencies including Regional Hospital Boards (and later in 1974 Area and Regional Health Authorities); New Town Development Corporations to launch a ring of satellite towns around the metropolitan areas of the country; and rural development agencies in Mid-Wales and the Scottish Highlands.

We argue that from the mid-1970s the range and scope of non-elected local government has grown. Severe financial constraints, and instability created by social and economic change, have encouraged institutional experimentation and a search for different forms of government on the part of both central and local authorities.

The Labour Government in 1975 created powerful economic development agencies in Scotland and Wales as a response to the increasingly sharp decline of these areas. A recognition of the massive loss of jobs, population and social facilities from some of our major cities led to the creation of a number of 'partnerships' – joint-working arrangements between central government, quasi-governmental agencies and local authorities – in declining inner areas. The Glasgow Eastern Area Renewal (GEAR) project was launched in 1976. Later similar schemes were launched in other inner city areas. The rationale for these partnerships was that a coordinated effort on the part of a range of public agencies was required if the tide of economic and social decline was to be turned. These initiatives were seen as valuable in terms of the resources that they channelled to deprived areas. In addition, they served the Labour Government as a statement of political commitment and concern.

The pace of institutional innovation accelerated after 1979. Despite an initial hostility towards appointed bodies, the Conservatives have made extensive use of such agencies as part of a wider attempt to by-pass local authorities unsympathetic to their aims. Examples which illustrate this strategy in operation include the creation of Urban Development Corporations to take over planning and development control functions in a number of cities and the expanded role given to the Manpower Services Commission to promote training and new education initiatives. The Conservatives have seen these non-elected agencies as more amenable to their policy influence. The use of such single-purpose agencies has also enabled the Government to maintain a general constraint on local authority spending, but channel through such agencies increased and substantial resources according to its priorities.

The Thatcher governments have also encouraged the growth of non-elected agencies through their attempts at restructuring and reforming the practice and performance of elected local authorities. Legislation in 1985 forced local authorities to create companies to manage their participation in bus and airport operations. The company format and associated legislative constraints, it was argued, would enable these facilities to be operated in a more efficient and 'business-like' manner. With their election for a third term the Conservatives are in the process of making it possible for public sector tenants and schools to 'opt out' of the local authority system. This will lead to the creation of a further range of non-directly elected local agencies to take over the responsibility for the management of these services from local authorities. Finally, as noted in Chapter 2, the greater use of non-elected agencies was a key outcome of the abolition of the GLC and the six metropolitan areas. Responsibilities have been divided between a number of joint boards, committees and quasi-governmental agencies.

The growth of non-elected local government has also been encouraged by local authority experimentation and innovation. Local authorities, like central government, have attempted to give themselves better instruments to meet the social and economic challenges of the 1980s. In economic development, for example, extensive use has been made of 'arms-length' agencies including enterprise boards, community business and cooperative development agencies. These agencies have proved attractive because they can act in ways not appropriate or open to local authorities. Enterprise Boards, in particular, can make direct provision of loans or equity funding to the private sector. These agencies have a flexibility and speed of reaction which normal local authority committee and departmental processes do not allow. Finally they can recruit staff with appropriate skills, perhaps from the private sector, and provide them with a working environment to their liking.

Local authorities have also experimented with institutional reforms aimed at giving a greater direct influence to users in the running and management of local authority services. The attraction of such schemes is that by bringing in users a more effective service may be delivered within budget constraints. The knowledge and commitment of users gives the service a greater responsiveness to the public. There may be 'knock-on' advantages in terms of an overall improvement in morale among local residents leading to a reduction in numbers of empty properties or levels of vandalism on, for example, housing estates managed by a committee of local residents. Housing and recreation have seen many initiatives which predate the Government's concern with 'opting out' provisions for certain local authority service users. Stewart (1986a, p. 32) comments: 'Despite (or possibly because of) the growing constraints on local authorities, initiative and innovation flourish. It is no longer assumed that local authorities can only act through direct service provision. Local authorities are learning [new] ways of governing in a turbulent environment'.

Finally both central and local government have encouraged experimentation with non-elected forms of government as a way of encouraging the greater involvement of major private corporate sector companies, banks and building societies in dealing with problems of urban and economic decline. Local enterprise agencies – sponsored by a mixture of local authorities, government departments and major companies – have been established to support the development of small businesses and advise on matters of environmental and economic development. Other public/private partnerships operate in housing and urban renewal. For public sector agencies the concern is to get access to private sector funds and expertise. For private sector agencies their involvement reflects a mix of motivations, ranging from a genuine desire to help, to a more 'public relations' concern to be seen to care about the localities in which they operate. There may also be a 'trade off' in terms of their relationship with government departments or local authorities. Participation and investment in one scheme may smooth the path to other more profitable opportunities. Thus, for example, a volume builder may agree to participate in an inner city renewal project in return for being granted planning permission for a suburban housing development.

Non-elected local government has grown in response to a diverse range of motivations and has drawn in a mixture of participants. Central government, particularly in the Thatcher years, has been a prime mover, through its creation of non-elected agencies to by-pass local authorities and its efforts at restructuring elected local government. Local authorities have, however, also innovated and experimented with non-elected forms to provide themselves with better instruments and provide opportunities for the more direct involvement of service users in local provision. Finally the desire 'to bring in' private corporate interests has fuelled the growth of the non-elected sector.

**The organisation of non-elected local government**

Our analysis of the growth of non-elected local government reveals a mixed group of organisations which draw on the resources and commitment of different participants and diverse rationales. In this section we identify six broad types of local non-elected agency on the basis of how they are financed (where the resources of the organisation comes from) and how they are constituted (who sits on their management committees). An outline of the key characteristics of the six types is provided in Table 3.1. Within each category various sub-divisions are made in an effort to increase our grasp of the complexity of the non-elected sector.

*Central government's 'arm's length' agencies*

These are organisations created and overseen at arm's length by central government. The British governmental system has a considerable range of such quasi-governmental agencies or non-department bodies. These quasi-governmental agencies are set up as independent organisations, free from direct government control, although they are subject to influence from Whitehall. They include organisations such as the United Kingdom Atomic Energy Authority, British Coal, the Independent Broadcasting Authority and the University Grants Committee. Most such quasi-governmental organisations operate primarily at the national level, and they form part of the broad 'non-local' governmental environment, considered further in Chapter 6.

Some elements of this quasi-governmental world, however, do focus their activities on particular localities and seek, to an extent, to tailor their policies and practices to meet the needs of particular areas. These organisations should be considered as participants in the world of non-elected local government. There is a major local

**TABLE 3.1  The organisation of non-elected local government**

| Type | Resource provision | Management committee | Examples |
|---|---|---|---|
| Central government 'arm's-length' agency | Mainly through central government | Composition largely dictated by central government | Health authorities, arts councils, urban development corporations, Manpower Services Commission. |
| Local authority implementation agency | Mainly through local authority | Composition controlled by local authority | Enterprise boards, local authority-owned bus companies. |
| Public/private partnership organisation | By public and private sector participants | Nominated by public and private sector participants | Local enterprise agencies, Stockbridge Village Trust. |
| User organisation | Mainly from public sector sources | Composition dominated by service users | Housing management cooperatives |
| Inter-governmental forum | As sanctioned by public sector participants | Composed of representatives from public sector participants | London and South-East Regional Planning Conference, Glasgow Eastern Area Renewal Project, and other joint committees. |
| Joint boards | By a precept raised from participant local authorities (subject to central government imposed limitations) | Nominees of participant local authorities (plus one third magistrates in police joint boards) | Police, Fire and Transport Joint Boards in metropolitan areas post-1986. |

dimension to their work which involves regular inter-action with local authority policy-makers. Four forms, at least, of such centrally-sponsored bodies can be identified: single-purpose service providers, promotional and grant-giving bodies, development agencies and strategic bodies.

Among the most important of the single-purpose service providers are the health authorities. The arrangements for the decentralised administration of health varies between England, which has a two-tier structure of 14 Regions and 192 Districts, and Wales and Scotland where single-tier structures operate. All these health authorities have their work overseen by an appointed board of members. In England Regional Health Authority (RHA) members are appointed by the Secretary of State for Social Services. The management board of District Health Authorities consists of four to six professional members and eight other members, known as generalists. These members are appointed by the RHA. Local authorities nominate the remaining four or five members of DHA management boards. The Secretary of State, in addition, appoints a chairman for the DHA. In Scotland and Wales a similar allocation system operates, with the respective Secretaries of State appointing the majority of health authority members and local authorities the remainder.

Health authorities have no significant independent sources of finance. Health services are funded directly by central government. Health authorities operate within the context of a hierarchy of command. In the English system the Secretary of State for Social Services oversees the work of the NHS Management Board, a central management agency. This board in turn allocates resources and gives directives to RHAs. The RHAs allocate resources and indicate priorities to the DHAs. The task of DHAs 'is to implement national and regional policies in a way that is appropriate to local circumstances and preferences'. Indeed the National Association of Health Authorities comments that 'health authorities have a particular responsibility towards the local community' (NAHA, 1986, p. 4, 3). In this sense they are non-elected agents of local government.

Another group of powerful single-purpose service providers with locally-orientated policy priorities is the water authorities. There are ten Regional Water Authorities (RWAs) operating in England and Wales. In Scotland elected local government remains in control of water, sewerage and drainage services. The work of the RWAs is overseen by an appointed management board. Initially following the establishment of RHAs in 1973 local authorities had majority nomination rights to these boards, a reflection of the fact that these responsibilities were formerly in the hands of elected local government. This system was changed in 1983 so that all board members are appointed by central government and no places are reserved for local authorities. The membership is smaller, with a salaried chairman, and organised more on the model of a private sector company.

These changes were seen as preparation for the Thatcher Government's proposed privatisation of water authorities. A number of legal and other problems lie in the path of this plan. RWAs are at the time of writing, at least, part of non-elected local government!

Promotional and grant-giving bodies that regularly interact with local authorities include the systems of Arts Councils and Sports Councils. The Arts Council of Great Britain was established in 1946. Later Scotland and Wales were given their own councils. In addition there is a system of regional arts associations in which local authority representatives are involved. These are independent of the Arts Council but work closely with it, providing a channel for its grant-aid and developing regional policies for promoting the arts. The Sports Council was established in 1965, with independent bodies set up in Wales and Scotland in 1972. The Sports Council has a system of nine regional offices with responsibility for implementing sports policies and developing strategies appropriate to the needs of particular areas. The regional offices work in consultation with nine regional councils for sport and recreation in which local authorities, various voluntary bodies and others participate. Both the Arts Council and the Sports Council receive their funds from central government (respective budgets £101m and £33m in 1984/5) and their national management bodies are composed of individuals nominated by the appropriate Secretaries of State.

The range of development agencies is considerable. Some are concerned with urban development, others with rural development and others more generally with economic development. They are influential organisations generally with power to give grants, assemble land and stimulate or undertake development. Some are permanent agencies such as the Scottish and Welsh Development

Agencies, the Highlands and Islands Development Board, the Mid-Wales Development Agency and the Development Commission on England (together with English Estates). Others are limited-life agencies including the New Town Development Corporations (most of which are in the process of being wound up) and the Urban Development Corporations (UDCs). The first two UDCs were established in 1981 in London's docklands (London Docklands Development Corporation) and Merseyside's docks. A further five were launched in 1986–7 in the West Midlands (Sandwell/Walsall), Tees-side, Tyneside, Cardiff Bay and Trafford Park (Trafford/Salford). The Government has established a further range of 'mini-UDCs' in Bristol, Leeds, Manchester and Sheffield. All of these organisations are primarily funded direct from central government and have their governing bodies appointed by central government. They can, however, 'self-finance' some of their activities through, for example, land sales. In 1986 the Scottish Development Agency self-financed about a third of its annual budget (SDA, 1986, p. 10).

Among the most powerful and influential of the strategic agencies working in the local political environment is the Manpower Services Commission (MSC). Its role and budget has grown substantially since its formation in 1976. By the mid-1980s its annual expenditure was above £2 billion and it operated through a system of 55 advisory Area Manpower Boards. In its role as a trainer and job creator it works closely with elected local government. Local authorities have been major agents for the programmes of the MSC, receiving financial support in return for providing work experience and training within the local government sector for young people and the long-term unemployed. Elected local government is the largest single provider of places under the Community Programme, with about 44 per cent of the total (Society of Chief Personnel Officers in Local Government, 1987, p. 12). The MSC has also worked with local authorities through the Technical and Vocational Education Initiative. By 1986/7 some 98 local education authorities were participating with this scheme which provides a major new education programme for young people and a restructured school curriculum. More generally, the MSC has been encouraged by the Conservatives to take over strategic responsibility for vocational and further education, with major future implications for local authorities (SOCPO, 1987).

*Local authority implementation agencies*

A second broad category of non-elected organisation is provided by arm's-length, implementation agencies appointed and resourced by local authorities. Many of these agencies have grown up in the field of economic development. They include some half a dozen large-scale enterprise boards including Greater London Enterprise, West Midlands Enterprise, Greater Manchester Economic Development Corporation, West Yorkshire Enterprises, Merseyside Enterprise Board and Lancashire Enterprise Ltd. The boards were originally established in the early 1980s by Labour local authorities to tackle the severe economic problems of their area. Conservative-controlled Kent County Council has established a similar board. The boards operate as substantial investors mostly in local manufacturing industries and the six original boards had by the end of 1986 invested a total of £35m (CLES, 1987, p. 2).

The enterprise boards are generally controlled by councillors or other nominees from the local authorities in whose area they operate. With the abolition of the GLC and the six metropolitan counties, the pattern of membership on boards has had to change. In most cases lower tier authorities have together taken on the overseeing role previously provided by the upper tier authority. The boards take the form of companies limited by guarantee and are responsible to their parent local authorities. Each has generally gone on to create a number of wholly-owned subsidiary companies. West Midlands Enterprise Board, for example, has about half a dozen such companies. The boards receive direct funding from their parent local authorities. In addition various funds from the private sector have been obtained in the form of loans or investments.

Beyond these major initiatives local authorities have launched a substantial number of smaller-scale, arm's-length agencies to pursue economic development policies. These include hundreds of cooperative development agencies (Macfarlane, 1986) and community business organisations (Keating and Boyle, 1986, Ch. 6; Teague, 1987). Cooperative development agencies as their name implies aim to promote industrial and other employment generating cooperatives. Community business organisations concentrate on providing job opportunites in areas of high unemployment. In many instances a two-tier structure operates with a holding company to identify and develop projects. Once a particular community business is established then a steering committee of local councillors, community representatives and possibly local businessmen is formed.

Some authorities have used arm's-length agencies outside the economic development field. Harlow District Council has an array of such agencies. Stirling District Council also has a well-developed approach and has launched at arms-length local sports and arts organisations.

Local authorities have also been forced to set up arm's-length implementation agencies because of central government-sponsored restructuring. The 1986 Transport Act obliged local authorities which owned bus operations to set up companies. The local authority retains ownership and can appoint up to seven non-executive directors. It would seem they are generally councillors. A similar requirement has been laid on local authorities responsible for the management of local airports by the 1985 Airports Act. Airport companies have to be established, again with the local authorities retaining ownership, a share in any profits and control by way of non-executive directorships.

*Public/private partnership organisations*

A third form of non-elected organisation involves a partnership between public and private corporate sector agencies. Resources to support the organisation and its activities are provided by both sets of participants and representatives from both public and private sectors sit on the management committee.

Economic development is again a key growth area for such organisations. A trail-blazing initiative was the Community of St Helens Trust established in 1978 as a result of the concern of Pilkingtons, the glass makers (Young, 1988). They realised that rationalisation and changes in technology would reduce the number of jobs they would be able to provide in the area and recognised the major impact this contraction would have, given their position as the dominant employer in St Helens. After consultations with the local authorities and other local businesses the St Helens Trust was formed with the aim of developing schemes for alternative employment. The trust provides financial advice and a consultancy service for existing small businesses and would-be entrepreneurs. It administers local authority grant aid and lobbies for the building of industrial estates and units.

Similar initiatives emerged in other parts of the country (Moore *et al.*, 1985). As these projects grew so too did the interest of the Thatcher government, local authorities and, indeed, the private corporate sector. In 1981 Business in the Community (BIC) was formed to promote and develop such initiatives and in 1983 a sister agency, Scottish Business in the Community, was launched. Since their formation about 300 local enterprise agencies have been established (Business in the Community, 1987). There are tax advantages available to local enterprise agencies if they register with BIC. Local authorities have been actively involved in launching many schemes. Strathclyde Regional Council, for example, has a policy that endorses the enterprise trust concept and has committed resources to an Enterprise Trust Development Fund. Indeed Keating and Boyle (1986, Ch. 7) suggest that for Scotland, at least, behind the rhetoric about the business-led nature of the schemes stands the reality of public sector intervention with the Scottish Development Agency and local authorities to the fore.

All local enterprise agencies provide free advice and counselling to support the setting-up and development of small businesses. In addition, a large proportion of agencies provide managed workshops, organise business skills training courses and allocate loan or grant funds. All are sponsored by a mixture of public and private sector agencies including local authorities, government departments and major companies operating in the area. Their management committees involve a mixture of public and private sector participants. Administrative and managerial support can involve secondees either from local authorities or major companies.

Public/private partnership organisations have also developed in housing and urban renewal. Among the first was the Stockbridge Village Trust in Knowsley, Merseyside. This was launched in 1982 to purchase and refurbish a run-down local authority housing estate. Its funds came from a mixture of public and private sector sources and its management committee included nominees from Knowsley Metropolitan District Council, Barclays Bank, Abbey National Building Society and some community representatives. Another private trust was launched in 1986 in Thamesmead to take over the management and renewal of a former GLC-owned estate. A White Paper produced after the Thatcher Government's third election victory proposes the establishment of a further number of similar organisation, to be called Housing Action Trusts (HM Government, 1987, pp. 16–8).

Other public/private organisations include the network of Groundwork Trusts which carry out environmental improvement to derelict land. The first trust was established in North-West England in 1982–3. A board oversees the work of each trust with nominees appointed from local firms, the voluntary sector and the MSC, as well as local authorities. Public/private trusts have also operated in the area of leisure and recreation. The Spectrum Project in Warrington provided an example until 1986 when it ran into financial difficulties and had to be disbanded.

Most of the public/private organisations described above are set up as limited companies or charitable trusts. They aim to provide a service to the public or run a project on a non-profit making basis. There are also, although less common, instances of public/private organisations operating on a profit-making basis. The Scottish Exhibition and Conference Centre Company provides an example (Young, 1988).

*User organisations*

These are non-elected agencies based on a partnership between service users and a government organisation. The agency is resourced from public sector funds but its management is shared with, or exclusively in the hands of, service users. An example of this form is the tenant management cooperative. The housing stock remains the property of the local authority, but the powers and responsibilities for management, maintenance and repair are handed over to a committee of local tenant representatives. As well as setting down guidelines for the establishment of the cooperative the local authority may establish other conditions (for example, no racial discrimination in the allocation of properties) as well as continuing to provide financial support and back-up in terms of the advice and expertise of housing department officials. A variation on the theme of housing management cooperatives is provided by the launch of three 'community ownership' schemes in 1986, inspired by Glasgow District Council. In these cases batches of about two hundred homes have been transferred to tenants not only to manage but also to collectively own. There are only about fifty housing management cooperatives operating in Britain in London, Birmingham, Glasgow and elsewhere (Downey, 1982; Clapham, 1985a). But this number seems likely to grow. Local authorities have shown an increasing interest in such initiatives (Clapham and English, 1987). A national federation of housing management cooperatives and a network of cooperative development agencies exist in order to encourage their formation. Moreover, the 1987 Housing White Paper proposes giving local authority tenants the right to choose a new landlord and notes that, 'tenants may if they wish be able to take control of their homes by forming a co-operative with their neighbours' (HM Government, 1987, p. 15).

There are other examples of user organisations taking on responsibility for local service delivery. They include joint management committees for sports and leisure centres, community colleges and schools, arts facilities and public parks. These committees are composed of users of the service but may also include local authority councillors, officials and staff. The local authority provides the financial support for the facility and will indicate any overall policy objectives it would like to see achieved.

Hambleton and Hoggett (1987, pp. 69–70) provide a particular illustration from Birmingham. Having purchased a playing field and sports facilities from a major local company suffering economic difficulties, the recreation department of Birmingham City Council called a public meeting to which all potential users of new facilities were invited. As a result, a steering committee consisting of casual users, organised clubs and representatives of statutory agencies was constructed to administer the facilities. Hambleton and Hoggett, in conclusion, note that 'user group involvement in the running of major facilities is now quite common' (p. 69).

Local authorities, then, have been the prime movers behind the development of user 'control' of local services. The Thatcher Government's interest in such initiatives in housing has already been noted. The proposals in the Conservatives' 1987 manifesto to allow schools to 'opt out' of local authority control could lead to the creation of another group of user organisations running a local service. Opted-out schools would be directly funded by central government but managed by a school council, composed of parents and other 'local interests', in cooperation with the headteacher and other teachers.

*Inter-governmental forums*

A fifth type of non-elected agency takes the form of a voluntary partnership between a range of public sector organisations. These agencies generally provide a forum for inter-governmental debate and policy formulation. They bring together representatives from local authorities, and in some instances from other public sector agencies, to oversee a particular policy area. These forums do not carry day-to-day responsibility for the management of a public service. But they may seek to set down guidelines and monitor performance in order to influence those responsible for implementation. Two sub-divisions within this form can be distinguished: the 'pure' joint committee and the 'mixed' joint committee.

A 'pure' joint committee is one where the management committee is composed solely of delegated councillors from participant local authorities. Generally local authorities have powers of recall over the councillors they place on such bodies. Such joint committees usually have only limited budgets of their own, and any major expenditure they incur has to be ratified by the parent authorities. These joint committees were a feature of local government in the pre-1974 reorganisation period. Many have survived into the 1980s including the Norfolk Museums Joint Committee, the Mersey Tunnel Joint Committee and North-East London Polytechnic Joint Committee (for a more extensive list see Flynn and Leach, 1984, Appendix One). One well-known joint committee that has survived since 1962 in several slightly different forms is SERPLAN, the London and South East Regional Planning Conference. SERPLAN brings together the local authorities of the South East, and its terms of reference include keeping the physical planning and transport issues affecting the region under review, establishing where appropriate feasible joint policies, and making recommendations to central government. As noted in Chapter 2, a whole series of joint committees was established after the abolition of the GLC and six metropolitan counties in 1985.

In 'mixed' joint committees representatives from local authorities are joined by central government and other public sector participants. An example is provided by GEAR (Glasgow Eastern Area Renewal) which was launched in May 1976. The project's task was to regenerate Glasgow's East End. A governing committee was established to oversee the general direction of the project. This committee consisted of senior elected members from the local authorities (Glasgow District and Strathclyde Regional Councils), and board members of other participants (Scottish Special Housing Association, Greater Glasgow Health Board, The Housing Corporation, Manpower Services Commission and the Scottish Development Agency), and was chaired by a Scottish Office Minister. The Governing Committee had no authority to instruct participating bodies to follow GEAR policies and it had no financial resources or budget directly under its control. The ultimate decision to spend money and undertake projects remained with the participants. What GEAR did was provide a format for agreeing priorities and gaining the commitment of a range of agencies to work in Glasgow's East End (Brindley *et al.*, 1988, Ch. 7). In this it was successful and had spent over £315m in current price terms before its disbandment in 1987.

Mixed joint committees have also emerged to steer the work of the seven English partnership areas designated in 1978 under Labour's Inner Urban Area Act. The partnership areas were Manchester/Salford, Birmingham, Liverpool, Newcastle/ Gateshead, Lambeth, Hackney/Islington and London's docklands. The latter was replaced in 1981 by an Urban Development Corporation, the London Docklands Development Corporation.

Mixed joint committees have also been formed to cope with the problems caused by steel closures in England and Wales. In, for example, Clwyd, Corby and Consett the relevant county and district authorities were joined on committees by BSC Industry (a division of the British Steel Corporation established in 1977 to create new jobs in areas affected by steel closures), MSC and other public sector agencies. In most instances the county councils took responsibility for chairing and servicing the committee (Young, 1987).

The discussion above has concentrated on the mixed joint committees created as part of inner city and economic development policies. A different example comes from community care where the responsibilities of health and local authorities overlap. In 1974 following the reorganisation of both services the two authorities were required to set up joint consultative committees to facilitate the collaborative development of services. Two years later joint financing was introduced, with central government money specifically earmarked for community care projects agreed after discussion between the two types of authority. The money has been spent mainly on services for the elderly and the mentally handicapped (Ham, 1985, p. 57).

## *Joint boards*

Joint boards differ from Joint Committees in a number of important ways. They are corporate bodies, generally created by order of a minister, with a legal identity in their own right. Joint boards have independent financial powers, including the power to borrow and obtain the money they need from constituent authorities by means of a precept (in effect an order to collect money on behalf of the joint board). They can hold land and property and employ staff. The constituent local authorities send their councillors to oversee the work of the joint board. The 1986 abolition of the GLC and the six metropolitan counties has created a whole series of joint boards. Details of the boards established were given in Chapter 2. In total some 20 joint boards have been launched. They provide important services including police, fire and public transport. The budgets for individual boards ranged between £20 and £80 million in 1986/7, with total expenditure in the region of £700 to £800 million.

These post-abolition boards were established with three distinctive features (Leach *et al.*, 1987). First although they have the power to precept they are precept-capped by central government for the first three years of their lives, and possibly thereafter. Second the constituent authorities are not free to nominate whomever they please. The majority party of the borough or district councils cannot send only representatives from its party; rather the council has to nominate in proportion to the balance of political representation involved in their authority. Thus for example if a council of 60 is composed of 40 Conservatives, and 20 Labour members and has three joint board places it would be required to appoint two Conservatives and one Labour member. Some anomalies emerged in the first round of nominations, with some minority parties finding arrangements unacceptable. It appears that a majority party is not obliged to allow a minority party to select its own representatives. Thus, for instance, Manchester City Council nominated a Conservative councillor unable to attend the day-time meetings of the Greater Manchester Police Joint Board!

The third major distinctive feature is that constituent councils have the power to recall delegates immediately if they are not behaving or voting in a manner which is viewed as appropriate. A number of authorities have exercised this right. For example, Labour-controlled Birmingham City Council in 1986 withdrew four Conservative representatives on the West Midlands Police Joint Board because of their support for a non-Labour chairman of the board. But although delegates can be recalled it is open to the authority to replace them only with members of the same party in line with the rules for compulsory proportional representation.

A final feature of the police joint boards is that a third of the representation consists of nominations from the local magistrates bench. This has had the effect of ensuring that in three out of the six joint boards since their formation no political party has been able to exercise control through having its councillors in a majority.

## Local politics and non-elected local government

Non-elected local government consists of a diverse set of organisations. The growth in its scope and range has important consequences for local government and politics. We cannot in this book fully explore the processes and dynamics of the non-elected sector. Lack of adequate empirical evidence, combined with the vastness and complexity of the sector, makes this too demanding a task. Below we explore a number of tensions and conflicts surrounding the different types of local, non-elected agency. We ask: Who influences these agencies? How is that influence exercised and to what effect?

### *Central government's 'arms-length' agencies*

These agencies pose a considerable challenge to local authorities. They have access to substantial resources, provide services and make decisions of importance to their localities. They are arms-length creations of central government. As such they can be expected to give precedence to the centre's priorities and policies. Yet these organisations have an 'internal dynamism' provided by their own bureaucracies and staff. This can provide a powerful momentum to policy-making and development. For example, the prestige of the medical profession and its direct control over clinical decisions have given the profession a major influence over health policy (Ham, 1985). Opportunities for influence to be exercised by local authorities over these centrally appointed agencies is limited. And the access of local interest groups to these bodies is often selective.

At best only a minority of nominees on the management boards of such agencies are local authority representatives. These representatives find it difficult to present effectively local views or priorities. Lack of time, legitimacy and resources can make the task difficult if not impossible. According to one DHA member nominated by a local authority, papers consistently arrive late, meetings are in unsuitable locations and no support exists for independent research or analysis by himself or his colleagues (Stoten, 1986; see also National Association of Health Authorities, 1986).

The Thatcher governments since 1979 have sought in a number of cases to further distance such non-elected agencies from local authority influence. Thus water authorities, as we noted earlier, have had their management boards restructured. Attempts have been made to pull health authorities closer to central government policies and priorities. The Thatcher governments have taken care to appoint nominees to RHAs and DHAs, particularly chairmen, who are sympathetic to their thinking. These chairmen and the core group of managers that surround them can form a powerful axis within health authority decision-making, squeezing out other health authority members from any decision-making influence (Saunders, 1984a).

If formal management structures do not provide effective mechanisms of influence for local authorities, can more informal and subtle strategies of influence be adopted? Stewart (1986b, pp. 8–9) argues that a local authority has a range of resources for influence available including its powers as a local authority, land and property, local information and knowledge, staff and skills, public legitimacy and funds. In dealing with any particular appointed agency the relevant resources will vary. 'They can be used as threats or promises. The important step for the local authority is to realise that it has resources for influence. The management of influence require their mobilisation'.

Keating and Boyle (1986) in their study of Scottish urban policy provide a number of illustrations of the successful management of influence by local authority over appointed agencies. They argue that local authorities do not feel threatened by the SDA and see area projects in particular as 'a means of gaining extra resources for economic development . . . at very little cost either financially or in loss of autonomy' (p. 106). The SDA views the involvement of local authorities as essential to its area initiatives in order to stretch its own limited resources as well as draw on the knowledge and information of local councils. The management of influence by a local authority involves a trade-off between what it can offer which is of value to the non-elected agency, what it has to give up in order to work with that agency and what it can gain in terms of resources or opportunities.

The management of influence is not without its dilemmas. Stewart (1986b, p. 13) suggests that 'the local authority must be ready to be influenced if it seeks to influence'. Local authorities may find themselves carried along in directions which they might not want to follow. Local authorities who have worked with the MSC in developing the technical and vocational educational initiative (TVEI) scheme have been warned that 'those who accept this type of funding are also accepting that in the long term, their policies and programmes could be determined neither by the needs of the area, nor by the strategies of the local authority but by outside bodies who have provided finance for a limited period. In effect, developments in services will be governed by what the Central Government organisation in question is prepared to fund' (SOCPO, 1987, p. 39).

Further, not all appointed bodies are amenable to influence. The London boroughs have adopted a variety of strategies in dealing with the London Docklands Development Corporation (LDDC). It would appear that Tower Hamlets has gone along with the LDDC, Southwark has adopted a stance of having nothing to do with the Corporation to express its defiant opposition, and Newham has sought to negotiate and bargain. Yet each admits it has had only a marginal impact on the LDDC. It remains to be seen whether local authorities will be able to exercise greater influence over the UDCs created from 1986 onwards.

Beyond local authorities a range of local interest groups may seek to influence the direction of centrally-sponsored, non-elected agencies. Indeed various consultative channels may exist. For example, health authorities consult with local or community health councils. They provide a channel for some community and voluntary groups to have an input, but on the whole appear to be 'weak and largely irrelevant' organisations (Saunders, 1984a, p. 40). Some centrally-sponsored agencies hardly go through the motions of consultation. This feature of the LDDC's style has been a source of public criticism (Docklands Consultative Committee, 1985). The LDDC specifically rejected the idea of a full-blown system of consultation arguing that it was too inflexible and time-consuming.

If the value of formal consultation is limited, centrally-sponsored agencies are sometimes open to more informal influences from particular interests, especially powerful economic or producer interests. The LDDC regularly negotiates and discusses its plans with major developers and builders. Stevenage New Town Development Corporation, it has been argued, was 'captured' by local industrialists, who directed its investment to provide housing for their 'key sector' workers and other supporting infrastructure (Mullan, 1980). Water Authorities work closely with producer groups including the CBI, the National Farmers' Union and Housebuilders' Federation (Saunders, 1984a, pp. 16–24).

The discussion above indicates that a range of non-local and local forces influence the action of central government arms-length agencies. Central government, the permanent staff and officials of the agencies, local authorities and powerful local interests vie with one another to steer these organisations.

*Local authority implementation agencies*

Local authorities can exercise direct influence through their control of the finances and the management boards of these agencies. However, in the case of bus and airport companies regulations imposed by central government, relating to levels of subsidy and other matters, restrict the choices available to local authorities. Even when the local authority is not faced by such constraints it can prove difficult to hold arms-length implementation agencies to account.

Local authorities with enterprise boards have sought to meet the challenge in a variety of ways. They have set out detailed guidelines, indicating the objectives that enterprise boards should pursue. There is often a close working relationship between enterprise board employees and local authority officers. Reports about enterprise board activities go to local authority committees and these activities are monitored by officials.

The ability to control nominations to a management board has also provided local authorities with a mechanism for influencing enterprise board activities. Yet these appointed directors may find it difficult to hold the staff of the enterprise board to account. (McKean and Coulson, 1987, p. 378). To fulfil their role satisfactorily, 'directors must not only exhibit a degree of business acumen but must also possess a high level of inter-personal skill and commitment'. This may be too much to ask. Directors may lack the expertise or time to effectively carry out their role. Moreover, staff working for enterprise boards may come from a private sector background 'where broader strategic issues are not considered when evaluating investment proposals'. The potential clients of enterprise boards, industrialists in economic difficulties, may demand confidential and closed discussions. Enterprise boards as a consequence are prone to having their direction dictated by their staff rather than by their sponsors. Enterprise boards are only likely to operate effectively from the viewpoint of their sponsors 'where the investment strategy has been well defined and operational guidelines and practices have been made explicit and established in practice'. The same can be argued for other local authority implementation agencies.

*Public/private partnership organisations*

For a local authority, involvement in a public/private partnership organisation carries with it a number of attractions including getting access to private sector resources and expertise, and bending those to meet the priorities of the local authority. But there are a number of dilemmas and risks.

Keating and Boyle, for example (1986, p. 157), warn that local authorities working with public/private enterprise trusts run the potential risk of having their social and employment objectives diverted into the simple securing of commercial expansion and profitability. Moreover, if a joint project runs into difficulties then the ultimate responsibility of local authorities as *elected* agencies means that it is they, rather than the private sector participants, who have to find a solution. Stockbridge Village Trust in Knowsley, which had taken over the management and ownership of a run-down council estate in 1982, suffered a severe financial crisis in Autumn 1985. It could no longer support a programme of investment and its revenue income was insufficient to cover daily management and maintenance costs. It took a year of protracted negotiations before a revised programme and resource could be agreed. In essence the private sector participants – Barclays Bank, Abbey National Building Society and Barratts, the volume builders – backed away from the scheme. Knowsley District Council, with central government support, had to find extra public resources to keep the trust and its renewal programme going. This caused a degree of resentment among Knowsley's officers and councillors (Brindley *et al.*, 1988, Ch. 8).

These two examples show that tensions may exist within a public/private organisation. The partners may have different priorities. The scope for local authorities to bend the priorities of private sector participants is limited by the private sector's ability to opt out.


*User organisations*

Tensions within users agencies can occur between the priorities of the users and those of the funding agency. A study of a housing management cooperative in Rochdale (Hambleton and Hoggett, 1987, pp. 71–3) highlights of a number of tensions over allocation policy. The cooperative departed from local authority policy in that it did not consider applications from single people. Its concern was with creating a balanced and viable community for its area. The local authority, in contrast, had an overall responsibility for meeting housing needs in the town. The cooperative's understandable concern to improve the environment of its residents led to allegations from some local authority councillors and officers of favouritism and of not meeting social need.

This clash of priorities can be underwritten by different conceptions of democracy. On the one hand, local people argue their case on the grounds that they have a specific interest in the service because they use it. They have a direct material interest in the service and their area. On the other hand, local authority councillors claim legitimacy as elected representatives. The debate is between direct and representative visions of democracy.

These different visions of democracy are by no means easy to reconcile. Yet some form of reconciliation is essential if user organisations are to operate effectively. Running a housing cooperative can make major demands on the time and lives of the tenants' representatives involved. Users are willing to organise and take on responsibilities providing the organisations in which they are involved 'directly relate to their interests and so long as they feel they are exercising real control' (Hambleton and Hoggett, 1987, p. 69). Officers and councillors have to recognise that unless people are allowed some real measure of control, user organisations will fail or be mere shams. At the same time, users have to recognise the legitimacy of the demands that a local authority or another funding agency might make given its broad responsibilities.

*Inter-governmental forums*

The politics of these organisations depend substantially on whether the participants can find sufficient common ground to make progress possible. Joint committees are most likely to operate smoothly if the activity involves information collection or provision of an already agreed service; if the financial commitment involved is modest; and if there is little scope for conflict between the participating authorities. If these conditions are not met conflicts and delays can grow. Joint committees rely on a willingness to cooperate and a broad consensus among the constituent elements. If these characteristics are absent they can prove to be cumbersome and ineffective (Flynn and Leach, 1984).

In Liverpool's inner city partnership committee overt conflict and disagreement emerged. According to a House of Commons report (1983, Ch. 4) problems resulted from disagreements between Liverpool City Council and Merseyside County Council and a lack of effective action from central government. No strategic approach emerged and there was an unwillingness among the 'partners' to work within the spirit of partnership. The partnership and its machinery were as a consequence allowed to atrophy.

The GEAR project in Glasgow's East End, in contrast, succeeded in bringing about a substantial degree of consensus and commitment among a range of public sector participants to the renewal of the area. Other inner city joint committees also achieved a degree of joint-working, although often on the basis of each participant obtaining funds for certain 'pet' projects. Young's (1987) judgement on the steel closure joint committees is that they worked only because the attitudes of the individual participants were 'constructive'. Leach *et al.* (1987) comment on the early experience of the joint committees established in metropolitan areas (excluding London) that common party loyalties have made joint-working possible to a limited degree. 'The ability of joint committees to agree has been very much aided since May 1986 by the Labour domination of the committees in all the areas other than Merseyside' (p. 3.26).

## Joint boards

Joint boards like joint committees are dependent on the co-operation of a range of participants. Again the early experience is of party politics 'oiling the wheels' of joint working. District councillors from different parties meet together in party groups and develop a shared perception of policies and priorities. With Labour able to dominate the joint boards in five out of six metropolitan areas, with the exception again of Merseyside, tensions and conflicts are being smoothed out. 'The forces of party politics are prevailing over the forces of localism and responsibility to districts' (Leach *et al.*, 1987, p. 3.21). In Merseyside, however, where two of the five districts are Conservative-controlled, 'conflict and tension between districts have been only too apparent' (p. 2.47).

The picture with respect to police joint boards is complicated by the presence of magistrates in a third of the seats. As a result three out of six of the police joint boards are effectively hung. This has caused some tension and conflict. For example, in the case of the West Midlands Joint Board, Labour despite having a substantial majority among councillor nominees has found itself out-voted on occasion by a combination of Conservative and magistrate representatives.

If one party is in the majority the potential exists for block voting and some form of manifesto politics in joint boards. But it is a shadow of the type of party control exercised in many elected local authorities. The evidence of Leach and his colleagues (1987) shows that manifesto commitments relating to joint boards are relatively rare. District councillors give a relatively low priority to joint board work. The pre-meeting briefings by officials are inadequate; as too are reporting back procedures to either district councils or party groups. As a result the power balance has shifted in favour of Chief Officers and other full-time officials of joint authorities who are exercising considerable influence over policy processes. Moreover, the joint boards are subject to 'precept-capping' imposed by central government, which in effect limits the amount of money that joint boards can spend.

A final point about joint boards, which applies equally well to most joint committees, is that public awareness of their activities is very limited. A survey conducted a year after the abolition of the GLC and the six metropolitan counties found that between only two and four per cent of people in metropolitan areas correctly identified joint boards as being responsible for police, fire and transport services. More generally over twice as many people found the post-abolition arrangements more difficult rather than easier to understand (Leach *et al.*, 1987).


### Conclusions

The range and depth of the interventions undertaken by the organisations of non-elected local government make it plain that if we are to fully understand the world of local government politics we cannot neglect these non-elected bodies. Local authorities remain the pre-eminent governmental agencies of the locality but they operate in an environment heavily populated by other governmental or quasi-governmental agencies. Local authorities are no longer the sole service providers or strategic organisations for their areas. These responsibilities are shared with other agencies. Local authorities have increasingly had to work through, alongside, or in competition with a range of non-elected organisations.

The growth of non-elected local government has undoubtedly increased the complexity and fragmentation of the governmental environment at the local level. As a consequence the scope for organisational conflict and tension has increased. The creation of non-elected agencies has been motivated by a range of contrasting rationales but which nevertheless share a common commitment to developing what are seen as more effective tools of government. It may be, however, that the cumulative impact of the growth of non-elected local government has been to weaken the overall capacity for local government. Certainly the rise of the non-elected sector brings to the fore issues of inter-agency working and coordination.

Our discussion of non-elected local government has conveyed its diversity and its various institutional forms. But it has only been possible to develop in a fairly patchy and limited way an analysis of the politics of the organisations within the sector and the conflicts and tensions associated with their relationship with elected local authorities and other local interests. In the remainder of this book we concentrate largely on the politics of elected local government. We are convinced however that further study and a better understanding of the non-elected sector of local government is essential.

# II LOCAL GOVERNMENT IN OPERATION

# 4 The Internal Politics of Local Authorities

To understand the operation of local government it is essential to examine the internal politics of local authorities. What goes on inside towns, boroughs and county halls is vital for at least two reasons. First the administrative routines, power structures and conflicts of interest within local authorities can affect policy processes by modifying and mediating external influences. Second they may provide an independent dynamic. The internal politics of local authorities reflect not only an ability to make choices in the context of external influences, but also a facility for taking initiatives and independent action on the part of officers and councillors.

Chapter 1 identified a number of changes in the fiscal, economic, social and ideological climate surrounding local government from the mid-1970s onwards. They included a squeeze on spending, processes of economic growth and decline, changes in the social structure and shifts in public opinion leading to a more assertive and demanding form of politics in both party and pressure group arenas. These changes have affected the internal politics of local authorities in a number of particular ways which will be illustrated at various points throughout the chapter. Their overall impact has been to create a greater complexity, a larger number of points at which tension, competition and conflict can occur. The established distribution of power has come under challenge in this period of uncertainty and instability. To understand the internal politics of local authorities we need to abandon hierarchical habits of thought engendered by classical theories of organisation, habits which encourage a view that policy is made at the top of an organisation and passed down to subordinates for implementation. In reality the span of control of any one group is limited and in complex bureaucracies, which local authorities are, there are likely to be a range of cross-cutting and conflicting influences on policy processes.

In particular it is necessary to challenge the academic consensus of the late 1970s and early 1980s which held that power inside local authorities was shared by a joint élite of senior officers and councillors. Cockburn (1977, p. 6), for example, on the basis of a case study of Lambeth argues:

> What had existed as a loose assembly of council committees and a multiplicity of small departments, their work barely co-ordinated, had become a tightly-knit hierarchy under the control of a board of powerful directors (senior officers), in close partnership with a top-level caucus of majority party members.

Saunders (1979), Blowers (1980), Green (1981) and Alexander (1982b) share, in broad terms, this vision of joint élite domination. These writers give too much credence to the impact of the introduction of corporate management structures. Following reorganisation in the mid-1970s the vast majority of local authorities appointed a chief executive and established a policy committee bringing together a range of senior councillors. This committee ran alongside a management team of chief and senior officers (Greenwood *et al.*, 1975). Yet it is important not to see the introduction of these new structures as necessarily leading to different forms of decision-making (Greenwood *et al.*, 1976; Clapham, 1985b). The establishment of corporate structures provided the potential for senior councillors and officers to seize the initiative in policy-making as 'close allies' (Saunders, 1979, p. 224) or 'partners' (Cockburn, 1977, p. 6). Yet this did not always occur. Moreover, as the changes in the environment began to have an impact so other forces and tensions came into play. A different approach to the intra-organisational politics of local authorities is required to capture this new complexity.

### A framework for understanding internal politics

To understand the internal politics of local authorities it is necessary to recognise the potential for multi-sources of influence. Six arenas of influence are to be considered in this chapter:

1. The 'joint élite' of senior officers and councillors;
2. The ruling party group and party caucuses;
3. Councillors as ward representatives;
4. Inter-departmental conflicts;
5. Intra-departmental relations;
6. Inter-party deals.

The role and likely impact of each will be discussed in the light of changes in the environment in which local authorities operate.

The second element of our analysis rests on the view that in the context of the growing complexity of intra-organisational politics the distribution of power is only more or less fixed, and is subject to continual attack and defence. To understand the internal political struggle it follows that a dynamic element is required in our analysis. This is provided through a focus on the perceptions, the resources and the 'modes of action' of the various competing participants.

Few would dispute that the way that 'different "actors" perceive and make sense of the world helps to explain organizational behaviour' (Barrett and Fudge, 1981, p. 28). Analysis along these lines has developed in the identification of role orientations for officers and councillors (Newton, 1976; Bristow and Stratton, 1983; Laffin and Young, 1985; Rosenberg, 1985) and more generally in the 'assumptive worlds of governmental actors' (Young, 1977; Young and Mills, 1980). The approach developed here, however, is limited to a more 'rough and ready' concern with some of the key differences in the perceptions held by local authority personnel within the six identified arenas of conflict. Moreover, there is a danger of both the 'role' and 'assumptive world' approaches not escaping from a static frame of reference. This is why we also focus attention on the resources mobilised and modes of action adopted by competing local authority actors. In this way a dynamic analysis of the intra-organisational politics of local authorities can be developed.

The range of resources available for competing local authority actors includes position in the hierarchy, control of information and the management of contacts and networks. In terms of modes of action – strategies and tactics of influence – five broad categories can be identified. The first is *negotiation* which involves an element of give and take or bargaining. A second is *persuasion* and is used to refer to attempts to influence others by way of reason, argument and evidence. A third is *manipulation* and includes a range of covert tactics of influence. The fourth and fifth modes of action are only available to those in positions of formal authority. They are *regulation* which implies the adjusting of other proposals to suit your own preferences and *coercion* which suggests the availability of sanctions and the ability to compel certain courses of action.

In the remainder of this chapter we attempt to fill out our framework by showing that each of the six arenas of policy conflict we have identified provides a source of influence which cannot be neglected.

### The joint élite

The joint élite comprise a small group of leading councillors and officers. The composition of this leading group will vary from authority to authority but is likely to be drawn from committee chairs and vice-chairs together with chief officers and their deputies. The joint élite must be incorporated into any realistic analysis of decision-making inside local authorities. Too often, however, the literature gives the impression of a unified, cohesive group. The introduction of managerial changes, as noted earlier, has in some instances strengthened the hand of senior officers and councillors. We would reject, however, the view that these organisational innovations have ensured a new unity among the élite. Our approach suggests that relationships within the élite are, in fact, frequently characterised by tensions and conflict.

At a very basic level senior politicians are free simply to reject officers' policy proposals which they do not like (providing they have the backing of their party group). There are a number of examples of such élite division in case studies of the 1960s and 1970s. Ambrose and Colenutt (1975, pp. 109–12) describe how Brighton's senior Conservatives ignored repeated official warnings about an over-expansion of office development. Dennis (1972, p. 239) is obliged to admit that, despite the overall influence of senior planning officials in Sunderland, they could get plans adopted but could not persuade senior councillors to release the funds necessary for redevelopment.

In the current period of more assertive party politics the tendency for councillors to challenge officers has increased. As the Widdicombe (1986b, p. 125) researchers found: 'in a situation where quite clearly the political environment of local authorities is changing . . . it is almost inevitable that frictions between . . . the worlds of members and officers will be created'. In a number of areas of officer–councillor interaction the researchers discovered a rise in tension and conflict (see Chapter 6). These areas included: the processes of agenda setting for committees; the redrafting of reports; and the appointment of officers – all of which saw councillors becoming more assertive. The briefing of a chairperson prior to a committee was in many authorities more of a two-way dialogue.

> Whereas in the past chairmen saw their role, in many instances, as that of persuading the group to accept lines agreed between themselves and the chief officers, they are now more likely to act as a channel in the opposite direction, from the group to the chief officer, advising that certain recommendations will not be accepted, or that alternative options should be investigated. (p. 130)

The Widdicombe researchers also found councillors increasingly likely to expect free access to all departmental officials rather than feeling obliged to operate through a chief officer. Finally, councillors showed a tendency to challenge the chief officers' 'right to manage' his or her own department. With, for example, some Conservative-controlled authorities in search of cost-cutting 'efficiency' savings demanding to probe internal management in detail.

In short the new challenges faced by local authorities have increased the likelihood of tension within the joint élite. In a substantial number of authorities senior councillors have become more assertive in their relationships with senior officers. As the Widdicombe researchers (1986b, pp. 124–5) comment:

> The reality in many authorities until the late 1970s or early 1980s . . . was one of a group of self-confident professional officers

facing a group of leading politicians with a less clear set of
political objectives than often now pertains, and a greater
predisposition to accept the guidance of officers. Since then . . .
in many authorities, politicians of all major parties have become
clearer about their political goals and priorities and more
determined to ensure that these are implemented.

On rare occasions senior councillors have gone as far as to entirely
by-pass the officer structure. Reference here can be made to
how a few leading councillors in Walsall pushed through a
decentralisation initiative in the early 1980s. They set the timetable,
they wrote reports and they sorted out the details of implementation (Seabrook 1984, Beuret and Stoker, 1984).

Many senior officers, however, accept that times have changed
and have worked with the more assertive councillors. When
alliances are formed it is likely they will be between senior officers
and councillors involved in the same committee or policy area. It
is clear they can be a powerful influence on local authority decision-
making as evidenced by the relationship between Council Leader
and Planning Chairman T. Dan Smith and Chief Planning Officer
Wilfred Burns who together dominated Newcastle's planning
atmosphere during the 1960s (Elliott, 1975; Davies, 1972, pp.
11–118). The willingness to form a partnership will inevitably be a
reflection of particular personalities. A common basis, however,
is shared outlooks: both may be committed to certain service or
policy developments.

Yet in pursuing their shared interests these chairmen–chief
officer alliances may come across opposition from other groups
of senior councillors and officers pursuing their own priorities.
Greenwood *et al.* (1977) point out the importance of cross-cutting
tensions within the leading group. We would suggest that in most
authorities there is likely to be no *single* centre of power among
senior councillors and officers. Rather, we would argue, there are
likely to be agreed spheres of influence and when disputes arise
they are overcome through strategies of negotiation, persuasion
or even manipulation. Mixed coalitions of councillors and officers
sometimes work against each other in favour of their own particular
policy preference.

This discussion of the role of leading councillors and officers has
confirmed their significance in influencing local policy processes.

There is, however, no automatic agreement on policy issues within the élite. Sometimes senior councillors and officers regard themselves to be in competition; sometimes they form alliances; sometimes there are cross-cutting tensions within each part of the leading group.

Our analysis has emphasised the growing assertiveness of senior councillors. It is important to recognise, however, that in many smaller authorities and those dominated by independents the nature of councillor–officer relationships has not changed dramatically, with senior officers still dominant and controlling. Moreover, even in 'politicised' authorities senior officers still have an important influence. They can facilitate new policy initiatives but they can also stand in their way. Senior councillors have their formal authority and, potentially, the voting strength of their controlling party group behind them, but if senior officers want to resist they have their professional expertise, their control of information and their full-time staff as resources. A complex strategic and tactical battle can ensue in such circumstances.

## *The ruling party group and party caucuses*

Our analysis of party influence disputes the view that politics in this arena is always both effectively dominated and manipulated by leading councillors. Rather, it is suggested, there are many occasions on which important inputs into council decision-making stem from the role of the ruling party group as a whole, not just its leading councillors.

In conformity with most findings in this area Green (1981, p. 62) sees Newcastle's Labour group as 'a receiving shop, serving to legitimise decisions taken elsewhere'. Neither Jones (1969) in his study of Wolverhampton, nor Bulpitt (1967) in his investigation of some North-West parties, could find evidence of party groups undertaking a successful policy formulation role. Other authors stress how party groups are effectively managed by leading councillors. Barker (1983, p. 17) describes Bristol's Labour group as 'manipulated and controlled by the leadership'. Saunders (1979, p. 221) argues that the purpose of Croydon's Conservative majority group meetings was 'to ensure that members formally fell into line behind their leaders'. Likewise, Dearlove (1973, pp. 132–3) depicts

Conservative majority meetings in Kensington and Chelsea as dominated by leading councillors.

We challenge this 'prevailing wisdom' and argue that it is important to consider the influence on policy processes that can be exercised by ruling group back-benchers in private party caucuses. Again the increasing politicisation of local politics is a key factor. More generally party groups are difficult institutions to manage. Differences in social characteristics – age, sex, class and ethnicity – can create conflicts and tension. So too can the issue of length of service. 'If these factors in turn are aligned with ideological factionalism, then group unity may be hard to achieve' (Widdicombe, 1986b, p. 88). Chapter 2 noted an increasing polarity of political ideology and policy preference not only between but also within party groups. For Labour the key distinction was between traditional elements, and the Urban Left. For Conservative groups, the key distinction was between the 'wet' and 'dry' elements. These labels are imprecise and their use varies from area to area. Nevertheless, they are seen as meaningful and relevant by many councillors.

It is quite possible for back-benchers to actually promote policy initiatives within the party group. Davies (1979 and 1981), in a study of Wandsworth describes how a small number of newly elected back-bench councillors in the controlling Labour group played a crucial role in developing a whole range of new planning and industrial policies. They persuaded party leaders and the party group to adopt the initiatives and subsequently took an important role in the process of implementation.

Such a pro-active role is rare. The norm is for party groups to adopt a reactive role, checking and considering initiatives stemming from elsewhere. This is indicated by the tendency for groups to meet mainly in pre-council or pre-committee situations, with special group meetings to consider major policy issues a much less widespread and infrequent occurrence (Widdicombe, 1986b, p. 82).

A key role for party groups, then, may be to scrutinise and test the policy initiatives that come to it. The scrutiny role is likely to be particularly important in a group committed to implementing a detailed manifesto. Generally Labour groups are more likely to emphasise the importance of the manifesto. Some indeed ensure that the policies contained in the manifesto are formally adopted at the first council meeting following their election. Efforts are then made to ensure that manifesto policies are implemented. Fudge (1981) provides one example of new practices. However, the Widdicombe researchers (1986b, p. 92) found that outside the larger authorities manifestos were 'very cursory affairs' and even within some politicised authorities it was clear that the manifesto was not in the forefront of the minds of either councillors or officers when it came to day-to-day decision-making.

There is, however, a more general sense in which the party group exerts influence; leadership policies need to be designed in order to conform with the core political values of the ruling party group. Green (1981, p. 74), despite his general emphasis on the power of the leadership, notes how 'traditional party values provided limits' to their influence. The leadership could not afford to challenge party commitments to council housing or a 'no redundancies' policy. Likewise, Saunders (1979, pp. 221–2) recounts the demise of a committee chairman who offended Croydon's majority Conservative group by proposing to abolish grammar schools in the area.

The increased political awareness of groups has reinforced this requirement for political sensitivity. As noted earlier, committee chairs now are more likely to see their task as explaining group preferences and sticking points to senior officers rather than vice versa. More generally boss politics have declined.

> The days seem to be fast disappearing when a leader could hope to deliver the group's vote without first consulting it in any way. Leadership styles still cover a wide spectrum from the ultra-democratic to the downright authoritarian. The trend however seems clearly in the direction of more open and consultative leadership under which discussions in group become a crucial, perhaps the crucial element in final decisions (Widdicombe, 1986b, p. 90).

This tendency is most developed in the Labour and Liberal parties. Leadership remains important but rather than being a prerogative of one boss figure it is provided by the inner circle of senior group members.

The group leader, committee chairman and other senior council-lors do have a number of resources at their disposal to ensure that party groups generally accept rather than reject the proposals they are presenting. These resources include: more ready access to advice and information from officers; greater time for council work available to senior councillors; their experience and sometimes their patronage in terms of control of committee jobs and other positions. They are thereby frequently able to persuade and manipulate back-benchers. But one resource which back-benchers do have is their formal authority. It is normally they who elect the leader of the group and, if they are in a majority, the committee chairs and vice-chairs. Party group members elect the group leader in 93 per cent of all authorities and the committee chairs in 69 per cent of all authorities (Widdicombe, 1986b, Tables 4.1 and 4.2, pp. 85, 87). Moreover, in the final analysis it is their votes that are needed to get policies through council meetings. Back-benchers *are* able to adopt a regulative stance, vetoing proposals that do not match their policy preferences.

In some instances this regulative role extends to party members outside the council. All the major parties allow for the attendance of non-council members at group meetings, though the practice is most common in the case of Labour. The Widdicombe researchers (1986b) recorded the presence of non-council members in 72 per cent of all authorities (Table 4.3, p. 99); but note that in only seven per cent of all authorities were these attendees allowed to vote (Table A.62, p. 308). In a few Labour authorities joint 'electoral college' arrangements exist for the election of leadership positions within the group, combining votes from the group, the district party and, perhaps, ward parties. In Liverpool in the mid-1980s it would appear that the council's financial strategy was essentially determined by the local district Labour party and its executive committee from outside the council chamber (Widdicombe 1986e, pp. 75–7). This situation was exceptional. In general even in highly politicised authorities, although the party group may seriously consult the party outside the council, it has considerable freedom of manoeuvre.

Our approach suggests, therefore, that role of the ruling party caucus in influencing the internal policy processes at local authority level cannot be neglected. While over many issues and for much of the time the group may simply endorse decisions taken elsewhere, at the very least senior councillors and officers must be careful not to offend the core political values and commitments of back-benchers. The role of party groups in local policy-making is, with the increased intensity of party ideology and organisation, a potentially crucial area for decision-making.


*Councillors as ward representatives*

It is often asserted that councillors as ward representatives are usually uninvolved in the policy processes associated with the taking of major decisions that affect their ward. A range of case studies provide supporting evidence (Elkin, 1974; Lambert *et al.*, 1978; Muchnick, 1970). This is supplemented by a more general argument that councillors with a policy focus develop it along city-wide lines, while those who see their role in ward terms are primarily concerned with administrative casework and lack a broader perspective (Newton, 1976). It is further argued that if councillors do attempt to use their position as ward representatives to influence major policy decisions they are likely to be ineffective. The efforts of majority party councillors are undermined by pressure to 'tow the party line' (Green, 1981; Dennis, 1975; Davies, 1972); while the demands of minority party ward councillors can easily be ignored.

These arguments can initially be challenged by noting some instances of effective intervention by ward councillors. Saunders (1979, Ch. 6) describes the close relationship between middle-class amenity groups and ward councillors in Croydon, who together successfully prevented high-density housing developments in order to preserve property values and the residential exclusivity of their areas. Another study describes how two Asian Labour councillors overthrew their party's policy and blocked a demolition plan in their ward (Stoker and Brindley, 1985). A campaign led by Liberal–Alliance ward councillors in Labour-controlled Manchester provides a further example of successful ward-based action. The Liberal councillors significantly affected the planning and redevelopment of their local area (Stoker, 1985).

These examples might be seen as minor exceptions to the rule of ward councillor non-involvement. There are, however, a number of reasons for not accepting that judgement. Firstly despite the increasing significance of party it is plain that in many authorities local loyalties still matter. In one shire county, for example, the ruling Conservative leader admitted to great problems in whipping some of his members from the rural areas furthest from the county town. These members were well entrenched in their communities and saw their task as one of defending local interests regardless of party loyalties (Widdicombe, 1986b, p. 89).

Secondly it is possible to identify a significant shift in the perceptions of both Liberal and Labour councillors which has led to a new breed of councillor who is much more willing to represent his or her ward on broader policy issues. These councillors may well have a history of activism in community groups or single-issue causes. In the case of the Liberal Party they are associated with the rise of 'community politics', with its emphasis on regular contact with voters and the skilful handling of local issues (Pinkney, 1983 and 1984). With respect to the Labour Party they are associated with 'local socialism' and its desire to develop a more participatory and open form of politics (Gyford, 1985).

Thirdly, there has been a growth in initiatives aimed at deliberately re-introducing an area dimension into policy-making. Examples include the establishment of area committees and neighbourhood forums. Administrative decentralisation to local offices, another area of increased activity, has also encouraged a ward-orientated consideration of policy.

The last two developments can be seen as responses to the rise of sectionalism within society and the increased assertiveness of some members of the public, noted in Chapter 1. In short, changes in the social structure and ideological environment of local government have fed through to internal operation of local authority politics. Moreover, once established administrative decentralisation can be used by the new breed of councillors to reinforce local loyalties and the area dimension in policy-making.

The above suggests that there are grounds for expecting a greater involvement on the part of ward councillors than the existing literature allows. But do ward representatives have any worthwhile resources at their disposal in order to increase their chances of being effective?

In answering this question it is necessary to draw a distinction between the position of majority and minority party members. In the former case a further division can be made between senior and back-bench councillors. Senior majority party councillors can and in some instances do seize the opportunities afforded by the membership of the joint élite (see earlier discussion) to protect and promote the specific interests of their ward. Back-bench majority party councillors are not so well placed, but by skilful private and sometimes public lobbying they may be able to show that what they want for their ward is in line with party policy or interests and therefore worthy of support. For opposition councillors publicity and political embarrassment can provide useful resources. In addition, behind the scenes work may enable influence to be exercised, especially where the majority party has no strong or clear views on the policy issue. A further resource is the potential of alliance with area-based officials which may provide valuable arguments and information as well as a direct feed into the bureaucratic/professional influences on decision-making. Ward councillors are not entirely resourceless if they seek to influence the broader policy processes of their local authority. They also have available a wide range of tactics. The emphasis is, however, likely to be on negotiation, persuasion and manipulation. Bargains may be struck with other ward councillors so that mutual support is obtained. Gyford (1978) describes an example based on his experience as a county councillor in Essex. Persuasion may take the form of public or private lobbying, while manipulative strategies may be adopted to play down an issue or present it in such a light that the risk of opposition is reduced.

This discussion has sought to show the importance of recognising that councillors as ward representatives can have an impact on local authority policy processes. The continued significance of local loyalties, particularly in the Conservative Party, and the rise of a new breed of Labour and Liberal councillor in some authorities, together with the introduction of an organised area dimension into decision-making, have created new opportunities for influence within this arena.

## Inter-departmental conflicts

Inter-departmental competition to increase or protect staff, budgets and responsibilities is a key feature of the intra-organisational politics of local authorities. It's effects are pervasive but a number of particular instances can be identified. First when a new responsibility arises inter-departmental rivalries can influence the design of the associated organisational structures. A study of Manchester (Stoker, 1985) shows how, in an attempt to appease various departmental interests, the major responsibilities for the housing renewal programme launched in the mid-1970s were split between housing, environmental health and architects departments. This fragmentation made the management and operation of the programme more difficult and contributed to the slow progress in housing improvement. A similar case is described by Davies (1981) where inter-departmental jealousy over Wandsworth's planners winning responsibility for a new industrial policy led to further functions associated with the policy being given to other departments.

A number of studies provide instances of inter-departmental conflicts leading to substantial delays in policy implementation (Malpass, 1975; Paris and Blackaby, 1979; Stoker, 1985). Further inter-department conflicts may simply undermine agreed policies. Davies (1981) describes how Wandsworth's estates department ignored a commitment by the council to support job-creating cooperatives. Another study outlines the collapse of a phased housing redevelopment project because of inter-departmental conflicts (Lambert *et al.*, 1978, Ch. 4). While Muchnick (1970) notes how a policy commitment to providing more social facilities by Liverpool City Council was by-passed by the housing and health departments, in opposition to the planners, in order to maintain the momentum of the slum clearance programme.

These examples of open conflict reflect an underlying tension in inter-departmental relations. The momentum for the policy struggle in this arena is provided by the perception of officials in different departments that they are involved in a competition. These perceptions have at least three sources. First there is what can be termed a 'bureaucratic rivalry' associated with the desire of departmental officials to protect and extend their administrative empires, manage their own programmes and maintain their own priorities. Second there are 'professional jealousies'. These exist, for example, between the technical departments involved in land development. Planners, architects, housing managers, valuation officers and engineers all claim an involvement and there is a long history of rivalry between these professions. Each department has an 'accepted action space', an area where their role and their decisions are left largely unchallenged, but there is also a considerable amount of 'debated territory' (Underwood, 1980, Ch. 6). Finally there are 'value clashes'. A study of Manchester reveals a whole series of conflicts between the city's estates and planning departments. The former drew on a free market philosophy which emphasised financial and commercial criteria in judging development schemes. The latter, in contrast, was generally looking to override market opportunism in order to meet broader planning objectives (Stoker, 1985).

An examination of the perceptions of local authority personnel, then, reveals a number of bases for inter-departmental conflict. It can further be suggested that the continued professionalisation of local authority service areas enhances the perception of departmental differences and fuels disputes over 'debated territory' between the professions. In recent years the more established groupings such as treasurers, engineers and lawyers have been joined by newer service providers – such as planners, housing managers, social workers – and economic development officers – in claiming the rights and responsibilities of professional status.

From the mid-1970s onwards the crisis of confidence in some professions and the challenge of developing new roles and ways of working led to further tensions and conflicts. Young (1988), for example, describes the shift of many local authority planners to a more entrepreneurial approach. More generally, Stewart (1986a) identifies the development of a 'new management' of local government which challenges past practices and responds to changes in society.

An investigation of the resources at the disposal of the participants leads to a further important point, namely that in general none of them has an agreed claim to exercise a formal authority over the others. Officials from the chief executives or treasurers departments come closest to holding such a resource. But notwithstanding corporate planning and other managerial innovations it is suggested here that in most cases no department is likely to be in a position to dictate terms to the others. This is not to deny that some departments are more powerful than others. There will generally be an unequal distribution of resources such as organisational status (a reflection of size and budget) and the degree of political support that the department's policies enjoy.

Finally it is possible to make some comments on the modes of action adopted in inter-departmental disputes. The first is a strategy of avoiding conflict through the establishment of what were described earlier as 'accepted action spaces' where a department's decisions remain unchallenged. When this breaks down, given the absence of the resource of formal authority, strategies of regulation and coercion are unlikely to be adopted. In general it would appear that inter-departmental conflicts are processed through negotiation and persuasion. Davies (1981) confirms this view commenting on how inter-departmental relations are developed by way of a 'complex networking process' pursued in meeting after meeting. As one senior Leicester City Council official put it in an interview in 1985: 'people are brought round and cajoled along'. On some occasions more manipulative tactics may be used. In particular an external imperative may be brought into the discussion in the form of 'what the councillors want', or 'what central government is demanding', or protests from community groups. Manipulation arises when the external imperative has been deliberately fostered or highlighted by one of the competing departments. Thus, for example, Muchnick (1970, p. 78) in his study of Liverpool shows how the planners deliberately stimulated community protest to support their case for greater social provision in redevelopment projects, and at the same time, in order to enable the protests to appear genuine they concealed the closeness of their relationship with community groups. Similar instances are recounted in the present author's study of Manchester (Stoker, 1985).

The above has provided the beginnings of an analysis of the dynamics of inter-departmental conflicts. There is clearly a need for further research but the significance of the arena in terms of the intra-organisational politics of local authorities has been established. It has also been argued that the trends towards the continued professionalisation of local authority service providers has reinforced the importance of the inter-departmental arena. Moreover, the crisis of confidence in some professions and the challenge of developing new roles in response to changes in the environment from the mid-1970s onwards have created new tensions and conflicts.

*Intra-departmental influences*

Dunleavy (1980, p. 119) has commented on 'our complete ignorance of the intra-departmental policy process in local government'. This is an exaggerated claim but nevertheless it is the case that there has been little attention given to, and no systematic analysis of, the subject. We have identified intra-departmental politics as an important and distinctive arena of policy influence. To establish this point we aim to show that while senior officials may exercise control over some departmental outputs their span of control is limited and that there are opportunities for very real influences to stem from junior ranking officials.

Modern local authority departments often display considerable complexity and diversity. An examination of the perceptions of officers reveals the basis of several sources of conflict and competing purposes within a department. The professionalisation of a service area guarantees a certain unity of view but it is limited by a number of factors. Conflicts may exist within the profession: a reflection of generational divisions, changed patterns of education and differences of ideological perspective. This point is discussed with respect to the planning profession by Underwood (1980, Ch. 3). The effect of national policy debates within professions and the 'national local government system' when fed into departments is likely to lead to differences in emphasis and approach (Dunleavy, 1980). Junior officers may be seen as the bearers of new ideas and senior officers as defenders of tried and established methods.

Further sources of tension can stem from administrative arrangements. Different sections may develop their own loyalties and priorities. In their study of one London borough Young and Mills (1983) found within a large planning department factions – combining groups of junior and senior officers – competitively promoting employment, housing and amenity priorities. Other authors provide similar pictures of broad intra-departmental debate (Davies, 1981; Underwood, 1980). With the creation of mega-departments administrative divisions of responsibility may be overlain with inter-professional rivalries. The potential significance of these has already been discussed in the section on inter-departmental conflict.

Intra-departmental divisions may also be associated with the introduction of an area or decentralised organisational element. Area-based officers may develop a joint loyalty, not only to the local authority but also to their area and its residents. Conflict may develop between area offices and central departments or between area bases (Paris and Blackaby, 1979, pp. 152–4; Stoker, 1985).

The above suggests that senior officers seeking to control their department will need to use skilfully the resources at their disposal. Yet we would argue that the control exercised by senior officers is limited and that as a result more junior ranking officials obtain opportunities for influence. The sheer volume of departmental work limits the potential for effective regulation. Divisions may also exist among senior officers which may be exploited by more junior ranking officials (Davies, 1981). In professionalised service areas, given advances in knowledge and new developments, senior officers may lack the necessary technical base to judge policy proposals. More generally, delegation means that operational control lies in lower-ranking hands. Malpass (1975) describes how in these circumstances Newcastle's architects of junior officer rank developed, shaped and determined various redevelopment schemes in negotiation with officers of a similar rank in other departments. As a result, suggest Young and Mills (1983), junior ranking officials are likely to react faster to changes in the policy environment and are more likely than their senior counterparts to have the imagination and energy necessary to develop new approaches.

Indeed in the context of the challenging environment faced by local authorities from the mid-1970s onwards the potential for junior officials to influence decision-making has increased. New difficulties and problems demand answers and place a premium on ideas rather than hierarchy. Senior councillors will accept or even encourage the stimulation of potential solutions from a wide range of sources, including the ranks of more junior officials. As noted earlier, councillors are now much more likely to expect access to the full range of departmental officials.

All this suggests that more junior officials are far from resourceless in intra-departmental politics. In the case of area-based officers additional potential resources are contacts with ward councillors (Young and Mills, 1983, p. 110; Underwood, 1980), and more generally relations with a range of community groups and outside interests. These can provide not only a valuable source of information but also can be used to raise issues in the wider political environment. A study of Manchester (Stoker, 1985) shows how junior planning and area-based housing officers, using a combination of the resources identified above, blocked unwanted developments, modified plans and created new policy initiatives in the period stretching from 1973 to 1983.

The strategies of junior officials rely on persuasion, negotiation and manipulation. The first two are made viable by the limits on the control exercised by senior officers outlined above. As for manipulation, in addition to priming ward councillors or community groups to raise issues junior officials may 'leak' information to the media. This, however, is a high-risk approach and less legitimate than the 'briefing' and 'placing of stories' that are on occasion practised by more senior councillors and officers. Beuret and Stoker (1984) provide one example of this latter activity when they describe an attempt that was made to improve the media image of Walsall's decentralised housing service.

The fiction that all proposals originate from the chief officer is 'religiously maintained' in many local authorities (Dunleavy 1980, p. 119). We have sought to show how, in contrast, a broader range of officials are involved including those of more junior rank. A number of case studies have been cited as supporting our argument. More generally it has been suggested that there are several bases of conflict within departments which give rise to a competition to influence policy processes. This competition may in many cases be controlled by senior officials if they muster their considerable resources, not least their formal authority, and pursue successful strategies. But the influence of more junior ranking officials cannot be discounted. The sheer volume of departmental work, the range of technical inputs, and the fact that operational control is often in their hands gives these junior officials opportunities to exercise influence. They can manipulate information, establish networks of support inside and outside the local authority and strike deals with others in order to promote their policy preferences. Moreover, given their position in the decision-making structure they are particularly well placed to react to changes in the environment and promote policy initiatives in response. Above all the turbulent environment faced by local authorities from mid-1970s onward has in many instances placed a premium on ideas rather than hierarchy. In these circumstances if junior officials offer 'solutions' they are more likely to be listened to by senior councillors and others.

*Inter-party deals*

The growing phenomenon of authorities subject to no overall party control makes it important to include inter-party deals as part of our approach. In 1985, as noted in Chapter 2, no one party had an overall majority in 18 per cent of all authorities. The rise of the Alliance and increased electoral volatility have made the major contributions to the spate of 'hung' or 'balanced' authorities. Inter-party deals are generally marginal to the decision-making processes of authorities where one party has a majority but in hung authorities they are often crucial.

Leach and Stewart (1986) in their study of the hung county councils – which following elections in 1985 numbered 25 out of 47 in England and Wales – identify three basic types of hung authority. First there are counties where partisanship is low and there is a strong tradition of independent councillors. In such authorities – Cornwall, Dyfed and Clwyd, for example – loose coalitions of Conservative or Alliance groups, together with a substantial block of independents, govern. In the second category of 'nominally' hung counties the Conservatives are the largest party and normally with the support of independent councillors can act as if they were a majority party. Examples include: North Yorkshire, Hampshire, Northamptonshire and East Sussex. The third and largest category is those county councils which are 'effectively' hung. In these authorities no single party can gain control even with the support of independents. The 'effectively' hung county councils included in 1985: Avon, Cheshire, Hertfordshire, Humberside, Lancashire, Somerset and Wiltshire.

It is in the 'effectively' hung authorities that the greatest amount of inter-party dealing is likely to occur. The degree of cooperation is likely to be affected by the strength of the party groups. According to Leach and Stewart (1986, p. 8) if the parties have roughly the same number of seats they 'are more likely to accept the reality of a hung county and try to make it work'. If, on the other hand, a third party holds the balance of power between two larger party blocks then there is less of a willingness 'to accept the realities of the situation'. Such authorities are more vulnerable to change through by-election results. Moreover, the influence of smallest party may be resented, causing tension and uncertainty.

Blower's (1977; see also 1987) experience in Bedfordshire bears this out. He notes that:

> . . . there were numerous instances of policies approved by committees being rejected by council or of conflicting recommendations by programme committees and the Policy and Resources Committee which reflected political balances (p. 309).

In the overwhelming majority of cases parties have refused any form of formal alliance. The prime reasons for this is a desire not to be held responsible for the policies of other parties. The closest arrangement to power sharing is in Oxfordshire and Bedfordshire where committee chairmanships were rotated on a meeting-by-meeting basis (Leach and Stewart, 1986).

The norm is for one party to form a minority administration. In the case of the county councils post-1985 this meant five Alliance-led, six Labour-led and five Conservative-led regimes. The minority party relies on the tacit support or acquiescence of usually one other party. When it comes to taking control the process can appear to be relatively smooth. In the case of Alliance-led Somerset, Wiltshire and Gloucestershire county councils Carter (1986, p. 13) notes:

> Control was not really negotiated in any of the counties. To generalise; the Alliance reaffirmed their commitment to increase expenditure, conceded to the Labour demand for one of the three seats on the ACC (Association of County Councils), and consented to various procedural reforms. Reassured by this, Labour willingly gave its support to Alliance nominations to Chairs.

In terms of the detailed development of policy within these minority administrations informal negotiation between the parties can be highly influential. In some authorities there are regular meetings between party leaders (Carter, 1986, p. 16). In others, specific items such as the creation of a special unit are the object of bargains. Mellors (1984, p. 285) notes as an example the audit and efficiency units established in a number of hung authorities as a result of Liberal pressure. Bargaining over the budget has often involved extensive informal negotiation and in some instances considerable brinkmanship. Leach and Stewart (1986) note that in Berkshire in 1982, the budget meeting lasted over 24 hours, with five adjournments!

With respect to those authorities where Labour or Alliance groups have formed administrations following long periods of Conservative control, senior officers are likely to notice a greater assertiveness, a willingness to probe and challenge officer advice (Carter, 1986). The atmosphere can become highly charged, especially if the officers are suspected of retaining a loyalty to the former Tory masters. In this respect a document produced by Cheshire in 1983 (known as 'the Cheshire Convention') is relevant. It sets out guidelines for officers and members in hung authorities dealing with such issues as access to information and officers, the handling of media statements, and so on. Similar conventions have been introduced in Essex, Hertfordshire, Warwickshire and Lancashire (Leach and Stewart, 1986, p. 9).

The rise of the Alliance and greater electoral volatility have created the conditions for increased numbers of hung councils. Inter-party deals can be a crucial element in decision-making within such authorities. This is an area of intra-organisational politics which will undoubtedly in the future attract considerable research interest.

**Conclusions**

This chapter has argued for a new approach to the study of the intra-organisational politics of local authorities. It has been possible to show how each of the six arenas of influence we identified can have an impact on a local authority's policy processes. In addition it has been possible to develop an initial analysis of core components of the dynamic struggle for influence which occurs in each arena. Defenders of the 'joint élite' model might be tempted to claim that key decisions remain in the hands of a small group of senior councillors and officers. Leaving aside the thorny issue of how to define 'key decisions' we feel that this chapter has assembled sufficient examples of influences on local policy processes stemming from outside the joint élite to support our argument that we need to broaden our horizons to develop a comprehensive understanding of intra-organisational politics.

The case for developing a broader approach is further supported if recognition is given to the impact of changes in the environment faced by local authorities from the mid-1970s onwards. In responding to these changes officers and councillors have challenged established patterns within local authority decision-making. In a more politicised environment senior councillors have become more assertive within the joint élite and the importance of majority party group caucuses has been enhanced. The rise of sectionalism within society has been met by councillors willing to take on and develop their role as ward representatives rather than simply remain on the sidelines. The crisis of confidence in some professions and the development of new roles and ways of working have led to increased tension in inter-departmental relations. The challenge of finding solutions in difficult circumstances has placed a new premium on ideas rather than hierarchy, giving junior officials new opportunities for influence. Increased electoral volatility and the rise of the Alliance parties has brought the role of inter-party deals into play.

Other developments, which have not been considered in any detail, have also added to the complexity of intra-organisational politics. These include the practice of co-opting non-elected representatives onto council committees, the appointment of politically sympathetic officers, the involvement of trade union representatives in decision-making and the role of information technology.

Of course the pace and extent of these changes varies from authority to authority. In some authorities, especially the smaller authorities in rural areas, senior officers still dominate the process of decision-making. Yet in larger authorities and those seeking to develop new ways of working intra-organisational politics is complex and influenced by a range of cross-cutting interests. Indeed this complexity provides an important explanation for the delays and frustrations faced by left-wing Labour councils in their efforts to establish new styles of working with respect to economic policy, women's issues, racial disadvantage and neighbourhood service delivery, or right-wing Conservative councils pursuing privatisation and 'value for money' audits.

# 5   Local Interest Group Politics

This chapter deals with the relationship between local authorities and local interest groups. It opens with a categorisation of local groups by their producer, cause community or voluntary sector focus. There follows an examination of a debate between pluralist and élitist positions which has dominated much analysis in this field. There are valuable lessons to be learnt from this debate but it is argued that it fails to capture the complexity of current patterns of local authority – interest group relations. The next two sections of the chapter examine how many local authorities have 'opened out', creating new, if limited, opportunities for participation from a wider range of groups. Attention is also focussed on an increased assertiveness, a spread of resources and a greater willingness by a number of groups to become involved in service provision. The implications of these developments for the diverse patterns of interest group politics in a range of localities are examined in the final main section of the chapter.

**The world of local groups**

According to Hampton (1987, pp. 129–30): 'the view is often expressed that if two Britons were marooned on a desert island the first thing they would do would be to form a club; and the second thing would be to elect a committee!' Evidence clearly suggests that a substantial active base of local groups exists in many areas. In his study of Birmingham, Newton (1976, p. 38, Table 3.2) identified some 4264 local organisations. There were over 2000 sports organisations, almost 700 social welfare groups

106

and 388 cultural clubs. The remaining organisations included trade associations, professional groups, social clubs, churches, youth clubs, trade unions and groups concerned with educational, health or technical and scientific issues. As Newton (1976, p. 36) notes this list was collected by a postal survey and as a consequence it included 'most of the best-organised, most visible, and permanent organisations, while probably under-representing the more un-stable, less organised, and more ephemeral groups'. A more recent study reveals a similar staggering range and complexity of clubs and associations even within small district councils (Bishop and Hoggett, 1986). In Kingwood, a local authority with a population of 78 000 in Avon County, the authors found that over a thousand individuals were actively engaged on local committees of one form or another. This level of activity challenges the presumption that only local government officers or politicians have experience of administration and organisation. Most local authorities operate in the context of a world of active local groups.

Many such groups will be concerned primarily with providing services, opportunities and contacts for their members or clients, or with simply pursuing their own activities. Our concern is not with this side of their operations but with their role in making demands on local authority policy and resources. The relationship between local authorities and local groups is our focus of attention.

To facilitate a discussion of this relationship we propose to draw a distinction between four types of interest group. The first category is producer or economic groups. It includes businesses, trade unions and professional associations. Organisations representing business interests range from individual firms or companies through to umbrella organisations, such as those relating to particular trades or articulating business concerns in a more general way. The most prominent of the general umbrella organis-ations are Chambers of Trade, Chambers of Commerce and Industry, Employers Federations, Country Landowner Associ-ations, the National Farmers Union and local branches of the Confederation of British Industry. Producer groups also include the trade unions and the umbrella organisation provided by local trades councils. Professional associations such as local branches of the National Societies of Architects, Chartered Accountants, Surveyors, Secretaries and Administrators also fall into this cat-egory.

The second category is community groups which draw on a distinct social base for their support. The main thrust of their activity is towards influencing decision-making and local state policy-making. Examples include amenity groups, tenants' associations, squatters' associations, ratepayers' associations, redevelopment action groups, hospital defence committees, women's groups and groups representing ethnic minorities. These organisations draw on particular social bases either in the form of residential communities or communities of interest. The latter category includes a range of groups with a shared problem and in particular this may relate to their shared access to a publicly or privately consumed service. In some instances more than one element is involved. Thus a tenants' association on a large council estate represents both a defined geographical area and a particular set of public service consumers. As Lowe (1986) notes there has been an increased level of activity from such groups at the local level as people have come together to defend or challenge the provision of public services and to protect their residential community.

A third type of interest group increasingly active at the local level is the 'cause' group, concerned to promote a particular set of ideas and beliefs rather than their immediate material interests. Examples include local branches of the Campaign for Nuclear Disarmament, anti-apartheid movements and solidarity campaigns with countries in Latin America and elsewhere in the world. They may ask the local authority to declare a nuclear-free zone, avoid using South African goods or twin with a town in Nicaragua as a gesture of commitment to the struggle for freedom by the people of that country. Groups campaigning against cruel sports may demand that local authorities in rural areas prevent fox hunting across their land. Cause groups have become increasingly active in the world of local politics.

A fourth category is the voluntary sector. Organisations in this category are established to meet a perceived need in the community on a non-commercial, non-statutory basis. The voluntary sector has enjoyed a considerable growth over the last decade in both numbers of volunteers and the scope of voluntary sector activity. Financial support from local authorities and other public sector sources has increased substantially. A distinction can be drawn between development agencies and those concerned more directly with service provision (Wolfenden, 1978). The former includes a range of voluntary agencies who act as umbrella organisations and seek to represent the voluntary sector and develop voluntary action within their local areas. Examples are the Councils for Voluntary Service (CVS), Rural Community Councils, Volunteer Bureaux, and Community Relations Councils. There are, for example, about 230 CVSs in England (CVS, 1983). Among the more direct service providers are a number of 'formal' voluntary agencies such as Barnardos, Age Concern, the local Churches, MENCAP and MIND which may employ full-time staff as well as drawing on volunteer effort. Their rationale is the provision of services to individual members of the community who are disadvantaged in some way through their personal circumstances, whether they be elderly, mentally ill or physically disabled. At the other end of the spectrum are thousands of more informal organisations which rely entirely on voluntary effort.

A 'striking development in the voluntary sector over the past 10 years has been the growing number and type of self-help organisations particularly in urban areas' (NCVO, 1985, p. 9). Self-help has been in evidence in rural areas in the past but has succeeded in establishing itself in many towns and cities in recent years. The major difference between these kinds of organisations and the direct service providers identified above is that instead of other people providing services to disadvantaged groups, those same groups are trying to help themselves and others like them. The urban self-help organisations also draw on a radical philosophy rather than the more traditional view of people taking individual responsibility for pulling themselves up 'by their own boot straps'. The rationale for this radical approach, according to the National Council for Voluntary Organisations, lies in the analysis of disadvantage put forward.

> Instead of disadvantage being seen as the product of individual misfortune, it is analysed as being the fault of political, economic or social circumstances. . . . Given this analysis the problems experienced by these sections of the community will never be wholly overcome through the provision of services by the same society or authority that is often responsible for the discrimination in the first place. The problem will only be overcome by, for example, black ethnic minorities forming their own organisations to provide relevant services for themselves

and to try and bring about change in society as a whole. (pp. 9–10)

This kind of approach is becoming increasingly prevalent in the voluntary sector. It is being developed by among others disabled people, working-class communities, women and ethnic minorities. It has also encouraged the more traditional formal voluntary organisations to recognise the need 'to change society's attitudes to their clients as well as continuing to provide their much needed services' (p. 10).

Thus lobbying and campaigning for a particular interest forms part of the activity of many groups in the voluntary sector, whether they are development agencies, direct service providers or self-help organisations. At the self-help end of the spectrum where groups of disadvantaged people combine campaigning activity with self-help, the voluntary sector plainly overlaps with the community group category identified above.

This suggests the dividing line between producer, community, cause and voluntary sector groups is not always clear-cut. Moreover there are plainly differences between the groups within any one category. Finally no particular claims are made for the comprehensiveness of this categorisation. There will be local groups that slip through the conceptual net provided. Some crude categorisation is, however, essential to enable us to begin to make sense of the complex world of local groups. The distinction between producer, community, cause and voluntary groups will prove its value in the discussion of the relationship between local authorities and local groups.

### Local interest groups: a pluralist/élitist debate

Much debate over local interest groups can be related to competing 'pluralist' and 'élitist' interpretations of group politics. Debate is perhaps an inappropriate term since the argument has overwhelmingly developed as a critique of a rather simplistic pluralist model. Pluralist theory is premised on the idea that interest groups help to articulate the specific interests of particular sections of society, and thus enhance local democracy. The pluralist 'straw man' is set up in the following terms by Dearlove (1979, p. 46). It is viewed as resting on: 'the idea that the interest group world is one of reasonably perfect competition, where the rules of the game ensure fair play and the equal access of all to the favourable decision of those in government'.

As we shall see a queue of writers, led by Dearlove, have sought to challenge this model. In its place they have offered an élitist picture, in which power is seen as concentrated in the hands of a few.

The élitist critique suggests that local authorities are enclosed organisations 'unresponsive, oligarchic and inward-looking' with 'influences from the mass of citizens . . . wholly or partly screened out of local policy-making' (Dunleavy, 1980, p. 150). Only a select range of external interests are drawn into decision-making and it is producer interests which are most likely to achieve this privileged access. This interpretation has unfolded in three waves each of which will be examined below.

*The initial challenge*

The first wave developed as an empirical challenge to simplistic pluralist interpretations. Researchers discovered that the main tenets of 'straw man' pluralism were contradicted by the reality of group influence in local politics. Dearlove (1973) in his study of Kensington and Chelsea found a local authority that was actively resisting, obstructing and excluding certain groups from decision-making. He argued that a local authority's response to groups would revolve around councillor assessment of the group's demands and communication style. The Conservative ruling group in Kensington and Chelsea had a clear picture of those groups they regarded sympathetically and those which they distrusted. Their support was given to groups that made acceptable demands in a proper manner and helped the authority achieve its own objectives. Unhelpful groups which made unacceptable demands were excluded from decision-making or over a period of time manipulated into changing their position so that they became more in tune with local authority wishes and concerns. Unhelpful groups face a 'catch-22' dilemma: either they modify their views to gain access to decision-makers or they preserve their principles but are ignored (Saunders, 1980, p. 131; Newton, 1976, pp. 86–7; Darke and Walker, 1977, p. 80). Saunders' (1980) study of Croydon, Dunleavy's (1977) study of Newham, Cousins' (1973, 1976) study of South London and Newton's (1976) study of Birmingham confirmed Dearlove's general findings.

Newton, in particular, extends the analysis in a number of ways. First he suggests that officers make similar distinctions between helpful and unhelpful groups. Second he argues that the resources available to interest groups to promote their concerns are distributed with cumulative inequality. Key resources include income, full-time staff, organisational and technical skills and an established position. The best placed organisations have access to all these resources. Newton (1976, pp. 76–9) found in his study of Birmingham that producer groups are most likely to be in this position with business and professional organisations leading the way in numbers and resources with trade unions taking second place. In contrast the City's ethnic minorities, for example, were under-represented and resourced. Finally Newton (pp. 83–5) argues that there is a lack of depth and diversity in Birmingham's local group world in terms of those groups that 'are willing and able to engage in political activity'. Thus, although there may be a diversity of social interests, those that mobilise politically are drawn from a much narrower range and may constitute a relatively 'small stage army'.

Overall these studies paint a picture of cumulative inequalities in the resources available to groups and the non-mobilisation of a substantial range of interests. The local authority is viewed as controlling and manipulating the local political environment. Interest groups are brought in on a very selective basis and only when they are in tune with a local authority's concerns and attitudes.

*Informal networks*

A second wave in the élitist interpretation builds on this platform. It focusses on informal networks of influence within localities. Dunleavy (1980, pp. 151–6) argues that such informal and social contacts develop between local political parties and certain external interests. In some instances it will even extend to directly corrupt relationships where rewards are provided in exchange for favours.

The informal network can also be observed in the 'burgher community' of councillors, some party activists and other local notables who meet together on the Magistrates Bench, the Rotary Club, school governing bodies and the management committees of various quasi-governmental agencies, such as the local health authorities.

The result of these informal influences is that some groups come to occupy an insider position in which their interests are built into the heart of the local authority. These groups become so well integrated that they hardly need to act because local authority councillors and officers share their values and perspectives. Saunders (1980, p. 235) describes this as a state of 'political communion'.

The process is given a certain legitimacy by the local character of these informal networks. In Conservative suburban Croydon the insider groups in political communion with the local authority are the local business interests and middle-class residents' groups. Sustained informal contacts, shared values and perspectives and a sense of common purpose underpin this communion (Saunders, 1980, Chs. 6 and 8). In Conservative rural Suffolk major farmers and landowners are strategically represented at all levels of local government. Agricultural interests and the public interest are viewed as synonymous. Informal contacts are maintained by 'playing golf, shooting pheasants or drinking gin and tonic with those in positions of power and eminence' (Newby *et al.*, 1978, p. 269). In urban and Labour Sheffield Hampton (1970) stresses the special relationship between the trade union movement and the ruling Labour group which found expression in the influence of the Trades and Labour Council on the local council's decision-making. The teachers' lobby was also influential and well-organised through trade union and professional associations.

What these studies suggest is that in particular localities there are narrowly defined sets of insider interests. The local authority reflects the dominant forces in the locality. These forces are generally producer interests: businessmen, landowners, farmers, trade unionists or professional teachers. Their influence is achieved by their informal contacts and the perceptions they share with leading councillors and officers. These informal networks screen out influences from the wider political environment and the general public.

*Local corporatism*

A third wave in the dominant interpretation argues that the privileged informal access of producer groups is increasingly being reinforced by the development of formal corporatist mechanisms. From the mid-1970s onwards a number of writers have identified the rise of local corporatism and point to the establishment of a range of local authority–producer group consultative forums, working parties and jointly managed projects, (see Chs. 5–8 in Grant, 1985). Producer interests are offered exclusive access to local authority decision-makers and the opportunity to influence policy in return for their cooperation in implementing policies. The result is 'additional privileges for already privileged groups in society' (Grant, 1985, p. 18).

The Thatcher Governments have forced some of this consultation onto local authorities. Since 1981 it has been a pre-requisite of inner city programme approval that local authorities should have consulted the private sector. The 1984 Rates Act imposed on councils a duty to consult non-domestic ratepayers.

On the other hand as local authorities have shown a greater interest in economic development, so too have some seen it as relevant to work through local Chambers of Commerce and other business organisations to ensure the effective implementation of policy. King (1983, 1985) describes cooperation in this field between Leeds Chamber of Commerce and Industry and its relevant local authorities. Grant (1983) found evidence of local authority–local Chamber of Commerce collaboration in Birmingham and Norwich. In the case of Norwich this extended to discussing all major land-use planning applications with chamber officials. Simmie (1981, 1985) suggests that the land-use planning is generally dominated by corporatist forms of interest representation. He argues that 'there has been a long-term drift towards corporatism in physical planning in Britain' (1985, p. 200). More generally Saunders (1985a, p. 172) suggests that local corporatism will grow in policy areas where pressure exists from producer interests such as landowners, developers, and commercial and industrial firms for relatively exclusive access to the responsible state agencies.

There are grounds for being sceptical about the strength and the extent of the development of local corporatism. Even one of its initial harbingers now seems more uncertain about its growth (Cawson, 1985). King, Grant and Simmie may have found evidence for corporatism in their case studies but others have searched for it in vain, in the areas of land-use planning (Flynn, 1983; Smith, 1983) and economic policy-making (O'Mahony, 1984). The Widdicombe researchers (1986b, p. 147) question the effectiveness of the statutory consultation with business interests established by the Thatcher Governments. In some instances the atmosphere is one of hostility, in others local government officers have found themselves explaining the complexities of local government finance to confused businessmen. Some councils have used the procedure as a public relations exercise and in some cases have extended the consultation over rates to tenants' groups, trade unions and community groups.

The élitist interpretation emphasises that there are cumulative inequalities in the resources available to groups, that relatively few interest groups are capable of effectively engaging in political activity and that local authorities are generally insulated from their local political environment. Local authorities are characterised as oligarchic, inward-looking institutions which grant privileged access to a restricted number of groups usually drawn from the producer category. This privileged access is seen as stemming firstly from the preferences of councillors and officers; secondly from the informal networks of influence which develop in particular localities, and thirdly from the growth of corporatist arrangements in the local political arena.

The remainder of this chapter challenges this interpretation. This is not to suggest a return to a simplistic pluralist mode of explanation. It is to argue that élitist interpretations do not match the complexity of current relationships between local authorities and local interest groups. The principal claim is that times have changed. The evidence for the first two waves of the dominant élitist interpretation relates to the experience of local politics before the mid-1970s. The case studies cited were undertaken more than a decade ago. With respect to the third wave, which deals with the development of local corporatism from the mid-1970s onwards, the argument is that it over-emphasises a relatively weak trend and overlooks a number of important counter trends.

The first step in developing this challenge is to show how at least from mid-1970s onwards many local authorities have created new opportunities for interaction with a wider range of groups including community, cause and voluntary organisations. A second step is to recognise an increased assertiveness, a spread of resources and a greater willingness to become involved in service delivery on the part of a wider range of groups. These two arguments occupy the next two sections of the chapter.

### The opening-out of local authorities

Several aspects of the opening-out of the organisational structures of local authorities have already been noted. Chapter 2 noted the influence exercised in some areas by parish and community councils. In Chapter 3 the involvement of local people in the management of leisure, housing and other projects was considered as one element in the growth of non-directly elected local government. In Chapter 4 the discussion of the role of ward representatives identified a number of other developments. The first was a shift in the attitudes of councillors, particularly within the Liberal and Labour parties, and their increased concern to develop a ward orientation. There are signs that this has led to a more active partnership between council members and local organisations. The second change is the introduction of an organised area dimension into local authorities decision-making structures. This has included the establishment of new political arenas in terms of area committees and neighbourhood forums as well as administrative decentralisation of service delivery to local or neighbourhood offices. The introduction of an area dimension in many cases has created new opportunities for public participation.

In addition to these developments there are other forces which have contributed to the opening-out of local authorities. These again can be divided into changing attitudes and new practices.

Parallelling the shift on the part of councillors it is possible to identify the growth of a 'community orientation' among some officers. Since the 1970s there has been concern expressed among land-use planners about involving non-joiners and disadvantaged groups. These attitudes have become widespread among planners, especially those in larger cities (Underwood, 1980) and have a limited but established base within the profession (Ravetz, 1980, pp. 207–11; Hague, 1985). A similar 'progressive' and 'community orientation' has developed among sections of the architectural, housing, social work, educational and community development professions. On the other hand, there is little evidence of a similar shift in attitudes among engineers and estates and valuation officers. In short, this shift of attitudes among officers has been patchy.

It is important not to view these developments as a fashion of the 1970s which has died away. The shift in attitudes may be limited but it is established within substantial sections of the local authority officer structure. Moreover, a second wave has begun to form during the 1980s with the advent of the 'public service orientation' debate within local government circles. This debate launched by Professor John Stewart and actively promoted by the Local Government Training Board calls on local authority managers to recognise that 'the activities of a local authority are not carried out for their own sake, but to provide service for the public' (Clarke and Stewart, 1985, p. 2; Clarke and Stewart, 1987). The public service orientation challenges the enclosed organisation of local authorities and argues for greater responsiveness to the public as customers and as citizens. It requires local authorities to look at their services from the viewpoint of the public rather than simply from the standpoint of the organisation. It also recognises an important role for the citizen as a participant in policy-making. This shift in management thinking is helping to encourage local authorities to open out. In some instances, however, the changes are cosmetic and in others they are very limited.

There have also been a number of developments in practice. Many local authorities now publish a regular newsletter and some have sophisticated information services. Labour-controlled Manchester City Council from 1986 has distributed to every household a detailed A–Z guide to its services and has established an information centre to provide a friendly, welcoming place for everybody coming to the Town Hall. The centre can provide answers to many questions, and where that is not possible its task is to guide people to the appropriate department. The Conservative-controlled London Borough of Westminster has a similar service.

Many authorities have displayed a commitment to open government which often pre-dated, and in practice goes beyond, the provisions of the 1985 Local Government Information Act.

Committees and sub-committees are open to the public. In Harlow this provision even extends to party group meetings! Efforts are made to ensure that papers and documents are relatively easily available. Manchester has a council bookshop which provides copies of all committee and sub-committee agendas. People wanting further information on reports written for committees are generally able to obtain what they need through bookshop staff.

Developments in practice, however, go beyond information-giving and the provision of access to local authority policy debates. Alongside the introduction of new organisational forms at the area neighbourhood level there has been a growth in consultation with outside interests. Local authorities have reached out not only to neighbourhoods but also to various communities of interest.

This point is recognised by Gyford in his research for the Widdicombe Committee (1986e, pp. 121–2):

> Increasingly . . . local authorities find themselves engaged in responding to the claims of a much wider variety of sectional interests . . . the trend seems to flow clearly in the direction of according recognition to sectional interests as can be seen by examining the range of consultations with such interests now being undertaken in various fields.

Among the areas noted by Gyford are social services, education, town planning, leisure and the arts, and housing. A survey by Smith (1985) of the practice of 88 local authorities provides empirical confirmation of the growth of public involvement. Local authorities have used public meetings, leaflets and opinion surveys to consult with interest groups. They have established consultative committees and co-opted people on to council committees or sub-committees. Some authorities especially the London boroughs and metropolitan districts co-opt quite widely. Other authorities, notably Conservative or independent-controlled shire districts co-opt few if any outsiders (Widdicombe, 1986b, p. 148).

Particular attention can be drawn to the growth of consultative mechanisms with ethnic minorities, women's groups and the voluntary sector. Gyford argues that for ethnic minorities 'the urban riots of 1981 had something of a catalytic effect upon both thinking and practice in this field' (Widdicombe, 1986e, p. 123). He identifies two particular types of consultative arrangement which have developed subsequently in some areas. They entail the setting up of race relations committees (and/or sub-committees and working groups) and the co-option of ethnic minority representatives onto council committees and/or sub-committees, etc. By 1985 there were over twenty race relations committees established. Some two dozen local authorities had established some form of committee dealing with women's issues by 1985. Such committees aim to put women's issues onto the local political agenda. In most cases race relations or women's committees have some form of officer support or policy unit to assist them in their work and to help ensure the effective implementation of policy. Thus, the concerns of these sectional interests have been built into the organisational structure of many local authorities.

The voluntary sector in many areas has also gained from consultative mechanisms. Inner city programmes and policies from the mid-1970s onwards have provided a stimulus to such developments (Williams, 1981). Johnson (1981, p. 117) argues 'that the advent of social services departments in 1971 engendered a more positive interest in voluntary services'. This is borne out by the appointment of full-time liaison officers with a special responsibility for working with volunteers and voluntary groups. In some authorities elaborate consultative machinery has also been established at a political level. Thus, for example, in Leicestershire a Voluntary Sector Liaison Committee meets twice yearly, and brings together the top members and officers of policy and resources, social services, and education and libraries committees and eleven voluntary sector representatives nominated by a county-wide forum of voluntary organisations (CVS, 1983, para. 34).

Cause groups have been provided with new opportunities by the tendency for local authorities to view their role as more than service delivery. Many local authorities have shown a willingness to extend the span of issues with which they concern themselves. This development is particular marked in those councils influenced by the 'Urban Left'. Councillors have used local government as a platform to present issues such as nuclear disarmament, nuclear power, third world development, animal rights and the conflict in Northern Ireland. In doing so they have worked with and alongside cause groups interested in these issues. The concern not to confine local political debate to questions of service delivery, however, extends beyond the Urban Left. Councils of various political outlooks have taken on issues such as crime prevention, poverty, A.I.D.S., food, ill-health and dietary change and have linked into a network of associated cause groups as a result.

It is important not to exaggerate the extent of the change that has occurred. Some local authorities have remained enclosed organisations. Nevertheless the trend has been towards 'a more overt commitment to the principle of consultation in local government' (Widdicombe, 1986b, p. 146). The practice of public participation, however, has been fraught with difficulties. As Boaden (1982, p. 179) and his co-authors indicate: 'though there have been great moves towards public involvement in local service provision in recent years . . . it has failed to achieve all that its proponents wished'. The ambiguities and conflicts associated with the trend are discussed further in Chapter 9 which focuses on the activities of those Labour authorities which have been the vanguard. Notwithstanding the difficulties a significant change has occurred. As Smith (1985, p. 23) argues: 'however badly some of them are being implemented, the range of new approaches currently being tried in local government represents something much more substantial than mere trendiness'. Many local authorities have opened out, providing access not only to producer groups but a wider range of community, cause and voluntary sector organisations.

### The strengthening of local interest group politics

Matching the opening-out of local authorities there has been a strengthening and a widening of the base of local interest group activity. Three elements in this process are singled out for attention below. First the increased assertiveness and diversity of political activity is recognised. Second it is argued that there is an increased availability of resources to support this activity. Finally it is suggested that there is an increased willingness on the part of interest groups and local authorities to share responsibility for service delivery.

Gyford identifies the general shift towards assertiveness and diversity among local groups.

The increasing need for local politicians to operate in a more open and responsive fashion can be seen as a direct reflection of social trends which are leading away from a rather quiescent and largely homogeneous mass society towards one that is both more assertive and more diversified. (Widdicombe, 1986e, p. 109)

From mid-1960s onwards a fundamental shift in British political culture occurred with traditional respect for and deference to public bodies and authorities being challenged by more questioning, sceptical and assertive attitudes. As Boaden *et al.* (1982, preface) comment: 'People are less willing than they were to accept authoritarian styles of leadership. Action groups and public protest have become a regular feature of policy development'. Within particular authorities the sea-change occurred at different times. In Manchester a series of strongly organised and vocal protests against its house clearance programme from the late 1960s onwards contributed not only to the end of that programme but opened the floodgates for a wider range of interest group activity. Lowe (1986, p. 4), drawing on the writings of Castells (1977 and 1978) among others, suggests that 'what happened in Britain was but a small part of a much wider post-war escalation of urban protest throughout the world, with an intensification in the 1960s and 1970s'.

Accompanying the increased assertiveness has been an increased diversity in the range of interest groups that have mobilised. There has been 'a proliferation of pressure groups at both local and national level, devoted to the achievement of quite particularised goals in such areas as pollution and the environment, sexual behaviour, media policy, animal welfare, homelessness, transport policy, energy policy and disarmament and defence' (Widdicombe, 1986e, p. 109). One leader of a London borough, faced by a complex range of interest groups seeking to influence council policy, commented ruefully to the Widdicombe researchers about 'pressure groups coming out of our ears' (Widdicombe, 1986b, p. 146).

In particular in contrast to the finding of Newton (1976), noted earlier, about the non-mobilisation of ethnic minorities in his study of Birmingham's politics, Ben-Tovim *et al.* (1986) emphasise the rise of ethnic minority organisation and mobilisation at the local level. Local politics has 'provided important sites of struggle particularly for local organisations committed to racial equality' (p. 169)

A second factor which has contributed to the strengthening of local interest group politics is the increased availability of resources to support its growth. Indeed, there has been a rise of a new 'professional' occupation – community work – whose rationale rests on its capacity for:

> . . . helping to relate the activities of service agencies more closely to the needs of the people they serve . . . and facilitating citizen participation to give 'life to social democracy'. (The Gulbenkian Foundation, quoted in Lees and Mayo, 1984, p. 3)

There are a range of activities undertaken by community workers. Some are employed by local authorities and others by various non-statutory agencies. The 'profession' grew rapidly and has an established position in both urban and to a lesser extent rural locations (Specht, 1975; Thomas, 1983). By the mid-1980s there were over 5000 community workers.

Some community workers are solely concerned with stimulating self-help and support amongst sections of society but for many an important aspect of their job is to stimulate the participation of disadvantaged groups in the policy process and to ensure that they have a greater say over the decisions that affect their lives. In particular it would seem that 'much community work involves helping groups influence local councils' (Smith, 1981, p. 1).

Some writers have suggested that community workers have acted as agents of social control (Corkey and Craig, 1978). Yet the evidence overwhelmingly suggests that on the contrary community work has proved an important stimulant to working-class community action, enabling fatalism to be overcome, and discovering latent skills and abilities among local people (Smith, 1978). A number of case studies emphasise the crucial role of community work support in local political struggles including Butcher *et al.* (1980), Henderson *et al.* (1982), Barr (1977) and Thomas (1976). Lees and Mayo (1984), in particular, show how a network of resource centres – operating in Glasgow, London, South Wales, Manchester and Tyne and Wear from the late 1970s to early 1980s – facilitated and developed a range of local political campaigns about social security, employment, housing and planning issues.

Other support mechanisms for interest group activity exist, although they are not so widely spread and established as community work. A network of law centres has been established to make legal expertise available to community groups as well as individuals (Lea and Young, 1984). In January 1973 the Town and Country Planning Association set up the world's first planning aid service. This national, London-based service has a nucleus of full-time staff. Some regionally based experiments have also been initiated (Bidwell and Edger, 1981). In 1983 the Association of Community Technical Aid Centres was formed. ACTAC claims to have 30 established groups and its aim is to bring planning and architectural expertise to serve the needs of the powerless. In order to increase awareness of community self-help and user control in the redevelopment of neighbourhoods (Doorly, 1983). Plainly, the support resources provided by these centres are patchy in their coverage and can only partially redress inequalities in access to technical expertise.

Finally, the local interest group world has been strengthened by a growing partnership with local authorities in service delivery. As noted in Chapter 3 private sector producer groups – including companies and building societies – have shown an interest in such involvement through public/private trusts. However, it is groups from the voluntary sector category that are to the fore in this activity. For a whole range of reasons many local authorities have sought to use voluntary sector agencies to provide services rather than providing services directly themselves. The Wolfenden Report (1978, Ch. 5) notes the development of this trend in the mid-1970s, and up until the mid-1980s the experience in many areas has been of dramatic growth in the funding of voluntary organisations (NCVO, p. 4). In its first full year of operation, 1965–6, the GLC awarded grants to the value of £427 000. By 1983–4 the figure had risen to £34 million (GLC, 1984). Between 1981–2 and 1983–4 alone the cash value of grants awarded by Camden grew by nearly 60 per cent, reaching a total of £4.5 million (Raine and Webster, 1984, pp. 7–8). The use of grant-aid to support voluntary and community organisations is a feature of the strategy developed by the 'Left' Labour authorities and is discussed further in Chapter 9. However, it is important to note that many non-Labour authorities have also increased their support for the voluntary sector. Conservative-controlled Westminster, for example, in 1986–7 gave just under £3 million worth of grants to groups in its area.

The implication of these developments in terms of the argument being developed here is that voluntary sector organisation has been greatly strengthened, although some groups are vulnerable to changes in the political climate if their political supporters lose their influence on council decision-making. Moreover, given the rise of self-help organisations within the sector and a more general willingness to engage in campaigning activity, the potential for and likely effectiveness of voluntary sector lobbying of local authorities has also been considerably enhanced. Indeed, this politicisation of the voluntary sector has attracted criticism from the right-wing Centre For Policy Studies with its warning about 'political bodies in voluntary clothing' (C.P.S., 1985). The National Council for Voluntary Organisations is careful to emphasise, however, that the key role is in debating and discussing local policy issues rather than direct involvement in electoral politics (NCVO, p. 22).

The changes that have occured in many areas since the mid-1970s have not so strengthened the operation of interest group activity that all the inequalities of income, staffing, organisational and technical skills (identified by Newton in his study) have been ironed out. What has been argued is that the balance has been redressed to a degree, so that community and voluntary groups have a greater access to such resources, although they undoubtedly remain generally disadvantaged compared to producer groups. What has also happened is that a wider range of groups have proved themselves to be willing and able to engage in political activity at the local level. Newton's 'small stage army' of active groups, dominated by producer organisations, has been swelled in many areas by a range of community, cause and voluntary sector organisations. Indeed, the world of local interest groups is closer now to a conscript army in its diversity, range of opinion, its disgruntled participation and propensity to rebellion!

### The diversity and complexity of local interest group politics

The pattern that emerges from our discussion of local authority–interest group activity is one of uneven development and diversity.

Some authorities are more open than others and some have more active and wide-ranging group politics. It is difficult to generalise but the following four categories would appear to capture important differences between localities.

First there are those urban areas where left-wing Labour authorities have come to prominence. Voluntary sector, cause and community groups are highly active and the local authorities have responded to and supported this development. In practice tensions and difficulties emerge but a closer and better relationship with a wide range of groups is seen as an essential part of councils' political strategy. Tenants', women's, ethnic minority and single-issue cause groups will be amongst those that are active. Good relations with local authority trade unions and other trade unions are also prized by councillors. Relationships with other producer interests notably business organisations may, however, be antagonistic and even hostile. The local authority may see itself as engaged in challenging the power of these interests and tipping the balance more in favour of voluntary, cause and community organisations.

Second there are urban areas where centre-right Labour- or Alliance-influenced authorities hold sway. The group world again is relatively active and diverse and there is a keenness on the part of the local authority to be seen to be listening. On the surface there is a commitment to good relations with a range of groups from producer, community and voluntary categories. The Widdicombe researchers identify such a Labour authority in a medium-sized provincial town which prides itself on maintaining good relations with 'what the Leader described as the "liberal establishment" – the lawyers, the doctors, the architects, the preservationists, the Towns Womens Guild – as well as with the Trades Council, the voluntary sector, the Chamber of Commerce and two or three major local employers' (Widdicombe 1986b, p. 146). The extent of the commitment to working with these groups is, however, limited and there may be suspicion of some organisations. For example, tenant associations may be viewed as dominated by extremists or residents' associations as selfish, middle-class organisations acting as a front for the Conservatives or other opposition parties. Cause groups, such as local CND branches, may also attract little or only muted support.

Third in suburban and rural locations where Conservative- and Alliance-influenced councils hold sway another pattern can be observed. The more formal end of the voluntary sector may be well organised. Farmer and landowner interests may be well established. The environmental and amenity lobby will have a growing voice, with issues being taken up by residents' organisations and parish councils. Something of the flavour of this sort of politics is given in the study of Berkshire, provided by Short and his colleagues (1986). In such localities some interests may never find a voice, for example agricultural workers or those who require housing for rent. Campaign organisations, such as Shelter (National Campaign for the Homeless), that take up their cause are likely to be given a hostile reception; as too may other unacceptable cause groups.

Fourth in urban and suburban locations where 'New Right' Conservative authorities dominate there is likely to be a willingness to work closely with a select group of middle-class residents' associations, amenity groups and business interests. However, these local authorities are actively hostile to any groups they consider left-wing. These might include CND, Shelter and many other cause groups, any feminist organisations or elements of the voluntary sector that are viewed as 'political'. Indeed the level of hostility towards such groups is reflected in the recommendation of a Conservative party research paper that the funding of single-issue cause groups by local authorities 'should be prohibited altogether' (Campey, 1987, p. 198).

These portraits of the differences between interest group politics in particular localities must be treated with some caution. The politics of militant-influenced Liverpool during the early 1980s does not fit easily into any of the categories. The Labour council in that case insisted on the dominance of an active party rather than interest group world. It saw the institutions of the Labour party as having the crucial role, with the local party acting as the guardian of the manifesto and ensuring that councillors carry out election promises. Sectional politics were seen as subordinate to class politics and interest groups only accepted in as far as their demands could be absorbed into the general order of party priorities (Ben-Tovim *et al.*, Chs 4 and 5). Moreover, in some areas interest group activity may be very limited. The Widdicombe researchers found that in some rural areas councillors were unsure about what interest groups were (Widdicombe 1986b, p. 148).

If we narrow down the focus to relations within a particular authority the theme of complexity again comes to the fore. The reality of interest group politics within a locality is often of different interests attracting support from different sections of the local authority. Thus particular parts of a Town Hall may have different constituencies in the community. As noted in Chapter 4 these constituencies may get called on in the intra-organisational political struggle within local authorities. It was argued that, for example, area officers may use their contacts with community groups to persuade them to raise issues and express demands for more resources for their area. Looked at from the other side interest groups will have a good idea who their main supporters and potential opponents may be within a local authority. The structure of allies and enemies may reflect differences within the ruling party group and divisions amongst officers based on their professional background, position in the hierarchy, or their areas of responsibility. In short, in many instances groups are likely to be faced with complex patterns of responsiveness which cut across and distort the dominant patterns of local authority–interest group politics identified above.

**Conclusions**

This chapter has attempted to move beyond the pluralist/élitist debate which has dominated the discussion of local interest group politics. We have argued local authorities cannot in general be classed as enclosed organisations and that while significant inequalities in the resources available to different groups remain they are not inevitably so overwhelming as to make competition untenable. We have suggested that the pattern of local authority–interest group relationships is one of uneven development and diversity. Some authorities are more open than others, some have a more active group base to deal with, and the nature of participating groups varies.

Our discussion has concentrated on very much a 'surface' picture of local interest group politics, on interest group activity. The pluralist/élitist debate is about different interpretations of this surface politics and the distribution of power associated with it. We have tried to move beyond this debate by identifying the uneven development and diverse patterns of local authority–

interest group interaction. But there is another face of power which needs to be considered if a complete picture is to be assembled. It rests on the view that groups gain influence not only through their political activity but also by their structural position within society. Both faces of power need to be considered in the study of interest groups (*cf.* March, 1983, especially pp. 21–2).

Certain interests – especially business interests – have such a crucial role in society that no government, local or central, can afford to ignore their interests. Their investment and their cooperation is required to provide employment, exports and goods and services demanded by society and needed by governments looking to maintain their popular support. In a market-orientated economy and a liberal–democratic political system such as ours these groups, therefore, have available to them an additional lever of influence. This power depends less on overt interest group activity and lobbying and rather reflects their ability to constrain the options available to government as well as the support they gain from dominant ideological forces (Lindblom, 1977). Thus, for example, Friedland (1982, p. 14) notes how in urban politics in the USA the influence of large business corporations stems from their control of many of the resources necessary to economic investment and growth. As a consequence they tend to be 'actively solicited by city fathers anxious to sustain the local tax base, employment and economic growth'.

Local authorities of all political outlooks will face pressure to accommodate the interests of such groups. Even left-wing Labour authorities committed to giving priority to cause, community and voluntary sector groups are likely to have a 'special' relationship with their areas' largest employers or be drawn into 'deals' with commercial developers in order to protect local employment opportunities or provide good shopping facilities.

Structural power, however, is not enjoyed continually by all business interests. Its impact is mediated by interest group activity and surface politics. We are not suggesting that the political activity on which we have focussed in this chapter is a mystification and that real power lies elsewhere. Local lobbying and interest group activity does influence the policy process but the impact of the structural power available to certain groups needs also to be considered if a full understanding of local politics is to be developed. This point is returned to in Chapter 10.

# 6 Central–Local Relations and Policy Networks

In this chapter we focus on the complex network of governmental and quasi-governmental relations in which local authorities operate. The first section identifies the constituent parts of Britain's governmental system. The second discusses how best we can conceptualise and understand the complex flows of inter-governmental influence. It introduces the idea of the national local government system and its associated policy networks. The remainder of the chapter examines the impact of the increasingly politicised and conflict-laden environment of the mid-1970s onwards. Attention is focussed in turn on the change in central–local relations, central government's attack and the strategies it has used, and the challenge facing some of the policy networks that have seen the greatest degree of innovation and controversy.

## The complex system of British government

Local authorities are one element in a complex system of government in Britain. They are influenced by and in turn exercise influence over this governmental world. To understand local politics we need to be aware of the governmental context in which local authorities operate. A comprehensive review is not possible. Below we simply note some of the key features of central government, the territorial ministries and the intermediate institutions of government. They constitute the main components of the British governmental machine. Account is also taken of the role of quasi-governmental organisations.

## Westminster and Whitehall: British central government

Much media and academic attention is focused on Westminster and Whitehall. They are the national political institutions based in the capital city and can be seen as constituting Parliament and central government.

British central government is characterised by its non-executant and fragmented nature. As Dunleavy and Rhodes (1986, p. 109) comment only one in ten public sector employees is a civil servant and only a fraction of them are based in Whitehall. Policy-level civil servants and ministers are largely concerned with allocating funds, regulating standards, processing legislation and identifying new problems and issues but they are not directly responsible for day-to-day service delivery and policy implementation. These tasks are the responsibility of local authorities and other governmental and quasi-governmental agencies. Thus although we live in a unitary state, in the sense that the power to delegate or revoke delegated powers remains in the hands of Parliament, the system is managed by a differentiated polity which leads to a complex and fragmented governmental system (Rhodes, 1988).

Along with recognising the non-executant character of central government we need to consider the fragmented nature of central government itself. As Rhodes (1988) argues the term 'central government' has to be understood as shorthand for a diverse collection of departments and divisions.

With diversity comes a number of conflicting interests. In local government expenditure, for example, there are, at least, three axes: the Treasury with its broad concern for budget restraint; the spending departments – such as the Ministry of Defence – with little direct interest in local government who may wish to see local government bear the brunt of any cuts; and finally, there are those spending departments with a major interest in local government – such as the Department of the Environment or the Department of Education and Science – who may advocate and seek to protect local spending. This example is just one illustration of inter-departmental conflict. In practice the divisions are more complex with the DoE, for example, combining its advocate role with that of a monitor and restrainer of local authority spending. Tensions also arise over rival service and policy interests. Strong corporate tendencies also operate, pulling together the various elements of central government, with the Treasury, Cabinet Office and the Prime Minister's Office often providing a focus for coordination. There is to a substantial degree a shared culture and a commitment to common values among the civil service giving central government the character of a 'village community' in the eyes of one set of commentators (Heclo and Wildavsky, 1974). Nevertheless the fragmentation of central government means that local authorities are often faced by a complex and shifting group of allies and enemies at the centre.

Fragmentation also exists within departments, helping to create a range of function-specific policy networks. The DoE, for example, is composed of a series of divisions which at various times over the last two decades have included water, transport, local government, housing, planning and construction. There is a tendency for these divisions to establish separate relationships with the governmental and quasi-governmental agencies and groups implementing and developing policies in their area. In this way different elements within local authorities get tied into a range of policy networks associated with the diverse interests within central government departments. Local authorities do not simply have a relationship with central government. Rather they are connected with a range of 'centres'. We shall return to this point later in the chapter.

## *The territorial ministries*

In Scotland and Wales (and also in Northern Ireland, although beyond the scope of this book) the pattern of government is also conditioned by the role of the territorial ministries. The Scottish Office is headed by the Secretary of State accompanied by several ministers and is based in Edinburgh. The Welsh Office has a similar system of political control and is based in Cardiff. They are responsible for their territories' interests in a broad sense and more specifically for a wide range of 'domestic' policies including housing, education and agriculture. Consequently for local authorities in Scotland and Wales they are not just one of many central departments but the prime port of call – 'their centre'.

The relationship between local authorities and these territorial ministries is conditioned by the dual character of the ministries. They are simultaneously of the centre and for a territory. According to Rose (1983, p. 105) the territorial ministries are much more of Whitehall than they are part of Scotland or Wales. They act as agents of centre: monitoring, encouraging and facilitating the implementation of the national policies of Westminster and White-hall. In Chapter 7 we describe how the Scottish Office pursued a policy of tough financial constraint for Scottish local authorities during the 1980s and in this way provided a test ground for legislative measures in England and Wales. As Goldsmith (1986, p. 154) comments about finance: 'the Scottish Office has been not only a keen follower of Imperial policy, but also a willing experimenter on behalf of the core'.

The territorial ministries also perform a lobbying/spokesperson function, in effect being the voice of their countries in Whitehall. This role, however, argues Goldsmith (1986) is less frequently adopted than might be expected, especially given the specific economic and social difficulties of Wales and Scotland. He goes on to draw a contrast between the Welsh Office 'which appears largely unwilling and perhaps unable to transmit the *Welsh* dimension upwards into Imperial policy debates' (p. 154) and the Scottish Office which is more likely to promote actively the *Scottish* interest. This is, in part, explained by the fact that the Welsh Office only dates from the 1960s. (For a more detailed discussion see Jones 1986.) The Scottish Office, in contrast, is a creation of the nineteenth century, and draws on a tradition of separate adminis-tration and a distinctive legal system (see Keating and Midwinter, 1983, Ch. 2).

In general, neither Welsh or Scottish Secretaries of State frequently fight for or win concessions in Cabinet. Westminster and Whitehall produce policies and legislation for all parts of Britain and the task of the territorial ministries is to implement these policies. The politicians and civil servants who manage the ministries are part of the national party and administrative systems.

Yet there is scope for discretion because the territorial ministries are expected to take responsibility for seeing through the policy process in their areas. As Bulpitt (1983) argues there is a tradition in Britain for the Imperial core to be most interested in the 'high politics' of defence, international relations and economic management, leaving the 'low politics' of domestic provision in housing, education, and so on to other agencies. This tradition we shall go on to suggest has been eroded to a substantial degree in the last decade, but in the case of the territorial ministries there remains an expectation that they should get on and manage areas of domestic policy.

What emerges in Scotland and Wales is a distinctive pattern of central–local relations in contrast to that generated in England. According to Goldsmith (1986) the smaller scale of the networks makes them more informal (especially in Wales). The people involved in the ministries and local authorities know each other well and are more likely to develop a mutual comprehension of policy preferences and constraints. In particular 'it seems clear that relations . . . do involve a greater sense of trust and understanding between individual local authorities and central departments' (p. 168). Thus although the territorial ministries generally seek compliance with national policies they do so in the context of the room for manœuvre which their territorial status provides and in the light of a more detailed sharing of knowledge and concerns than is often the case in central–local relations in England. Goldsmith's general characterisation seems plausible. Although as he recognises in the arena of financial constraint the territorial ministries have pursued their local authorities as hard if not harder than those in England.

*Intermediate institutions*

All central departments have some form of sub-central structure. Rhodes (1988) suggests the use of the phrase 'intermediate institutions' to refer to those deconcentrated structures. He describes these agencies as forming a 'complex mosaic', with regional organisation varying not only between departments but also within departments.

In order to bring some order to this complexity Rhodes identifies three main roles pursued by intermediate institutions. They manage tasks handed down from the centre and in doing so coordinate the activities of the various other agencies. Regional Department of the Environment offices, for example, administer Housing

Investment Programmes and bring together the various 'Estate Action' bids within their areas. A second role is monitoring and facilitating the implementation of central government policies. A third role is representing territorial interests to the centre. Using the example of the DoE it is clear that these last two roles can contradict one another. As Young (1982, p. 90) comments:

> The regional offices are . . . in an ambivalent position. They represent the region's interests to the centre, but try to retain a sense of balance and objectivity when arguing Marsham Street's views and ministers' arguments in the region.

From the perspective of local authorities the regional offices for Departments of the Environment or Transport are the 'eyes and ears' of central government; yet at the same time potential allies in campaigning for more resources or new policy initiatives. Local authorities need to establish relations with the regional offices in order to manage a range of policy measures in their areas. For example, to know whether certain capital schemes will be approved. Some regional officials will thereby gain a detailed knowledge of particular projects or initiatives. But generally local authorities are uncertain about how much information to provide and to what extent they can afford to be open. There is, then, regular contact between officials of intermediate organisations and local authorities. But in England, in contrast to the territorial relations of Scotland and Wales, there has not been a full sharing of knowledge or trust (Houlihan, 1984).

## Quasi-governmental organisations

Local authorities, then, operate in the context of a complex governmental system comprising of central government, territorial ministries or intermediate institutions. In addition, as noted in Chapter 3, they operate alongside a quasi-governmental world of appointed bodies, non-departmental agencies, single purpose authorities and mixed public/private institutions. In particular we identified and categorised those agencies with a local dimension or which regularly interact with local policy-makers. We referred to them collectively as non-elected local government. They form a further element in the environment in which local authorities operate. Yet as Dunleavy (1980, p. 103) notes, beyond those quasi-governmental organisations which have regular relations with elected local authorities there is a vast number whose interventions are episodic and specific in character. (For a further discussion of these institutions see Rhodes, 1988; Barker, 1982; Hood, 1983.) They too form part of the context in which local authorities make policy, and their interventions can have a dramatic effect. Dunleavy quotes the example of the nuclear power industry looking for suitable sites for generation or disposal. Quasi-governmental organisations plainly form an important part of the governmental system of Britain.

### Conceptualising inter-governmental relations

There has been an increasing interest shown in the problems of conceptualising and comprehending central–local relations and more generally inter-governmental relations (see Dunleavy, 1980; Rhodes, 1981 and 1988). The key point to emerge is that we need to move beyond a narrow focus on relations between central and local government towards an understanding of the 'national local government system'. According to Dunleavy (1980, p. 105):

Councils are located and locate themselves in what may be termed the 'national local government system'. This may be taken to describe the complex web of inter- and supra-authority relations which can exert a strong influence on the policies pursued in particular localities.

The attraction of this definition is that while central–local relations rightly remain a prime topic for analysis the wider organisational networks and influences of inter-governmental relations are brought into focus. The term 'central–local government relationship' can be misleading if it encourages a narrow focus on the interaction between central departments and local authorities. In practice a range of other organisations cut across the relationship, including the local authority associations, professional organisations, party institutions, quasi-government organisations and trade unions. 'This constellation of actors and organisations deter-

mines the parameters within which local authorities operate'
(p. 105). Thus while the influence of central government on local
authorities is substantial and cannot be neglected attention should
also be directed to ideas and influences coming from other
organisations within the national local government system.

The national local government system influences and is influenced by local authorities. It is an important source of ideas
and values. It provides an environment in which local authorities
situate themselves and their problems and an arena for them to look
for new initiatives or policy solutions which may be appropriate to
their needs. As Dunleavy (1980, p. 106) comments:

> The local government press (both the general and professional
> outlets), the functional service associations and their publications
> and activities, the apparatus of local government professionalism
> and the regular conferences, seminars and meetings which play
> such a large part in the nationalisation of local policy change –
> all these define the boundaries of policy consideration and
> debate, in local authorities as a whole.

At the same time, individual local authorities contribute to this
policy-making environment. Their innovations in particular service
areas add to the national picture. The development of local
economic initiatives or equal opportunities strategies involved the
spreading of networks of innovation and discussion among a
limited number of local authorities to a wider audience. Ultimately
ideas and policies such as these may be taken up and promoted
by central government. Indeed Dunleavy goes as far as arguing
that 'central government policy changes of a substantive or
innovative kind, such as the introduction of new standards or
methods of service provision, are thus most frequently generalis-
ations of existing local authority practice or responses to demands
produced by local authorities' practical experience, rather than
ideas originating with government departments' (p. 105).

Rhodes (1988) has developed this vision of a national local
government system by identifying a range of policy networks that
operate within it. These networks reflect a series of discrete policy,
service or area interests within the national local government
system, and draw together the organisations that interact within
particular fields. Below we briefly identify six types of network in

which local authorities are involved. Empirical studies about their operation are also noted. Rhodes provides a more detailed analysis of both the characteristics of the networks and a review and a comparison of the available case study material.

Amongst the most closely-knit of networks are the territorial and policy communities. The territorial communities are based around the territorial ministries, local authorities and other governmental organisations of Wales, Scotland and Northern Ireland. Something of the flavour of the relationship has been given earlier in the chapter (in addition to the references cited there see Midwinter, 1984). Policy communities are based around a shared policy and service delivery responsibility. Policy communities exist in many areas (for a useful overview see Ranson *et al.*, 1985 and Laffin, 1986). Later in the chapter we discuss the education and housing renewal policy communities. A third, although less tightly integrated network, is the 'national community of local government' in England, in which the main representative bodies are the Association of County Councils (ACC), the Association of Metropolitan Authorities (AMA) and the Association of District Councils (ADC). This type of network is referred to as inter-governmental by Rhodes, who has provided the most detailed analysis of its operation (Rhodes, 1986).

The next two types of network are defined by their dominant or pre-eminent participant. They are professionalised networks such as those associated with health care and personal social services (Webb *et al.*, 1986), and producer networks which deal with a particular industry (Davies *et al.*, 1984; Wright, 1987). The final category of network is the most loosely integrated. Issue networks generally contain a large number of participants with a limited degree of interdependence. Inner city partnerships are cited as an example (Leach, 1985; Parkinson and Wilks, 1986).

The discussion of the national local government system and the policy networks in which local authorities are involved opens up a field of investigation and analysis which cannot be fully developed here. Sufficient references have been provided for the interested reader to pursue.

Local authorities can be involved in any of the range of policy networks. Their participation provide opportunities for exercising influence and presenting their localities' concerns. It also enables local authorities to learn from the experience of others and gain access to new ideas and innovations from specialist sources. A recognition of policy networks adds to our understanding of the complex web of inter-governmental relations in which local authorities are situated.

The focus of the discussion in the remainder of the chapter follows the approach developed elsewhere in this part of the book. Our concern will be on how the national local government system has changed in the context of the socio-economic shifts and increasingly politicised environment that has developed since the mid-1970s. Broadly we will argue that the Thatcher Governments have attempted to short-circuit the national local government system, and its associated policy networks, in many substantial areas of the policy process. In particular we will analyse the nature of central government's attack; examine some of the key strategies used by the centre; and finally consider the shattering effect this challenge has had on policy communities in housing renewal and education.

### The nature of central–local relations, 1979–87

There is overwhelming agreement amongst those writing on the subject that from the mid-1970s onwards, and in particular since 1979, there has been a major shift in the nature and direction of central–local relations (see, for example: Jones and Stewart, 1983; Rhodes, 1988; Walsh, 1986; Loughlin, 1986). Central government has increased the intensity and strength of its interventions. In Chapter 7 we discuss in detail the struggle over local spending. In Chapter 8 we examine the Conservatives' attempts to promote privatisation through, for example, the sale of council houses. In this section we provide a backcloth to these detailed studies by considering in general terms the nature of central–local relations during the period of the first two Thatcher Governments.

The pattern of central–local relations has changed substantially in a number of respects in the Thatcher years. First the intensity of the Government's concern with the behaviour and performance of local authorities is more marked. This finds expression not only in the volume of legislation, circulars, advice and in some cases abuse directed at local government, but also in the willingness of the centre to interfere with particular authorities through, for example, rate-capping. Second the strength and force of the weapons that central government has given itself marks a departure from earlier years. The range of strategies used is considerable as we shall see. Legislation and other measures have been used to reduce local authority discretion and choice in education, housing, finance, transport, land-use planning and many other policy areas. This contrasts with enabling and empowering legislation which characterised much of central–local relations during the years of growth in local authority service delivery. In contrast to the negotiation and compromise which underlay much of post-war central–local relations, the Thatcher Governments have developed a style of setting for local authorities arbitrary and non-negotiated goals and targets. This point will be illustrated in the chapter on the struggle over local spending.

It is clear that the Conservatives' concern with local government has reflected not only a desire to reduce public expenditure but also a concern to restructure local policy-making. The Government has been concerned to redirect policies in education to meet its perception of what is required in a changing industrial society. It has attempted to redefine the nature of housing renewal policy by emphasising that the dominant role should be taken by the private sector. These two examples are considered in more detail later in the chapter. For the present they illustrate that the Conservatives' concern has not simply been with holding back public expenditure but has also involved a desire to intervene in policy and redefine the purposes of local authorities. Thatcher's response to the challenges posed by the socio-economic changes of the last decade or so has moved beyond fiscal austerity.

It would be unwise to view central government's attack during this period as the working out of a pre-determined philosophy. The recent history of central–local relations is more realistically seen as a process of action and reaction, rather than the cumulative implementation of a clear ideological standpoint. As Ian Aitken has commented: 'the most extraordinary feature (of Thatcherism) has been the extent to which a supposedly ideological government has evolved its alleged principles of action by accident rather than design' (*Guardian*, 27 July 1987). One of the most startling examples on this phenomenon is the emergence of proposals to abolish the GLC and the six metropolitan counties. They appear to have been the product of a Cabinet committee originally set up to devise an acceptable alternative to the rates. The inclusion of these proposals in the Conservative manifesto of 1983 bears the hallmarks of a last minute insertion, at the behest of the Prime Minister herself, based to a degree on her antipathy towards the policies and propaganda of the GLC and her personal dislike of its leader, Ken Livingstone (see discussion in Chapter 1).

In general the metaphor of a chain reaction is appropriate when looking at central–local relations during this period. The setting up of the Widdicombe Committee to examine the conduct of local authority business was in turn a response to the publicity campaign launched by the GLC in its unsuccessful attempt to stave off abolition. The committee was there to provide a legitimate basis for introducing legislation to prevent 'political propaganda' but also was given a wider remit to investigate local politics. This report in turn seems likely to lead to further legislation, since, according to the 1987 Conservative manifesto, the Widdicombe Report 'painted a disturbing picture of the breakdown of democratic processes in a number of councils' and the manifesto promises remedial action. The chapter in this book on the struggle over local spending illustrates the chain reaction nature of policy development, with one set of measures following another, on the basis of the perceived inadequacies of earlier legislation.

This action/reaction cycle in part reflects the fact that central government has faced resistance from local authorities. As Dunleavy and Rhodes (1986, p. 126) comment:

> The Thatcher governments have time and again confronted problems raised by their inability to secure the active cooperation of local government in meeting new priorities which have arisen in the 1980s.

Many local authorities do not share the same perception as Thatcherism when it comes to finance, education, housing or inner city problems. Yet at the same time the Conservatives' require the cooperation of local authorities in these and other areas, because they carry day-to-day responsibility for service delivery and have the detailed knowledge and information which goes along with this operational experience. This is the dilemma for central government built in by its non-executant character. The result is that central government can intervene and influence but it has to be selective, concentrating on those policy questions which are most important to it. To intervene effectively it has had to resort, as we shall see, to a complex web of assertive strategies. Even then many local authorities have evaded measures they dislike. Moreover, local authorities have not remained passive but, in the context of greater central pressures and new social/economic circumstances, have responded with policies which are either unknown or unwelcome to the centre. The strategies of Urban Left local authorities, for example, are considered in Chapter 9.

Thus although central intervention has increased – that is the sheer number of times that Whitehall interferes – it is far from clear that central control has been achieved in the sense of the centre achieving its objectives. The successes and failures of central intervention in finance and privatisation are discussed in Chapters 7 and 8 respectively. What emerges is a picture of increased control but over a narrow range of matters. Along with control has come unintended consequences, ambiguity and uncertainty. Resistance from local authorities has also been stiffened and politicised.

The Conservatives have attempted in a number of key areas to by-pass the national local government system and its associated policy networks. This has proved to a degree effective but at the same time it has destabilised a complex system making it more difficult for central government to achieve its objectives. Unilateral action by one member of a network creates disruption and uncertainty. Indeed Rhodes (1988) argues that ministers and their civil servants have failed to comprehend the nature of the differentiated polity in which they operate. They have opted for the easy rhetoric of control and direction and in practice created confusion and resistance. 'The phrase policy mess encapsulates the period more accurately than centralisation'.

Rhodes' depiction of the experience of the first two Thatcher Governments is valid. Yet as we shall argue in Chapter 11 the cumulative impact of the Conservative attack has been considerable. Moreover, further measures promised in the 1987 manifesto indicate that central–local relations and the role of local government face further and radical reconstruction. Finally, there would appear to be a growing coherence to the Thatcherite attack. Out of the struggles of 1979–87 there is an emerging vision of the future of local government in which elected local authorities will have a much reduced role. This discussion must wait, however, until later in the book. In the next section we identify some of the various strategies used by the Thatcher Governments during the period 1979–87.

### The centre's strategies of intervention, 1979–87

*Legislation*

During the first two Thatcher governments over 40 major acts were passed with significant implications for local government. Legislation, plainly, has formed a vital element in central–local relations during the period. Loughlin (1986, p. 195) argues that the Conservatives have sought to structure local authority action through formal legal procedures. At the same time, legislation has extended the discretionary powers of central government. Local government law has been reformalised to direct and control local authorities and give greater freedom to the centre to enable it to pursue its objectives.

This aggressive use of the law has led to the collapse of the traditional legal relationship which provided a flexible structure within which central and local authorities could bargain and negotiate. The result has been the 'juridification of the central–local relationship' (Loughlin, 1986, p. 193). The legal relationship between centre and locality which in the past was a matter of minor concern has become a critical issue, as both parties have sought to establish the other's legal powers and duties. Given the uncertainties of the law in this sphere local authorities and central government have used the courts to promote or defend their interests (see also Grant, 1986). This trend has caused difficulties given that the courts were relatively ill-equipped in terms of design and culture to cope with these new demands. Moreover, as Loughlin (1986, p. 198) notes, although some adaptions have been made by the courts the adjudication of disputes between public bodies remains problematic given the absence of a written constitution specifying what responsibilities are held by which body.

Indeed, it would appear that central government has increasingly attempted to place itself beyond judicial review. Where local authorities have won victories the Conservatives have been prepared to pass new legislation to nullify the decision and often specifically exclude any further challenge through the courts. A striking example is provided by the Local Government Act 1987. Section 4(1) provides in relation to rate support grant:

> Anything done by the Secretary of State before the passing of this Act for the purposes of the relevant provisions in relation to any of the initial years or intermediate years shall be deemed to have been done in compliance with those provisions.

Section 4(6) continues:

> Subsection (1) above shall have effect notwithstanding any decision of a court (whether before or after the passing of this Act) purporting to have a contrary effect.

As Graham and Prosser (1988) comment: 'so much for limited government under the law!'

*Minimal consultation*

This has been another characteristic of central–local relations during this period. Rhodes (1986) describes in detail how the Conservatives shunned the networks of consultation established in earlier years in England. The local authority associations 'saw their special position slip away'. The Consultative Council of Local Government Finance became a forum not for negotiation but for ministers to announce hard and fast decisions about local spending. Some of the technical working parties 'remained important in spite of increasing restrictions of their work' and some policy networks survived better than others. But otherwise 'virtually all of the local government organisations at national level have been permanently on the defensive, stigmatized by Whitehall as promoters of profligacy rather than as potential allies or partners' (p. 377). The Thatcher Governments have shown little faith in consultative mechanisms. Indeed, they have been prepared to engage in major constitutional changes with the minimum of consultation. The proposals to abolish the GLC and the six Metropolitan Counties were pushed through without any public inquiry; let alone the Royal Commissions and public debate which have accompanied previous reforms of local government. The criticisms and submissions from local authorities and other bodies were brushed aside (Flynn *et al.*, 1985).


*Targeted funding*

The Conservatives have used to an increasing extent specific and supplementary grants in an effort to exert greater influence over local spending on individual services. For England and Wales these targeted grants have risen from 17.6 per cent of total central government support in 1981–2 to 23.6 per cent in 1986–7 (Douglas and Lord, 1986, p. 29). As their name implies specific grants are earmarked for particular purposes. They cover a fixed percentage of the costs of the service, leaving the local authority responsible for finding the remainder. The largest specific grant (1394 million in 1986–7) is directed at spending on the police, which the Conservatives have favoured. Other specific grants operate in education, social services, civil defence, magistrates' courts and urban regeneration. The Urban Programme in particular has increased its size in real terms, with local authorities in inner city areas losing rate support grants but having the opportunity to make up some of the difference through this targeted funding. Parkinson and Wilks (1986, p. 300) estimate that within four years of 1979 the proportion of urban programme funding used by partnership local authorities had doubled. This shift led to increasing conflicts over priorities, with central government attempting to encourage projects which stimulated an enterprise culture or supported business and local authorities favouring other groups and interests or looking to plug gaps left by cuts in rate support grants.

A further example of targeted funding is provided by the introduction of what came to be known as 'Estate Action' support. In this case, however, the targeting is a 'permission to borrow' rather than central government grant. Under the scheme a proportion of the annual Housing Investment Programme in England and Wales is 'creamed off' to be re-allocated to local authorities who submit projects for the renewal of public housing estates which meet the approval of central government. These projects often involve some elements of privatisation or new management structure, which reduce the role of the local authority (see Chapter 8). Under this scheme £75 million of potential spending was allocated in 1987–8.

## By-passing local government

The Conservatives have shown a willingness to by-pass local government policy processes. Examples of this strategy include the granting of planning permission to developers on appeal, after they have been turned down by local planning authorities. The Conservatives have encouraged greater use of the appeals system by developers and have upheld a greater proportion of appeals. Their aim has been to make the land-use planning system more responsive to market forces (see Brindley *et al.*, 1988).

Another example of the by-pass strategy is provided by the establishment of 'task force' teams of civil servants in a number of inner city areas. The approach was first adopted in Merseyside in the early 1980s. In 1985 City Action Teams were established in the seven inner city partnership areas to coordinate and target government effort. And in 1986 a programme of small task forces within particular inner city communities was launched with projects in the Highfields area of Leicester, Moss Side in Manchester, St Paul's in Bristol and Handsworth in Birmingham among other places.

The by-pass strategy, as noted in Chapter 3, has also involved the increasing and extensive use of appointed public bodies by the Government. The rationale is that these bodies are more susceptible to central direction. The establishment of Urban Development Corporations is a striking example. The role of the Manpower Services Commission has also been expanded greatly. The importance of these agencies and the way that the Conservatives have used them to re-direct local policy priorities has already been discussed in Chapter 3.

## The reorganisation and reform of local authorities

In pursuit of their objectives the Conservatives have also shown a willingness to reorganise local authorities. The abolition of the

GLC and six Metropolitan Counties is the major reform. In their place, as noted in Chapter 3, a system of joint boards and joint committees has been established which has been less susceptible to local authority control.

The Conservatives have also shown an interest in the internal operation and management of local authorities. Proposals relating to contracting-out and de-regulation are discussed in Chapter 8. The role of the Audit Commission is considered in Chapter 7. Other measures include the 1985 Local Government (Access to Information) Act which provides for public access to council meetings, reports and documents and requires local authorities to publish details of councillors. A similar measure, however, has not been taken in the case of central government! The 1986 Local Government Act placed restrictions on the type of publicity that local authorities could produce. As noted earlier further measures on the conduct of local authority business have been promised following the Widdicombe Report.

### The impact on policy networks

The Conservatives' increased commitment to central intervention and its pursuit of new policy approaches has in a number of areas had a substantial impact on policy networks. Some have survived relatively unchanged such as those associated with environmental health and trading standards (Rhodes, G., 1986) and others which have not aroused much political controversy (Laffin, 1986). But in other sectors the political and ideological challenge posed by Thatcherism has had a shattering or disintegrating effect. Rhodes (1986) analyses the collapse of the 'national community of local government'. Parkinson and Wilks (1986) describe how the issue networks connected with inner city partnership degenerated during the 1980s. Below we briefly review the challenge to the policy communities associated with education and housing renewal.

The centre's concern fundamentally to re-direct education dates back to the mid-1970s. Several issues are involved including that of falling school rolls, the alleged 'anti-industry' bias of schools and a concern about standards and whether all school leavers are being properly equipped for employment. The centre committed itself to a greater degree of intervention and to an attack on what it saw as the insulation of the education policy community and its dominance by the teaching profession. 'The concern has been to weaken local government and the profession in school and the LEA' (Ranson *et al.*, 1986, p. 272). Various legislative measures, the increasing use of the Manpower Services Commission to provide training, the introduction of the Technical and Vocational Education Initiative, the move towards a national curriculum and direct intervention in schemes relating to school closures and restructuring have all been part of the attempt to 'rationalise the government of education' and redirect it in line with the Conservatives' priorities.

The assault has had the effect of creating 'a seige mentality' within the education policy community (Rhodes, 1988). The Thatcher government has challenged core assumptions and values. The idea of partnership in education between central government, local authorities and teachers has been challenged and in its place a growing emphasis has been placed on a nationally run and administered system. Vocationalism has also been promoted with attempts to re-introduce streaming and social classification. Core values have, thus, been challenged 'as the concern for opportunities and personal development' has been forced to 'give way to vocational preparation and the needs of employers' (Ranson *et al.*, 1986, p. 271).

Our second example of a policy community that has found itself seriously challenged is provided by the area of housing renewal policy (Brindley and Stoker, 1988). For much of the post-war period policy in this area developed in a bi-partisan way, led by professional debates regarding the most appropriate techniques and approaches and premised on local authorities taking a dominant role in the process. The 1950s and 1960s saw massive slum clearance and redevelopment programmes. During the 1970s, encouraged by a variety of factors, the emphasis in the policy shifted to gradual renewal which relied to a much greater degree on continuous improvement and repair, combined with small-scale redevelopment. Nevertheless despite this shift the 1974 Housing Act still envisaged that the major and dominant role would be that of the public sector, with the local authorities leading area-based renewal schemes. But during the 1980s the Conservatives have argued that the public sector's role should be reduced and that instead private owners and the private corporate sector should be the main agents of renewal for both the private and to an increasing extent the local authority owned stock. More details of the policy is provided in Chapter 8. For the present we simply wish to argue that this policy of privatisation has fundamentally challenged the assumptions of the policy community surrounding housing renewal.

The rationale of past policy was provided by the environmental professions and was based on the idea that progress towards a civilised society was tied up with the continual *physical* improvement of housing conditions. Privatisation challenges this rationale, and with it the entire legacy of town improvement since the nineteenth century. It openly accepts a reduction in minimum housing standards and plays down concerns with housing conditions. It accepts the logic of the market, that a correlation will exist between low income and poor housing. The Government's approach in this field of housing policy is dominated by the promotion of owner-occupation. Progress is no longer to be measured by improved physical conditions but by the extent and growth of owner-occupation, the measure of the policy's success.

The policy network associated with housing renewal has at times reacted angrily, and at times expressed disbelief, at this shift in policy stance. It has had some success in challenging the Government's assertions about the ease with which private owners, builders or building societies will be able to take over housing renewal. The universally hostile reception given to a Green Paper (DoE, 1985) on home improvement led to proposals for legislation to be dropped. The power to delay remains but the policy community participants appear to have lost the power to exert a positive influence on Government thinking. The 1987 White Paper on housing shows that the Government's position has remained broadly unchanged in this field. Many of the environmental professionals, local authorities and housing pressure groups now feel it is no longer possible to make the Government listen. Their frustration is reflected by Malpass (1986, p. 239):

> To identify disturbing tendencies in housing conditions and to expose the deficiencies of the housing system . . . and to make suggestions about what should be done to improve the situation is ultimately irrelevant if the Government is not listening.

These examples from education and housing renewal indicate

that Thatcherism has in a number of key policy areas created a fluidity of ideas – made the unthinkable become the probable – and in this way challenged the consensus among associated policy networks. It has stimulated a series of crises in policy networks in which local authorities have been major participants. Old approaches and ways of working have been challenged, as have the direction and aims of policy.

**Conclusions**

This chapter has concentrated on the most politicised and controversial aspects of inter-governmental relations. It is worth noting that in many areas and over many issues calmer and more consensual relations prevail. Nevertheless the focus on conflict is justified by the increased intensity of central intervention during the period of the first two Thatcher governments and a desire to comprehend that assault and its effects. We have seen old assumptions and perspectives challenged as central government has sought to by-pass the amalgam of organisations within the national local government system and the associated policy networks. The centre has pursued strategies premised on control and direction rather than consultation and negotiation. However, as the next three chapters will show it has not been totally effective in achieving its policy goals and has stimulated a great deal of resistance, antagonism and resentment.

# III  KEY ISSUES FOR LOCAL GOVERNMENT

# 7 The Battle over Local Spending

This chapter examines the battle over local spending during the period of the first and second Thatcher governments (1979–87). The focus is on the conflict between central government and local authorities, especially those under Labour control. This conflict had at its roots several major issues including the appropriate level and direction of public spending, the constitutional position of local government and the future of local democracy. These issues have been extensively discussed elsewhere (Jones and Stewart, 1983; Newton and Karran, 1985; Blunkett and Jackson, 1987) and are not considered in detail here. The focus is rather on the way the conflict over local spending was fought out which, in practice, primarily revolved around complex legislation and administrative manœuvres. Popular mobilisation and public campaigning played a part but were dominated by a technical struggle between Department of the Environment officials and local authority treasurers, both supported and encouraged by their political masters. The aim of this chapter is to provide some insight into this battle and the strategies and tactics adopted by both sides.

The background to this struggle over spending is set by the growing reliance of local government on central financial support during the years of post-war expansion, particularly from the mid-1960s onwards. It was noted in Chapter 1 that the contribution of central government grants to local authority income for current expenditure increased from 35 per cent in 1953/4 to 45 per cent in 1974/5. During the same time the contribution of rates declined from 33 per cent to 24 per cent. When in the mid-1970s economic difficulties led to calls for financial constraint the then Labour Government ministers used the Consultative Council on Local

Government Finance, established in 1975, to exhort and encourage local authorities to curtail their spending. This policy had some success with current expenditure budgets coming to a virtual standstill after years of growth, accompanied by a substantial reduction in capital expenditure.

These achievements were considered to be inadequate by the incoming Conservative Government in 1979. Their concern was not simply a matter of limiting public expenditure. They wished to restructure public expenditure patterns and spend more on defence, law and order and social security (as a cushion for the rise in unemployment) and less on housing, education and social services. As Travers (1986, p. 80) explains:

> Therein lay a difficulty which plagued the Government from 1979 onwards in its relationship with local authorities. The Conservatives were committed to cutting spending on services which were not under direct central control. Local authorities had the power to raise any rates they chose within the law and could, if they chose, spend more than the new administration wanted.

In addition to this organisational dilemma the Conservatives increasingly faced sustained ideological opposition from a range of radical Labour councils, committed not just to protecting existing local government provision but determined to develop new policy responses to social and economic ills in a direct challenge to the approach of the Conservatives.

This chapter examines the struggle between central and local government in four sections. Most attention is directed to the struggle in England and Wales which is divided into two parts dealing with the periods 1979–83 and 1984–7. There is a brief comment on Scotland and a concluding section which assesses the struggle over local spending and outlines the Conservatives' plans for further changes in the system.

### The early exchanges: a dishonourable draw?

This section examines, in turn, the strategies used by central government to control local spending and the defence tactics of local authorities during the years 1979–83.


*Central government attack*

The Conservative attack on local spending came in three waves. First the Government introduced a new system for allocating central government financial support under the 1980 Local Government, Planning and Land Act. This act also contained a number of other important measures; some relating to local government finance, and others dealing with the operation of local authority direct-labour organisations and of the planning system, which will be considered in Chapter 8.

The 1980 legislation replaced the old system for supporting local authority current expenditure by a new Block Grant. Simplifying greatly, the old system operated on the basis of existing patterns of expenditure among local authorities. In other words, on the basis of local assessments of what was needed to be spent. The new Block Grant was distributed according to centrally-determined, grant-related expenditure assessments, or GREs for short. Grants were to be distributed on the basis of an assessment of local need made by central government. This was a change 'of fundamental importance' (Newton and Karran, 1985, p. 117). It was accompanied by a provision for 'grant taper' to discourage local authorities from spending much above the central assessment of their spending needs. This was soon followed by an automatic penalty-zone for authorities which spent more than ten per cent (on average) above the assessed need figure. This 'extra' expenditure would have to be financed to an increasing extent out of the rates rather than from central government funds.

The Local Government, Planning and Land Act also changed the Government's controls over local authority capital spending. As Travers (1986, p. 137) explains: 'up till 1981–2 the Government had controlled authorities' powers to borrow money to fund capital expenditure. From 1981–2 onwards control was exercised over expenditure'. The ability to spend on capital works was cash-limited within a particular financial year. Central government gave local authorities permission to spend, or block allocations, for education, personal social services, transport, housing, urban and (from April 1984) other services. In addition, the centre might grant additional allocations for individual projects. Local authorities were also able to use profits from trading undertakings and a proportion for net capital receipts (for example from the sale of land or council houses) prescribed by central government. The system operates, then, on the basis that local authorities raise money for capital works by borrowing and other means and that they are constrained in the amount they can spend by the allocation system run from the centre. These controls and the general economic climate proved on the whole an effective deterrent to local capital expenditure during 1979–83. Indeed at the end of 1982 the Government became so worried about the impact of declining capital expenditure on the construction industry that it asked local authorities to increase their capital spending! As a result there was, for example, a short-lived 'mini boom' in expenditure on housing improvement grants and other capital projects. By 1984–5 Government concern had again shifted back to limiting capital expenditure (see Table 1.4).

It was with respect to current spending that the Conservatives met more substantial difficulties. Government ministers even in the first year in which the new Block Grant system operated (1981–2) decided that the controls it offered over local spending were insufficient. This view led to a second line of attack.

The second wave in the Conservative offensive involved the introduction of a system of targets and penalties, as an additional element grafted onto the block grant scheme. The first targets for spending were set for every authority in England in January 1981 and later in the year targets were produced for Welsh authorities. The targets were established on a different basis from GREs and were backed by a system of penalties. If an authority chose to spend above target its Block Grant would be cut. These penalties were known as 'holdback'. The precise system used to set targets was changed every year (even within a year sometimes) and the superimposition of those targets and penalties on the basic block grant system made the arrangements extremely complicated. The penalties were made increasingly severe each year so that by 1983–4 many authorities were in the position of receiving less grant in absolute terms, at higher spending levels. Some, for example ILEA and the GLC, managed to spend their way out of any entitlement to grant.

The shifting system of targets and penalties made it extremely difficult for local authorities to plan effectively (Audit Commission, 1984). It was also subject to political manipulation so that Conservative councils were 'let off the hook' and penalties were most severely imposed on Labour authorities. For example, in 1983–4 Conservative-controlled councils incurred penalties of £24 million, and Labour councils incurred penalties totalling £217 million (Boddy, 1984a, p. 221).

The third wave in the Conservative attack was signalled by the 1982 Local Government Finance Act. This act followed the failure of an earlier bill which had proposed that local authorities should hold a local referendum if they wished to raise a supplementary rate. Conservative back-bench MPs and others expressed concern about the constitutional implications of such a proposal and the bill was dropped. The act which replaced it contained three important elements. First it legalised retrospectively the system of targets and penalties introduced in 1981–2 by the Government, and discussed above. Second it dealt with the issue of supplementary rates and precepts (see later discussion) by simply abolishing the right of local authorities to undertake those activities. Third it established the Audit Commission to oversee the auditing of local authority finances and encourage 'value for money' from local spending.

It is important to consider the role of the Audit Commission in fulfilling the Government's general strategy of reducing local spending. The Commission is nominally an independent body but its governing body is appointed by central government. In its work it has rather narrowly concentrated on issues of economy and efficiency and has tended to lend ideological support to Conservative Government claims about 'waste' in local government (Kline and Mallaber, 1986). On the other hand, it has been critical of the arbitrary and complex nature of central interventions (Audit Commission, 1984).

The Conservative attack on local spending between 1979 and 1983 was accompanied by rhetoric about 'overspending' councils and 'value for money'. It stopped local authorities raising additional revenue during a financial year by abolishing supplementary rates and precepts. But its main weapon was the withdrawal of central government grant support and a system of penalties for those authorities designated as over-spenders. Between 1981 and 1984 a total of £713 million was 'held back' from authorities in England alone (Travers, 1986, p. 132). The proportion of local authority revenue expenditure supported by central government grant fell from 48.5 per cent in 1979–80 to 35.9 per cent in 1982–3 (Travers, 1986, p. 211).

## Local government defence

The attack launched by central government was greeted in a number of quarters by a spirited defence of democratic local government (see especially Jones and Stewart, 1983). The Local Authority Associations were highly critical and complained bitterly about the centralisation and loss of local autonomy associated with the Government's proposals. There was stiff opposition to major elements of the Local Government, Planning and Land Act, even when the Associations were Conservative-controlled. The 1982 Act was also vigorously opposed, with some minor concessions rung from the Government (Travers, 1986, pp. 88–90, pp. 111–12).

Among some left-wing Labour councils there was support for a local counter-offensive (Preston, n.d.). Defensive strategies such as putting up the rates to maintain services were seen as electorally dangerous and unacceptable since the costs of central government financial cuts would simply be passed on to ratepayers (Bassett, 1981, pp. 50–1). There was talk of the need to develop a new alliance between councillors, local authority trade unions and community groups to oppose local spending reductions (Labour Co-ordinating Committee, n.d.). Lambeth launched such a campaign in the early 1980s but it petered out. The key defensive weapons used by local authorities during this period proved not to be popular mobilisation.

The law courts became an increasingly used instrument in central–local relations. Loughlin (1986) argues that in this period of retrenchment disputes between central and local government were not merely dealt with by traditional administrative and political channels but were fought out in law courts, as the nature and limits of respective powers and duties were tested. He cites the challenge of Brent and other London boroughs to central government financial orders made under the 1980 Act as marking 'the commencement of a new era in legal relations between central departments and local authorities' (p. 37). He notes how Hackney challenged the legality of its 1984–5 target and how some Conservative London boroughs charged the Labour-controlled GLC of the early 1980s with breaching its fiduciary duty to ratepayers by spending at levels which incurred such high penalties (pp. 42–3). The law courts were used by both sides to pursue the struggle over local spending. Central government and its supporters generally had the advantage given the 'nineteenth century individualism' which dominates legal culture and the generally 'conservative stance' maintained by the law courts. Moreover, central government if defeated had the option of creating new legislation to meet its needs (see Loughlin, 1986, Ch. 9).

The main weapon adopted in practice by local authorities wishing to resist cuts in services during the period 1979–83 was to increase their rates. As Table 7.1 indicates these years saw substantial increases in domestic rates. In addition some authorities in 1981, including the GLC and Lambeth as well as some Conservative-controlled counties, used supplementary rates in order to enable them to fulfil their programmes. It was such strategies which stimulated the abolition of this option in the 1982 Act. Individual rate rises were often spectacular, especially if an authority was badly hit by 'hold-back'.

Local authorities putting up their rates were able to limit the electoral damage by blaming central government cuts in grant for high rate demands. 'Sheffield Council, for example, put its rate up by 41 per cent in 1980 and 37 per cent in 1981 and was still supported at the polls' (Blunkett and Jackson, 1987, p. 154). A public opinion survey conducted in 1982 showed that nearly 60 per cent of respondents blamed central government for rate increases. The figure rose to 76 per cent among Labour voters (Weir, 1982, Table 5, p. 346). Moreover, this survey and others which followed showed both a widespread support for many public

TABLE 7.1  **Domestic rate increases in England 1980–4 (per cent)**

| 1980–1 | 1981–2 | 1982–3 | 1983–4 |
|--------|--------|--------|--------|
| 27 | 19.4 | 15.4 | 7.3 |

Source: CIPFA *Financial and General Statistics* 1980/81–1983/84.

services and a willingness within limits to pay for them (Game, 1984; Taylor-Gooby, 1985). Raising the rates was not as electorally unpopular as some had feared.

What of the other issue raised by left-wing Labour councils: the burden placed on working-class and poor families by rate increases? Here Labour councillors and others were able to draw some comfort from the growth in social security payments which underpinned increases in domestic rates (see Table 7.2). Rebates under the social security system are funded from central government finances. As Gibson and Travers (1986, p. 5.15) comment, despite the problems of producing comparable figures for the whole time series, it is clear that rebates have become a significant proportion of domestic rates. For the poorest families rebates mean that their rates bill is, in effect, zero. Indeed, as noted in Chapter 2, this feature of the social security system led the Conservatives to express concern about representation without taxation.

In addition to putting up their rates the other main weapon used by local authorities involved 'creative accounting'. From 1981–2 onwards in order to protect themselves from the uncertainties of block grant targets and penalties local authorities began to build up their rate fund balances (Travers, 1986, p. 133), which gave them some room for manœuvre. Special funds were also established and are described by Douglas and Lord (1986, p. 38) 'as the most widely-used kind of creative accounting'. The advantage of special funds lay in the fact that they enabled local authorities to manipulate the incidence of spending as between years. Thus money could be placed in a special fund in one year but spent in another year, thus avoiding penalties as far as possible and maximising income from central government grant. As Blunkett

**TABLE 7.2  Domestic rate income and rebates in England 1979–86 (£ billion)**

|                         | 1979–80 | 1980–1 | 1981–2 | 1982–3 | 1983–4 | 1984–5 | 1985–6 |
|-------------------------|---------|--------|--------|--------|--------|--------|--------|
| Domestic rates (gross)  | 2.6     | 3.4    | 4.2    | 4.9    | 5.3    | 5.6    | 6.1    |
| Less rebate             | 0.1     | 0.2    | 0.3    | 0.5    | 1.1    | 1.2    | 1.3    |
| Domestic rates (net)    | 2.5     | 3.2    | 3.9    | 4.4    | 4.2    | 4.4    | 4.8    |

Note: Changes in the social security system during 1982–3 affected comparisons.
       Rebates for 1979–80 to 1982–3 are understated as compared with later years.
Source: Gibson and Travers (1986) p. 5.15.

and Jackson (1987, p. 155) put it, creative accounting 'became a major form of political opposition'.

The struggle between central government and local authorities in the years 1979–83 has been described by a senior local authority officer as 'a dishonourable draw' (quoted in Travers, 1986, p. 145). Financial experts have described the Government's approach as 'inept' (Gibson, 1983, p. 19) and 'ill-thought out' (Travers, 1986, p. 147); although a DoE economist has defended the Government's record (Heigham, 1984). The Government used rhetoric and more specifically grant cuts and penalties to achieve its objectives. Local authorities replied with their own propoganda but relied in practice on rate increases and creative accounting to protect local spending levels. Capital spending was reduced but current spending was not significantly cut. The Government succeeded to an extent in transferring the burden of paying for services from central government to local ratepayers. Local authorities were in many cases able to protect and in few cases improve the standard and quality of the services they provided.

## Rate-capping and beyond: from campaigning to creative accounting

This section examines the struggle over local spending during the period 1984–7. It examines the public campaign against rate-capping and assesses its failure. It goes on to show how the struggle then returned to the level of technicalities, with local authorities using creative accounting to protect services and the Government devising a range of different administrative and legislative procedures to facilitate its control over local spending.

### The campaign against rate-capping

The Government retained its commitment to controlling local authority expenditure on its re-election in June 1983. Indeed it stepped up its propaganda against the overall level of local spending and the behaviour of particular Labour authorities who were seen as 'overspenders'. The abolition of the GLC and the six metropolitan counties, under the 1985 Local Government Act was in part justified by the Conservatives on the basis of the supposed wastefulness and profligacy of these authorities. Central government also maintained and tightened the system of targets and penalties, first introduced in 1981–2. This period also saw the introduction of a further weapon in the Government's armoury: rate-capping.

The 1984 Rates Act gave the Secretary of State for the Environment the power to limit both the rates of named authorities and reserve powers to limit the rates of all authorities. Only the former power, however, was used, and in June 1984 the Government published a list of 18 authorities who were to be rate-capped in 1985–6 (see Table 7.3). All but two of the councils were Labour-controlled; the two were Portsmouth (Conservative) and Brent (Labour–Alliance coalition).

The rate-capped Labour authorities together with Brent, supported by some heavily penalised but not rate-capped authorities (in particular Liverpool), launched a major campaign against rate-capping. With the option of raising rates to cover the loss of central

**TABLE 7.3   Rate-capped local authorities 1985–8**

| 1985–6 | 1986–7 | 1987–8 |
| --- | --- | --- |
| Basildon | Basildon | *As 1986–7 list with the* |
| Brent | Camden | *addition of:* |
| Camden | Greenwich | Brent |
| GLC | Hackney | Brighton |
| Greenwich | Haringey | Middlesborough |
| Hackney | Islington | Newham |
| Haringey | Lambeth | Gateshead |
| ILEA | Lewisham | North Tyneside |
| Islington | Liverpool | Sheffield |
| Lambeth | Newcastle | Tower Hamlets |
| Leicester | Southwark | *and the removal of* |
| Lewisham | Thamesdown | *Liverpool* |
| Merseyside | *plus* | |
| Portsmouth | All the joint boards | |
| Sheffield | created following the | |
| Southwark | abolition of the GLC | |
| South Yorkshire | and the six metropolitan | |
| Thamesdown | counties, as well as the | |
| | re-organised ILEA | |

government grant no longer open these authorities decided that the time was ripe for concerted and public mobilisation against the Thatcher government's policies.

Three factors form important elements in the context of the anti-rate-capping campaign. First soon after the June election over 70 local authorities and all the major public sector unions had joined together to form what became known as the Local Government Information Unit. It became an important focus for co-ordinating campaign activity. Second there was the propaganda victory achieved by Liverpool in mid-1974. After protracted negotiations, which involved the authority refusing to set a rate, the Militant-influenced Labour councillors claimed they had won substantial extra central government financial support for their city. A claim which proved to be exaggerated but Liverpool's success was, at the time, widely perceived as a major political defeat for the Government. Third the miners' strike was putting considerable pressure on the Government and anti-rate-capping campaigners felt that they, like the miners, were defending the living standards and future of their communities (Blunkett and Jackson, 1987, p. 167). In short, the time seemed ripe for a major and public campaign against the attack on local spending.

In July 1984 the involved authorities agreed 'a strategy of non-compliance' and committed themselves to adopt one of two tactics: either refusing to make a rate for the next financial year or deficit budgeting (which involves deliberately planning a level of expenditure which cannot be met by known income). The campaign had both national and local dimensions.

Nationally an unprecedented degree of coordination was achieved by the campaigning authorities. Over the autumn of 1984 and the winter of 1984–5 the leaders of rate-capped authorities and other sympathetic councils met regularly. In public an impressive degree of unity was displayed and a number of highly successful campaign activities were launched.

Local campaigns were aimed at drawing together three elements – the council, the workforce and the community. This was by no means a smooth exercise as the description of Sheffield's campaign by Blunkett and Jackson (1987, pp. 176–8) makes clear. They note how councillors 'learned much about the difficulty of defending local government services given the long-held feelings of frustration among many users and workers'. Nevertheless, a wide range of community groups and local authority workers were drawn into the protest. The changing relations between some local authorities and local interest groups, noted in Chapter 5, bore fruit in many of the local campaigns. It culminated on 6 March 1985 in a lively London demonstration which involved over 70 000 people.

By November 1984, the threatened local authorities had decided to adopt the 'no rate' rather than the 'deficit budget' strategy. But behind this apparent unity there was growing evidence of division (Lansley, 1985; Blunkett and Jackson, 1987). There was uncertainty about the objectives of the struggle. Some were looking to wring substantial concessions from the Government in the application of the Rates Act; others wanted to force the Government to withdraw the act and restore central government financial support to previous levels. There were also growing doubts, though not publicly spoken, about the ability of the Labour leaders to deliver votes for a 'no rate' strategy in their Labour groups. The fear of acting illegally and the threat of surcharge and possible personal bankruptcy, which hung over councillors, was beginning to have an impact.

In order to maximise unity the local authorities decided to shift their position from not setting a rate to agreeing to defer setting a rate in an act of collective defiance on 7 March 1987. A different position arose, however, in the case of the precepting authorities: Merseyside, South Yorkshire, GLC and ILEA. They were required by law to set their precept by 10 March and it was among these authorities that the pressures first told.

South Yorkshire and Merseyside set their precepts by 10 March. So too did the GLC after days of wrangling in public between Ken Livingstone, the leader and John McDonnell, his deputy. ILEA followed suit.

Although in total fifteen authorities deferred setting a rate on 7 March the collapse of the precepting authorities marked the beginning of a disorderly retreat. By 5 June all the authorities had set a legal rate, with the exception of Lambeth and Liverpool. These authorities finally set their rates in July, and their Labour councillors were served notice by the District Auditors that they were to face surcharges and expulsion from office. The defiant stand of the councils had collapsed.

*An assessment of the campaign*

The campaign against rate-capping failed because of miscalculations about what could be achieved, both in denting the resolve of the Government and maintaining unity and commitment among the Labour authorities. The Conservative Government was able to stand firm behind its legislation and its mandate. It obtained a reasonable degree of information and knowledge about the state of the local authorities' campaign. Crucially in February 1985 it revised upwards the rate limits of six authorities – ILEA, Hackney, Islington, Leicester, Lewisham and Haringey – thereby lessening the necessity for the councillors from these authorities to maintain a position of outright defiance in order to protect their local spending levels.

The weakness of the Labour authorities revolved around two factors (Lansley, 1985; Smith and Wheen, 1985). First there was the failure of the parliamentary party leaders to provide effective leadership to the campaign. Party leaders did not wish to be associated with a strategy which they feared could lead to law-breaking. This left relatively inexperienced local leaders fighting on their own and unsupported by a wider challenge to Thatcherism. Second there was a considerable lack of frankness and honesty among the local government leaders. On the one hand, it soon became clear that most of the Labour councillors involved were extremely unwilling to act illegally and thus occur surcharges, loss of office and possibly an end to their political careers. On the other, the dire consequences of rate-capping were greatly exaggerated for the purposes of campaign. At least in the short term it became increasingly clear that many rate-capped local authorities could survive even with a legal rate. Jobs and services could be maintained by a combination of creative accounting and other techniques.

For some the anti-rate-capping campaign was a product of left-wing wishful thinking which further damaged local government's image and esteem. Blunkett and Jackson (1987, Ch. 8), in contrast, comment that although the campaign failed to achieve its stated objectives it did raise local consciousness about public services and helped to bring into focus the Conservatives' attack on local democracy. They point to lessons gained about national and local campaigning. Public opinion they claim was moved in favour of the rate-capped local authorities. Finally the campaign strengthened the resolve of local authorities to resist cuts. 'If they had given up meekly during the financial year 1984–5, they would have adjusted to the government's view on local public spending'. Instead the 'political pressure exerted by the campaign forced politicians and officers to break new ground and extend the boundaries of financial ingenuity' (p. 189) in order to defend local services.

### Beyond anti-rate-capping

In the aftermath of the failed campaign local authorities switched their opposition from public campaigning against the Government back to creative accounting. In addition to the techniques mentioned earlier there are a range of options that have been used (see Douglas and Lord, 1986, pp. 38–9). These include the sale of mortgage debt, land and other council assets to produce income which can be used for capital spending. Several local authorities have re-scheduled their existing debt pushing off into the future the repayment of the principal and thus reducing their costs in the short term. Another technique is capitalisation which involves recording as capital spending items which in the past have been viewed as current expenditure – such as repairs and modernisation of council property. This ploy helps to avoid grant penalties on current expenditure levels. Deferred purchase schemes have also been devised using a finance company as an intermediary: an authority may undertake capital spending in one year but pay both capital and interest in future years, with initial repayments being small and later repayments covering the bulk of the cost. This devise is a more expensive way of funding capital work because of the capitalisation of interest (see Table 7.4 for an illustrative example). Nevertheless it has proved attractive to a substantial number of authorities.

Finally various 'lease and leaseback' schemes have been devised. According to *The Sunday Times* (12 April 1987) Manchester City Council has a plan to raise £200 million through a leasing deal with the Manchester Mortgage Corporation which is wholly owned by the City Council. The council will long-lease 32 civic buildings, including swimming pools, art galleries and an abattoir to the

**TABLE 7.4   Illustration of a deferred purchase scheme**

Capital expenditure implications of Leicester City Council's scheme to fund modernisation of 'Boot' houses

| Financial Year | Deferred Purchase (£ million) | Normal System (£ million) |
|---|---|---|
| 1986/7 | | 4.5 |
| 1987/8 | 0.6 | 5.3 |
| 1988/9 | 1.7 | 5.4 |
| 1989/90 | 2.8 | 5.3 |
| 1990/1 | 3.8 | 5.1 |
| 1991/2 | 4.9 | 2.7 |
| 1992/3 | 5.7 | 0.2 |
| 1993/4 | 6.0 | |
| 1994/5 | 6.0 | |
| 1995/6 | 6.0 | |
| 1996/7 | 4.8 | |
| 1997/8 | 3.7 | |
| 1889/9 | 2.6 | |
| 1999/2000 | 1.6 | |
| 2000/2001 | 0.5 | |
| | 50.7 | 28.5 |

Note: 'Boot' houses are so-called after their builder. They suffered from what became know.ז as 'cement cancer' and required almost total re-building.
Source: Leicester City Council, Report to the Housing Committee, 4 February 1986.

corporation in return for the money. The corporation in turn will raise £200 million in the City using the buildings as security. The council will invest it to bring in interest of £15 million in the first year. It will be used to support local service delivery and jobs. Manchester will lease the buildings back but because it can dictate its own terms will not start paying rent for two years. *The Sunday Times* estimates that Labour local authorities may have in effect borrowed some £5 billion by such schemes, although other estimates are more modest.

The Government has reacted by attempting to outlaw such schemes. The 1986 Local Government Act restricted the sale of mortgage debt. Deferred purchase arrangements were outlawed from midnight on 22 July 1986. In early 1988 the Government moved to block 'lease and leaseback' schemes. Schemes which put off payments into the future have an inherently limited life since ultimately substantial payments have to be made. They were, in effect, a delaying tactic used on the part of Labour authorities in the hope that they might be dealing with a more sympathetic central government in the future.

The Conservatives have also kept the pressure of rate-capping. In 1986–7 12 local authorities were selected plus ILEA and the non-directly elected joint boards established after the 1986 abolition. For the financial year 1987–8 the list of rate-capped local authorities swelled to 19 (see Table 7.3). Again, these hit lists were overwhelmingly of Labour-controlled local authorities or in the case of the joint boards in areas where Labour had previously been in control. The only exception is the selection for 1987–8 of Liberal-controlled Tower Hamlets.

Alongside this continued assault the Government made a number of 'concessions'. First some of the rules associated with rate-capping were loosened so that in 1986–7 several of the affected authorities were able successfully to appeal against the expenditure levels they had been set. As a result of what is known as 'redetermination' these authorities had their expenditure levels increased by between 2.2 per cent and 7.7 per cent. Second from 1986–7 onwards the Government abandoned the system of targets and penalties separate from the basic block grant mechanisms. Instead, the two systems were to be integrated so that a local authority would lose central grant at a substantial rate if it spent at a level significantly above GRE. Finally the grant settlement for 1986–7 was relatively generous, enabling the Government to cushion the impact of abolition and the second year of rate-capping to be coped with by a number of authorities (Travers, 1986, pp. 184–6).

It would, however, be mistaken to suggest that the Thatcher government had lost its commitment to intervening in local spending. Rather it had become more realistic about what could be achieved (Gibson, 1987). Indeed the 1987 Local Government Act pushed through just before the end of Thatcher's second government retrospectively legalised the Government's past decisions relating to local authority spending, and removed the right of appeal and the right of judicial review of past and present ministerial decisions about the allocation of grants and accounting practices.

For both local authorities and the Government after the brief flowering of public campaigning in 1984–5, the struggle over local spending was largely fought out in a range of complex technical, administrative and legislative manœuvres. Moreover, the struggle was hard-fought. The Government relentlessly pursued its task; taking new measures, closing loopholes and granting the occasional concession. Local authorities have found themselves under considerable pressure. As Table 1.4 indicates after a minor 'boom' in 1983 and 1984 local authority capital spending fell back. Current expenditure, on the other hand, continued to slightly increase in real terms between 1984 and 1987. A number of Labour but also other authorities clearly continued to defy the Government in their commitment to protect, and even expand, the services that they provided.

**The struggle in Scotland: a brief comment**

The struggle in Scotland took a different form given differences in legislation and circumstance. The early years of the conflict are described in detail elsewhere (Midwinter, 1984, especially Chs. 2–3). In general it would appear that the Government took more far-reaching powers in Scotland. In addition to cutting back central financial support the Government acquired two major new weapons. The 1981 Local Government (Miscellaneous Provisions) (Scotland) Act 'marked a significant advance of central control' (Travers, 1986, p. 137). It allowed the Government to intervene selectively in the expenditure decisions of individual councils by giving the Secretary of State the power to reduce grant during the course of a particular financial year and prohibited authorities from making up any lost grant by extra borrowing. Cuts in grant would thus have to be funded by reduced spending. Selective action was announced in 1981–2 against seven councils, seven again in 1982–3 and five in 1983–4. Lothian, Stirling and Dundee were in the forefront of the campaign against the Government's attack (see NUPE, 1983).

The second major weapon taken by the Government was Local Government and Planning (Scotland) Act 1982. This legislation supplemented the power to reduce central government grant by allowing the Secretary of State to decide whether to reduce an authority's grant or to require the authority to reduce its rate and to reimburse its ratepayers, or to combine a cut in grant with a cut in rates.

Yet despite these draconian powers and selective attacks on particular authorities the Government's measures in Scotland have failed to deliver substantial reductions in overall levels of local spending. Indeed Midwinter (1984, p. 98) doubts whether the centre has 'any stomach for the redundancies that would be necessary to achieve large-scale cutbacks'. As in England and Wales 'local government has been resilient to central pressure, and shown a capacity for survival'. What has occurred, has been a transfer of the financial burden for local services from central government funds to locally raised rates.

Concern over this shift was heightened in Scotland by the impact of a revaluation of the rate base in 1985–6 which led in some cases to considerable increase in the rates demands faced by both domestic and non-domestic ratepayers (although it resulted in reduced demands for others). The Government under pressure provided short-term financial support to reduce the effect of change. This incident also encouraged the Government to consider further radical measures to replace rates by a community charge and the uniform business rate.

### Conclusions: paying for local government

The struggle over local spending illustrates some of the general features of central–local relations noted in Chapter 6. Despite their determination and legislative action the Thatcher governments 1979–87 found themselves constrained by their lack of direct control over local government. Many local authorities – through their manipulation of financial information, creative accounting and by raising their rates (subject to selective limitation) – were able to fight a sustained rearguard action against central government. The battle was mostly fought out on technical grounds at the behest of opposing political masters. As Blunkett (1986, p. 12) comments:

Of all the groups employed by local authorities in the past few years, it is ironical that . . . often dubbed the most reactionary . . . – the Treasurer or Finance Officer – which has shown the greatest ingenuity and initiative . . . It has in fact been the imagination and ability of politicians together with the professional initiative of officers, combatting wave after wave of government legislative and financial attacks, which has most protected the delivery of services in those areas.

The Thatcher governments were able to pass more of the burden of paying for local government on to local ratepayers and away from central government but they did not succeed in substantially reducing local current spending. Indeed, on the contrary, local authority current expenditure has continued to slightly increase in real terms (Table 1.4).

The Conservatives have kept capital spending under control, continuing the trend established by the Labour Governments of the 1970s. Capital spending on housing, schools and road maintenance by local authorities has remained at a low level compared to the pre-1975 period. Some minor shifts in the pattern of local authority current expenditure have occurred in line with the Conservatives' priorities. The proportion of current spending devoted to law, order and protection services, for example, increased from 12 per cent to 14 per cent in England between 1978–9 and 1984–5. Yet the Government itself claims that overall it has only achieved modest success in holding back local spending and that its efforts have been 'accompanied by a worsening of the relationship between central Government and even the moderate and responsible local authorities' (HM Government, 1986, p. 5).

A recognition of these factors, plus concern over the problems associated with the rate revaluation in Scotland, led the Conservatives to commit themselves to a further wholesale reorganisation of local government finance. This time the main target was the abolition of domestic rates. The Green Paper *Paying for Local Government* (HM Government, 1986) proposed that domestic rates would be replaced by a 'community charge' which, in practice, would be a poll tax levied from every adult in the authority. A community charge proposed by an authority could be subject to 'capping' if central government felt that it was excessive. Non domestic rates would be set by central government rather than local authorities. The yield from this rate would then be handed back to local authorities as a payment per adult. Further changes to the block grant system and more far-reaching controls over capital expenditure were part of the package. Finally there was a proposal that people supported by welfare payments should be obliged to pay at least a proportion of their community charge themselves. Legislation to introduce the new community charge and other associated measures in Scotland was passed during the 1986–7 session. To provide a similar scheme in England and Wales was a Conservative manifesto commitment for the 1987 election, despite considerable professional and other criticism of the impracticability and distributive consequences of introducing those financial reforms.

With the Conservatives winning power for a third term those Labour and other local authorities who adopted creative accounting devices to keep up their spending levels have had to reconsider their position, and engage in some rapid budget pruning. The financial position of several London boroughs and other authorities, including Manchester and Liverpool, would appear to be critical. Substantial cuts in services and job losses are on the agenda of the Labour authorities. In Chapter 11 we examine the debate over the community charge and the Conservatives' other measures and consider the impact of these reforms on the operation of local government.

# 8   Privatising Local Government

In combination with the struggle over local spending the first and second Thatcher governments also saw considerable conflict over proposals to 'privatise' local government holdings and activities. Privatisation is taken here to refer in a general way to policies which aim to limit the role of the public sector and increase the role of the private sector. These policies are linked with fiscal austerity since advocates of privatisation claim that local authorities and their ratepayers would gain from such policies by savings in running costs and by obtaining new sources of funds. But privatisation is more than a response to fiscal constraints. The complex range of motivations behind privatisation emerge as a key theme in this chapter.

The discussion starts with an examination of the different forms of privatisation and the underlying factors which give some coherence to Thatcher's privatisation strategy. The bulk of the remainder of the chapter is taken up with discussing in detail each of the various approaches to privatisation during the 1979–87 period. The main issues addressed are the impact of privatisation and the nature of the conflict that has occurred over its implementation.

## The nature of privatisation

There is considerable confusion about what privatisation means. Following Heald (1983, p. 298) we see privatisation as 'an umbrella term for very many different policies loosely linked by the way in which they are taken to mean a strengthening of the market at the expense of the state'. Young (1986, p. 236) provides a similar definition:

> In very broad terms 'privatisation' can be seen as a term used to describe a set of policies which aim to limit the role of the public sector, and increase the role of the private sector, while improving the performance of the remaining public sector.

He goes on to comment that 'privatisation takes a variety of forms and is a complex phenomenon. Separate and apparently unconnected threads of government policy appear, on examination, to be part of an overall privatisation strategy' (p. 237). Let us consider these arguments in more detail.

In local government three forms of privatisation have come to prominence. First there is the sale of local authority assets. The sale of council houses is the most obvious manifestation here. Second there are initiatives aimed at introducing 'market discipline' into local authority service delivery. The contracting out of services such as refuse collection – with public sector providers forced to compete with private contractors – is a key development. The 'deregulation' of bus services provides another example. Third there is the encouragement of private sector substitute provision and investment. A host of initiatives reflect this trend including the rapid growth of private-sector homes for the elderly and other dependent groups, the rise of enterprise trusts to provide business advice and other services and the whole process of 'leveraging' the private sector into investment projects in deprived areas.

Having identified three forms of privatisation relevant to local government the next issue that needs to be addressed is in what sense do these various initiatives form 'an overall privatisation strategy'? Dunleavy and Rhodes (1986, p. 141) claim that 'the privatisation label gives a bogus unity to disparate policies connected chiefly by the ideological prejudice that "private equals good" while "public equals bad", and the electoral calculation that intensifying public/private conflicts and "rolling back the state" provided a long-term boost to Conservative electoral support'. They are right to suggest that 'gut politics' and electoral considerations have played a part in stimulating Conservative interest in privatisation. Yet they go too far in suggesting that the relationship between the various elements of privatisation is bogus.

There are several underlying themes which give the privatisation strategy an overall coherence.

First the strategy has developed in and is a response to a period of fiscal austerity. The receipts from council house sales have been used to reduce pressure for public sector borrowing. Contracting-out and deregulation advocates make claims in terms of the savings that can be achieved in the running costs of service delivery. The use of private sector substitutes brings in new resources and funds in a period of public sector restraint. The financial pressure on local authorities has given the privatisation strategy a cutting edge.

Second privatisation draws on the distinctive philosophy of the Thatcher Governments. Each of the forms of privatisation has helped to create new markets and greater opportunities for the private sector. This corresponds with the Conservatives' belief in the need to change the way the economy works by releasing market forces. Furthermore, each of the forms of privatisation have contributed to the Conservatives' attempts to fundamentally reduce public expectations about what the state should do and what it should be responsible for. The commitment to a market economy and a limited role for the state are key elements in 'New Right' thinking. 'Public choice' theorists also provide intellectual support for privatisation with their criticisms of the stagnation and inefficiencies of public bureaucracies. We will consider these arguments in more detail in Chapters 10 and 11. For the present we have sought to establish that each form of privatisation is consistent with key elements in New Right thinking.

As Young (1986, pp. 246–7) suggests privatisation was based on a philosophy worked out when the Conservatives were in opposition. Once in power the philosophy stimulated a large number of potential schemes; some have been dropped but others have been pursued with vigour. As new problems have emerged so the privatisation philosophy has provided a guide to action. Thus, for example, after the 1981 Liverpool riots Heseltine's response was to take private sector investors on a tour of the city.

The pace and direction of particular initiatives have varied over time in response to a complex of factors, including practical problems, questions of priority and the strength of political opposition. The implementation process and the impact of each form of privatisation provide a focus of attention in the remainder of the chapter. What has been argued this far is that although there are different forms of privatisation the Conservatives' privatisation strategy has gained an overall coherence from its development in the context of financial constraints and its association with key elements of New Right philosophy.

## Selling off local authority assets

*The sale of the century?*

The two key areas for public sector asset sales relevant to local government have been the sales of council-owned land for private development and the sale of council houses. Some authorities have sold other assets. Conservative-controlled Westminster City Council in January 1987 disposed of three large cemeteries to a company with the delightful name Cemetery Assets UK Ltd! However, in 1988 it moved to buy them back because of local protests.

As Poulton (1984) notes the sales of council-owned land increased markedly during the early 1980s. The 1980 Local Government, Planning and Land Act obliged local authorities to produce registers of unused or under-used land in their ownership and the Secretary of State took powers to order the release of certain sites. This power has provided the basis for formal warnings and informal pressure. Concern with providing sites for industrial development has also acted as an encouragement to sales. But in the releasing of land for private sector house building the greatest impact can be seen. Local authorities and new towns sold sufficient land to private house builders in England between April 1979 and March 1986 for around 52 000 houses. 'Building under licence' schemes by private builders in partnership with local authorities produced a further 16 500 houses for sale, and local authorities in Great Britain also built for sale some 7000 low cost homes (Social Trends, 1987, pp. 145–6, Table 8.18). Many of these schemes required extensive public sector subsidy (a point we will return to later). They have had a dramatic effect on the physical appearance of some major cities, most notably Glasgow and Liverpool where over 2000 homes have been completed in each city. This level of activity, however, pales in significance in comparison to the impact of council house sales.

The Conservative manifesto (1987, p. 6) proudly boasts that

'more than a million council homes have been sold in Britain since 1979'. About two-thirds of these sales have been to sitting tenants under the 'Right-to-Buy' legislation. The remainder are made up of sales of vacant dwellings and acquired properties, with increasingly whole estates being handed over to property developers for refurbishment and re-sale. Council house sales are the most pervasive privatisation policy in terms of the number of individual households affected. Moreover, capital receipts from the sale of council houses dramatically outweigh those from other asset sales and have become an important element in public expenditure planning. For these reasons, we focus our discussion of local authority asset sales on the council house sales policy.

## *The origins and motivations of 'Right-to-Buy'*

Bassett (1980) identifies a number of interlocking factors that contributed to the development of the Conservatives' policy on sales. The pioneering efforts of some local Conservative councils, such as Birmingham in the 1960s, combined with the local leaders' active promotion of sales probably helped push the issue onto the national agenda. Thereafter the policy had the advantage of attracting support from a wide range of opinion within the Conservative party – from Peter Walker to Keith Joseph. The two key motivations associated with other forms of privatisation were present: a concern to limit the role of the public sector and increase that of the private sector and claims about the financial benefits of sales in an era of fiscal austerity.

An additional motivation was undoubtedly the perceived electoral advantage of the sales policy. During the 1970s a sale programme was increasingly seen as an election winner, among national Conservative party leaders. Some Conservative local authorities also seem to have deliberately developed policies aimed at shifting tenure patterns in an effort to maintain their local power. The example of Wandsworth will be considered in the next section. Although as noted in Chapter 1 there is some debate as to whether the impact of tenure location on voting behaviour is strong and clear-cut the perceived electoral advantage of council house sales made it a priority element in the Conservatives' privatisation strategy.

The Conservatives in opposition between 1974 and 1979 became not only more convinced of the value of a sales policy but became committed to making it obligatory for local authorities to facilitate tenant purchase. Since the inter-war years local authorities have been able to sell dwellings with ministerial consent. Few local authorities took advantage of this provision until the 1960s and with the active encouragement of a Conservative Government in 1972 council house sales reached the level of 46 000. But it declined thereafter and, whether justified or not, much Conservative criticism was addressed towards 'recalcitrant, oppositional local authorities' (Forrest and Murie, 1985, p. 16). Frustration and a concern to actively promote sales led to the 'Right-to-Buy' legislation.

The 1980 Housing Act gave tenants of three or more years standing the right to buy at 33 per cent less than market value, with a further one per cent discount for each year of tenancy up to a maximum of 50 per cent or £25 000. The discount would have to be repaid if the house was sold again within five years. These carrots were combined with the stick of enforced rent increases. Loss of central government subsidies pushed up rent levels, with the average weekly rent in England jumping from £8.18 in 1980–1 to £13.59 in 1982–3 (McCulloch, 1987, pp. 58–60).

*The struggle over council house sales*

Central government from the outset took an active part in implementing the 'Right-to-Buy' policy. It launched a publicity campaign and spent in total £2.3 million (up until May 1985) on promoting council house sales. It also engaged in extensive scrutiny of the performance of local authorities. By December 1983 the government was in contact with about 200 mainly Labour-controlled local authorities about aspects of their practice relating to 'Right-to-Buy'. As Forrest and Murie (1985, p. 32) note 'this represented a much more active and interventionist stance than had generally applied in the housing area in the past'.

The resistance from local authorities took overt and covert forms, and was not entirely confined to Labour authorities. Some Conservative councils were concerned about the impact of sales and followed the advice of their officers in an effort to restrict the number of sales, as in Rugby during the early 1980s (McHale,

1984). Among the more covert tactics adopted were the use of delay in the handling of 'Right-to-Buy' applications, an insistence on explaining the financial disadvantages as well as the attractions of owner-occupation, and in at least one Labour authority the implied threat that a 'problem family' would be moved in next to households purchasing their homes! The opposition was in some authorities led by councillors. In others, for example Lambeth, representatives of NALGO were to the fore (Ascher, 1983).

Sustained overt and campaigning opposition came from about two dozen Labour authorities. Greenwich, a number of other London boroughs, Sheffield and other major urban authorities were in the forefront of this campaign. The Labour party nationally committed itself to repealing the 'Right-to-Buy' legislation and to legislate to ensure that all future sales would be at the discretion of local authorities and at full market value (Labour Party, 1982). Behind this firm stance, however, there was considerable uncertainty, which weakened the base of Labour's opposition. For some the perceived electoral appeal of council house sales made it an unwise policy to attack and they felt there was little chance of mass opposition from tenants. For others the issues were more fundamental and related to whether council housing was a particularly socialist form of tenure and whether in practice – in its current operation – it was worth defending (Jacobs, 1982). As Forrest and Murie (1985, p. 7) put it: 'It was certainly questionable whether an unqualified resistance to sales was a struggle for the working class or the preservation of local paternalistic, bureaucratic empires'. They continue: 'despite some initial aggressive posturing few local authorities chose to go anywhere near the wall when Right to Buy was introduced'. Final warnings, which were needed, were sent by the Department of the Environment to Sheffield, Greenwich and a few other authorities. Only against Norwich did central government decide to use its full powers to intervene.

The case of Norwich is described in detail in Forrest and Murie (1985). What emerges is that Norwich's opposition was based fundamentally on a localist position, the right of local authorities to make their own decisions about their housing stock. Norwich was selected for attention by central government to set an example to other authorities. On 4 December 1981, after a prolonged period of dispute, Section 23 powers were invoked which enabled the DoE to take over the administration of Norwich's council house sales policy. Norwich's challenge in the courts against this intervention eventually proved unsuccessful and as a result they agreed to cooperate with the DoE official sent in to take over. Forrest and Murie comment that without Norwich's cooperation 'the lack of experience of DoE . . . could have seriously exposed the intervention'. The episode showed the strength of central government but it also indicated a potential weakness: 'the risk that the competence of central government would be exposed by being left to carry out local administration' (p. 120). In the short term, however, the capitulation of Norwich signalled a triumph for the Conservatives.

Not every local authority was reluctant or resistant. Some Conservative administrations pursued sales policies with enthusiasm. Wandsworth boasts over 9000 sales including a high proportion of flats between 1978 and 1987 (Beresford, 1987). Many of them were under 'Right-to-Buy' but in addition the council has pursued an active policy of site sales, sales of individual vacant properties and the disposal of entire estates to private sector developers. The local authority has used publicity to promote sales, door-to-door canvassing and has established a special unit to coordinate the policy. These activities combined with an active improvement grants policy, which appears to have encouraged a degree of gentrification, has resulted in a dramatic shift in the tenure pattern of the authority. The owner-occupied sector has grown from 27 to 48 per cent of the stock between 1978 and 1985, with the proportion of council tenants and private tenants falling respectively from 40 to 34 per cent and 29 to 14 per cent. Indeed this policy seems to have been pursued as a deliberate attempt to shift the electoral preferences of the authority and ensure continued Conservative rule. Judging by local election results in 1982 and 1986 and the gaining of Battersea by the Conservatives in the 1987 general election this policy appears to have had some success.

### The impact of 'Right-to-Buy'

Notwithstanding the Wandsworth example the political impact of 'Right-to-Buy' is difficult to assess. It was widely felt to have contributed to the Conservatives' electoral success in 1979 and 1983. Certainly the Labour party shifted its ground after its 1983 defeat and went into the 1987 election supporting the 'Right-to-Buy'. At a national level both Labour and Alliance leaders appear to be trapped by their perception of the popularity of the Conservatives' home ownership policies. They regard housing as a 'lost cause'.

It would not be appropriate to engage in a full discussion of the effect of the sales policy on the public sector stock (see Clapham and English, 1987; Forrest and Murie, 1984). Broadly since 1979 the local authority stock has been in absolute decline as sales have exceeded new building. Better quality dwellings and houses rather than flats have been the most likely to have been sold. There is an increasing proportion of council tenants who are semi-skilled or unskilled, on low incomes or reliant on welfare benefits. This trend suggests that a decaying council housing stock is increasingly providing accommodation for the poor and welfare dependents. Council house sales have contributed to this process.

There is a distinctive regional pattern to sales, crudely following a North–South dimension. The areas which achieved the highest sales are in the South, especially in less urbanised areas on the fringes of cities. These areas generally had a smaller proportion of local authority stock to begin with. Beyond this factors such as the buoyancy of the local economy, the nature of the stock and the availability of alternative opportunities for owner-occupation have produced complex local variations in the propensity of council tenants to buy. Broadly, though, the uneven spread of sales is linked to the uneven impact of economic restructuring and decline (Forrest, 1987).

The impact of these economic factors is reflected and reinforced by the political control of local authorities, with Conservatives dominant in the buoyant South and Labour's main strongholds in the North.

The policy of council house sales has proved to be a major success for the Conservatives. Yet after an initial surge to over 200 000 public sector sales in 1982 the annual rate of sales has dropped back to about half that number. Further incentives in the 1984 Housing and Building Control Act had little impact. The 1986 Housing and Planning Act provided further discounts and incentives targetted especially at flat sales. There are some signs of renewed tenant interest and the DoE had meetings during 1987 with several Labour-controlled London boroughs to urge them to step up their rate of 'Right-to-Buy' sales. Nevertheless it seems unlikely that sales to individual tenants will enable the Conservatives to reach the target of 80 per cent owner-occupation. As Forrest comments we have seen 'a stubborn refusal by the vast majority of tenants to be cajoled into exercising their rights'. Lack of income is one factor in explaining this phenomenon among others. For this reason the Housing and Planning Act turns its attention to other forms of privatisation involving the disposal of whole estates to private developers and the taking-over of management functions by non-local authority agencies. We shall consider these developments later in the chapter.

## De-regulation and competitive tendering

A second form of privatisation rests on the Conservatives' commitment to bringing the discipline of market competition to bear on local authority service delivery. It is argued that opening up public service deliveries to private sector producers creates an environment which can lead to improved efficiency, innovation in service delivery and a greater awareness of consumer requirements. A number of initiatives have flowed from these views. They can be placed under two broad headings: de-regulation and competitive tendering.

### *The de-regulation of bus services*

In terms of local government it is in the provision of bus services that de-regulation has had the greatest impact. Since 1930 passenger transport had been subject to a strict regulatory system with local bus service providers requiring an operator's licence to ensure safety standards and a road service licence to run a particular service, with controls on fare levels and stopping places. The provision of bus services, in part as a result, has been dominated by public sector operators.

The 1980 Transport Act made it easier for new and private sector operators to gain licences to provide bus services. But it left considerable powers in the hands of established operators who could cross-subsidise and divert considerable resources in the short term in order to see off 'up-start' competitors. An example of this process in operation is provided by Evans (1985) in an analysis of Cardiff City Council Transport's response to a private sector challenger. The 1980 Transport Act also established three trial areas in which it was no longer necessary for operators to obtain a road service licence before providing a bus service on a particular route. This experiment in de-regulation had little impact in two of the trial areas (Norfolk and Devon), but in a third – Hereford – there was a growth of some private sector interest and competition (Evans and Hayes, 1984).

The 1985 Transport Act extended this regime of de-regulation throughout Britain, excluding London. The system of licensing was abolished and replaced by a streamlined registration system. In addition the act sought to promote competition by undermining the dominance and monopoly position of public sector operators. The Passenger Transport Executives and district councils operating bus undertakings had to form their operations into companies (see Chapter 3). These companies were to operate according to market principles as viable businesses. The National Bus Company was to be privatised and broken down into small commercial units. The act gave local authorities and other transport authorities a general duty not to inhibit competition but rather to promote value for money in transport provision. Finally the Act allowed subsidies to be provided by local authorities only to support unprofitable but socially desirable routes and only after bids to operate the route had been the subject of a competitive tender. (For a more detailed discussion see Loughlin, 1986, pp. 88–92.)

The act came into operation in the Autumn of 1986. Between 70 and 80 per cent of the old route system is being operated under the new commercial regime, but off-peak and Sunday services on these routes have been reduced. Relatively few new private operators (some 200) have come forward to work in the commercial market and then typically on a very small scale. As for tendered services the early signs are of even less new blood among operators. However, the level of public subsidy support has fallen by some 30 per cent. One visible impact has been the increased number of mini-bus services, more than 200, according to the 1987 Conservative manifesto.

From the customer viewpoint the results from Bus Watch's Survey suggest that 'deregulation does not seem to have improved matters overall' (Hoyle, 1987). The loss of off-peak, Sunday and rural services, and uncertainty about timetables, has made life more difficult for those dependent on public transport. Some 70 per cent of bus passengers are female, so it could be argued that de-regulation has done little to improve choice and opportunities for mobility among women. Moreover, de-regulation has failed to deliver an expansion of services in urban areas capable of attracting car users onto public transport. The other main losers appear to have been the employees of former local authority and public sector operators where there have been considerable redundancies and a worsening of wages and conditions for those left in employment.

### Competitive tendering

Competitive tendering in its most common form involves private contractors competing for the contracts to undertake, for example, public sector building or supplies. This form of competition and use of private contractors has long operated in local government. Indeed Chapter 1 argued that local authority purchasing in this way has a crucial impact on the local economy and employment market. Since 1979, however, a different form of competitive tendering has grown in prominence within British local government. These tendering exercises have involved services previously provided by in-house workers. In most cases, the in-house workforce has been asked to compete against interested private bidders. If it wins the work then the contract price becomes its budget and it operates as if it were an arms-length organisation servicing the local authority. If it loses then the service is contracted out to a private company and the direct labour force is disbanded. This form of competitive tendering has 'grown up as a central plank of the national government's privatisation programme' (Ascher, 1987, p. 21). It has been applied in central government and the National Health Service as well as local authorities.

The motivation behind contracting-out reflects the general thrust behind other privatisation initiatives. Forsyth (1982) argues that both ratepayers and businesses are winners in the contracting-out game. Ratepayers are winners because of 'the one great fact about privatised services: they are cheaper'. Businesses are winners because the contracting-out of services 'offers them the chance of extra business'. The contractor 'finds opportunity for enterprise, development and profit in the new activity' (p. 988).

There is an additional major factor which has stimulated the drive towards contracting-out by the Conservative party: a desire to weaken public sector trade unionism. Ascher (1987, Ch. 2) traces the origins of the present competitive tendering debate in local authorities back to the 'winter of discontent' in 1978–9. Local authority manual workers were in the forefront of strike action during this period, which brought home to many the power that such workers wielded over key public services.

> Competitive tendering and contracting out fit into the Conservative Government's comprehensive and sustained attack upon trade union power. In particular, they offer scope for reducing the 'stranglehold' that the Party attributes to public sector unions. (p. 47)

A private sector contractor's employees are less likely to be strongly unionised. Even if the service stays in-house the position of the trade unions is severely weakened.

The drive towards competitive tendering has developed at both local and national levels. At the local level Southend led the way in the early 1980s with the contracting-out of its refuse collecting and street cleaning services. But the London Borough of Wandsworth pushed ahead most aggressively with contracting-out. Between 1982 and 1987 the borough 'checked' 32 activities against the private sector and has subsequently contracted out 15 services and established a further eight in-house teams following a competitive testing exercise. Savings totalling £24 million, running at about £6 million annually are claimed (Beresford, 1987, pp. 9–10).

At the national level the 1980 Local Government Planning and Land Act contained a commitment to introduce market discipline into the operation of councils' direct labour organisations (DLOs). An overall rate of return on capital of five per cent would be required for DLOs. In addition, competitive tendering for a certain percentage of work was required. Central government has progressively increased the amount of work that has to go out to tender. Several Labour councils devised ways to limit the impact of the legislation on their DLOs and encouraged expansion into new areas such as asbestos removal and damp proofing. In general though there has been a considerable reduction in the size of DLOs with a 22.5 per cent fall in numbers of employees from 156 606 to 121 381 and a 17.7 per cent drop in the value of output from £1.8 million to £1.5 million between 1980 and 1985. DLOs have had to reorganise to survive, with some proving more successful at improving efficiency than others.

Government interest in competitive tendering was reinforced by sustained lobbying activity by the right-wing Adam Smith Institute (Forsyth, 1980) and consultants funded by major contracting companies. Two Conservative MPs, Michael Forsyth and Christopher Chope, were prominent campaigners for contracting-out. At first it appeared that the Government, even after its re-election with a large majority in 1983, was reluctant to extend mandatory competitive tendering to a range of local authorities services. But the campaigners were rewarded in February 1985 by the publication of a Government consultative paper (DoE, 1985c) proposing to make competitive tendering mandatory for a variety of local authority services including refuse collection, street cleaning, internal building cleaning, ground and vehicle maintenance and catering. Legislation to carry out these changes was expected in the parliamentary session 1986–7 but was delayed. Following the Government's re-election in 1987 appropriate legislation will be operational by 1988.

That legislation has had to be considered reflects the limited impact of contracting-out on local authorities. Annual Surveys by *Local Government Chronicle* (17 June 1983, 22 June 1984, 5 July 1985, 3 July 1986, 3 July 1987) show that while some authorities have sought to contract out voluntarily, the majority have not. There was a boom in interest in privatisation in the early 1980s with 150 authorities considering contracting-out between 1982–3. Yet only 37 authorities eventually contracted out a service in this period. Later surveys showed a decline in local authority interest. Although some authorities continued to contract out services the value of contracts was small, less than £120 million for 1986–7. After an initial number of major refuse collection and street cleaning contracts the trend shifted to small-scale activities such as toilet cleaning, grass-cutting, catering and rodent control. Rather like council house sales there has been a North-South dimension to contracting-out. Conservative-controlled councils in the South of England have shown the greatest interest. Labour authorities have shown the least commitment and Scottish authorities have hardly privatised anything. As Ascher (1987, pp. 227–8) notes by as early as 1985 contractors were disillusioned with the lack of growth in the market and withdrew from promotional work at the local level.

Explanations for this relative failure of contracting-out vary. Propagandists for contracting-out blame the vested interests of local authority trade unions and bureaucrats and the weakness of councillors (Butler, 1985). Trade unions sources argue that privatisation has failed because its benefits are more imaginary than real; and that savings, even if they are achieved, are at the expense of reduced employment and working conditions and decreased quality in service delivery (SCAT, 1985).

In the propaganda battle it would appear that after an initial push by the contractors the counter-attack by the trade unions made considerable headway. The publicity that the union campaign gave to contractors' failures 'caused many authorities to think twice about contracting out' (Ascher, 1987, p. 225).

Where contracting-out has developed it has relied on a heavy degree of political support and commitment, usually from Conservative councillors. Wandsworth is a prime example (Beresford, 1987). In some instances senior officers have been enthusiastic supporters of the process, in others they have not. The reaction of the trade unions has varied too. In highly unionised and militant areas, suggests Ascher (1987, p. 245), unions have refused to cooperate with management and attempted to use industrial action and public campaigning to oppose privatisation. In other areas unions have found themselves working to win the contract for in-house employees. Both strategies have major disadvantages. Unions run the danger of losing localised oppositional campaigns, while 'playing the contracting game' can lead to cooperation in a process of job cutting. Many councils have used threats of privatisation to re-establish firm control over their in-house staff and trade unions. The tendering process has in a number of cases been used by local authority managers to reassert their right to manage.

In as far as savings are achieved during the tendering process they are at the expense of trade unions and their members. Local authority workers from the manual sector have been the main target. For them 'job losses, reductions in pay and deteriorating conditions of service are the most visible outcomes of the tendering process'. Not only has their material position worsened, 'any sense of security, importance or belonging has been undermined' (Ascher, 1987, p. 111). As the focus of tendering activity has shifted from refuse collection to cleaning and catering services so a gender dimension to the conflict has grown. Contracting-out has posed a particular threat to women's jobs and conditions of employment.

Ascher (1987, Ch. 8), referring to work by Williamson (1975), argues for an approach to contracting-out which breaks from the highly politicised debate of the last few years and instead focusses on the different conditions under which internal or external provision may be appropriate. This wish is unlikely to be granted given the Government's commitment to the compulsory tendering of key local authority services. Competitive tendering and contracting-out are destined to grow in local government but in the context of highly charged political interventions led by central government.

## Encouraging private sector provision and investment

There has been a substantial growth in initiatives aimed at encouraging private sector provisions of services. Apart from private schools and hospitals there has been an expansion of private sector homes for disturbed adolescents, the mentally ill and handicapped, and of nursing homes for the elderly (Laurence, 1983). We have already discussed in Chapter 3 the role of the private sector in supporting the rise of enterprise trusts and their provision of business advice. More generally as Young (1986) notes private sector institutions have been encouraged to extend their sponsorship of the arts, youth and community projects.

We concentrate below on the attempt to extend private sector support for investment schemes associated with urban renewal. This form of privatisation that has attracted little attention but it represents a considerable policy shift. Various schemes have sought to substitute private sector for public sector resources in the provision of local faculties and services.

There are many manifestations of this privatisation policy for urban renewal. There is the operation of Urban Development Corporations in London and Merseyside and the further UDCs announced from the end of 1986 onwards. Private Housing Trusts have been established in Knowsley and Thamesmead. These institutions were identified in Chapter 3 as part of non-elected government.

Other initiatives have operated through local authorities including various schemes aimed at stimulating low-cost homeownership and the increasing numbers of estate sales to private sector developers for refurbishment. Figures of low-cost homeownership land sales were given earlier in the chapter. For estate sales a TV Eye Survey broadcast on 31 October 1985 identified some 13 000 dwellings in over 30 different local authorities that had been or were being sold. Since then Salford City Council alone has been involved in selling off 2000 former council houses. As noted earlier the 1986 Housing and Planning Act is in part aimed at encouraging such schemes. There are also the industrial and commercial investment incentives provided by enterprise zones and urban development grants. These various initiatives differ widely in emphasis and detail but share a common objective: a concern to use a small amount of public sector money to 'lever in' a larger amount of private sector money.

The rationale for these schemes matches that of other forms of privatisation. Advocates of bringing in the private sector as partners make their case substantially on the basis that public sector sources of investment have been reduced and that private sector funds are needed to fill the gap. This is the view of central government (DoE, 1985a and b), private developers (Wimpey, 1987) and consultants. For example, Mallinson (1987, p. 18) comments:

> Many councils will have to rely on a contribution from the private sector if they are to maintain – or indeed increase – their available resources for new building and to cope with the huge demand for resources for repair and modernisation.

Fiscal austerity, then, has played its part. So too has a concern to create new market opportunities for the private sector. The whole approach is premissed on the view that with public sector involvement and subsidies it is possible to create new private sector interest in areas and conditions where little has existed before. Indeed, private builders such as Wimpey, Wates, Leach, Barratts and Ideal Homes have all established urban renewal subsidiaries in response. As noted in Chapter 3 the Nationwide and Halifax Building Societies have combined with builders Y. J. Lovell to establish 'Probe', an enabling agency commited to partnership in urban renewal.

There is perhaps an additional element in the Government's concern to press the banks, building societies and volume builders to take up a major role in urban renewal: a desire to stimulate corporate responsibility. The Conservative privatisation strategy, in this field, rests on a long-term attempt to cajole and tempt companies into thinking that they have a responsibility to the community at large as well as to their shareholders. Heseltine (1983, 1986) has been a key promoter of this view. Yet it sits rather uneasily alongside the emphasis on the need to create a competitive, profit-orientated enterprise culture.

We have assessed in more detail elsewhere the impact of this privatisation strategy in terms of housing and urban renewal (Brindley and Stoker, 1988; Brindley and Stoker, 1987a and b). We argue that while an increase in corporate sector investment can be expected it will not replace the public expenditure lost from building and repair programmes since the early 1970s. The strategies' market orientation leads to a rather narrow range of land-uses: office building, housing for owner-occupation and, in the retail field, 'exclusive' shops or large hyper-markets. These developments do little to meet the housing and shopping needs of many inner city residents. Nor do they provide easy access to the job market for these groups. The politics surrounding privatisation initiatives often lack local accountability, with both involved local authorities or active central government agencies, such as the LDDC, often behaving in a high-handed manner. Since the strategy rests on dealing directly with the private corporate sector other actors who might challenge the investment criteria and proposals of the private sector tend to be excluded from negotiations.

In urban renewal the Conservatives encouragement of private sector substitute investment is unlikely to meet effectively the needs of the poor and inner city residents. It has, however, enabled the Government to 'ride out' a crisis in housing investment and more generally inner city policy. It is a placebo policy since it enables the Government to claim that it is concerned and to appear to be doing something.

**Conclusions**

The Government's privatisation strategy for local government has three components: the sale of local authority assets; the introduction of market disciplines into service delivery through competitive tendering and de-regulation; and the encouragement of a greater role for the private sector in investment projects and service delivery. During the 1979–87 period the Conservatives' policies in each of these fields has developed in response to a combination of ideological commitment and more pragmatic considerations. Council house sales 'free' tenants from local authority landlords and also create a new potential group of Conservative supporters as well as providing substantial financial receipts for the public exchequer. Contracting-out and de-regulation introduce the discipline of competition into service delivery and at the same time help to undermine the power and strength of public sector unions. The encouragement of greater private sector involvement in investment projects and service delivery demonstrates that it is unnecessary for the public sector always to assume responsibility and has the added attraction of making limited public sector funds appear to go further.

The progress of privatisation has been substantial. In broad terms the Government's 'successes' in the field have been greater than those achieved in controlling local public spending. The resistance from local authorities has been strong in some instances but it has not been possible to assemble broad alliances of opposition across a range of authorities. Political uncertainty about council house sales, the conflicting interests of local authority managers and unions and the pressure of financial restraint have helped to undermine resistance. The campaign against council house sales never really took off; local authority opposition to bus de-regulation has been muted and increased private sector investment and activity has met a welcome from a wide range of authorities. Only in competitive tendering has local authority reluctance substantially slowed down the process of privatisation. As a result legislation to make competitive tendering mandatory for a variety of local authority services has been introduced in the 1987–8 parliamentary session. The implications of this provision will be examined in Chapter 11.

# 9  Labour's Urban Left: The Challenge of Local Socialism

A key development in local government during the 1980s has been the rise of a different style of Labour-controlled local authority. Councillors from within these authorities have been labelled the 'Looney Left' by their opponents but see themselves as building a new political force and imaginative solutions to society's problems. The rise of 'local socialism' reflects a concern to provide not only an alternative to Thatcherism but also a challenge to the conservatism and paternalism of some traditional Labour politicians. It is also premissed on the belief that the rapid social and economic changes experienced in this country require a radical response. This chapter provides some insights into the practice and perspectives of the Urban Left.

A focus on the Urban Left is justified by its alternative agenda for local politics and the scale of the often hostile reaction it has produced among party opponents and also within the Labour party. The Urban Left have stimulated a lot of angry debate and argument. To assess their performance during the period 1979–87 it is necessary to move the debate beyond the misleading vision of the Urban Left as a 'looney fringe' – obsessed by the promotion of gay rights, non-sexist language and anti-racist nursery rhymes – or an 'enemy within' – opposed to democratic institutions and in league with the Soviet Union. We argue in the first section of the chapter that the Urban Left's concerns are both more substantial and more tied to the tradition of British radicalism than these caricatures suggest. The Urban Left's strategy revolves around the twin aims of, on the one hand, mobilising the power of local government to challenge established interests and redistribute resources and, on the other, reforming local service provision and democratising local politics. The pursuit of those aims through a considerable range of diverse initiatives and practices provides a focus of attention for the middle sections of the chapter. Having established a picture of the Urban Left's strategy and practice the chapter closes with a critical assessment of the group's achievements. A number of difficulties and dilemmas have weakened and undermined the progress of local socialism.

## Contrasting themes in the approach of the Urban Left

The Urban Left are not a homogeneous group nor are they an organised political faction. They are rather a diverse group incorporating younger Labour councillors, community activists and radical professional local authority workers who came to prominence in local government in the early 1980s. The origins of this emergence of local socialism can be traced back to the events and shifting ideas of the late 1960s (Gyford, 1985, Ch. 2). The particular form of local socialism has varied according to local circumstances and conditions. Despite this diversity it is possible to identify a number of shared concerns among the Urban Left.

First they have a commitment to the value of local government. For much of the post-war period the Labour party has looked to national government as its main instrument (Sharpe, 1982; Gyford and James, 1983). At best, local authorities have been viewed as agents for the implementation of nationally instigated policies, in need of administrative and managerial reform in order to improve their performance of this task. At worst, local authorities have been viewed as bastions of resistance to be overcome so that progressive policy measures can be developed. Nationally-led initiatives and legislation have been the linch pins of Labour party policy-making. This centralist faith has been challenged and much greater attention has been given to the value of local government.

Second the Urban Left sees itself as faced by a major breakdown in social and economic organisation to which a radical response is necessary. This issue was touched on in Chapter 1 but it is worth emphasising the rapid pace of change and its impact on particular areas. Two examples will suffice. Sheffield's steel and heavy engineering base has collapsed since 1971. At that time some 139 000 people (about half the working population) were employed in manufacturing industry. By 1987 the number had slumped to 58 000, with manufacturing firms continuing to shed over 200 jobs each month (Sheffield City Council, 1987, p. 7). Haringey's multicultural community presents a major challenge to its local authority in the provision of education. The 1981 census showed 85 non-UK countries of origin and a Schools Language Survey showed 87 identifiably distinct spoken languages (Ranson and Walsh, 1986, p. 6). Similar experiences and issues confront many towns and cities. The Urban Left's approach represents one response to this challenge.

The fact that the Urban Left's response emerged at the level of local government, in part, reflects the fact that since 1979 Labour's only effective power base has been at the local level. It also corresponds with the close relationship between the Urban Left and a range of community-based and campaigning organisations. The rise from the 1960s onwards of the women's movement, black groups, ecological and environmental organisations, peace campaigners, the shop stewards' movement in industry and inner city community action contributed to a changed climate of ideas. The Urban Left committed itself to working with these 'fragments' (Rowbotham *et al.*, 1979). It is no accident that many of the officers and councillors of the Urban Left have been, and in many cases remain, involved in these community-based and campaigning political movements.

In part because of this relationship with community politics there has been an emphasis on the Urban Left's commitment to non-bureaucratic and accessible forms of public administration, and its concern to open up the political process to a wide range of groups (Gyford, 1985, Ch. 4). This aspect is certainly one element of the Urban Left's programme but another, equally important element, is to mobilise the power of local government to challenge established interests and redistribute resources. Hain (1983, p. 41) calls for:

a new synthesis of socialist strategies which on the one hand recognises the problems associated with the state, and on the other sees the need to use parts of the state machine to challenge the power of private capital.

Blunkett and Jackson (1987) argue for a local politics that is 'both active and responsive, democratic as well as purposeful'. In short, there are two key elements in the 'new Left's' programme. The Urban Left is motivated by a concern to devolve control over local government *and* a desire to mobilise the power of local government to challenge established interests. The potential conflict between these two objectives is considered later in the discussion, for the present they are presented as the core components in the Urban Left's approach.

Both elements reflect a critical analysis of the past role of the state in socialist reform programmes. On the one hand the concern to develop new administrative and political forms indicates a recognition of the problems of existing public provision in some areas. As Blunkett and Green (1983, p. 2) argue no one can 'easily defend a socialist principle (like for example direct labour) if it is encapsulated in a service (like council housing repairs) which is paternalistic, authoritarian or plain inefficient'. The community organisations associated with the Urban Left have themselves criticised the existing forms of public provision, made demands for greater personal and popular control over key political and social decisions and emphasised in their own organisations the need to find non-hierarchical and participative ways of working. The Urban Left took aboard these criticisms and sought to translate them into new practices for local government since that was where they were in positions of leadership (McDonnell, 1984).

The other element in the Urban Left's programme emphasises the need to bring into play the latent power and authority of the state. It is critical of the failure of traditional Labour politicians to use the power of the state effectively. They are seen as too willing to acquiesce to the power of business and other established interests. Thus, for example, in the realms of local economic initiatives mainstream policies are seen as ultimately underpinning private enterprise by subsidising production costs. The radical policies, in contrast, are viewed as challenging the power of private capital and its dictation of the terms of economic activity. They aim to support trade unions and workers in their workplace and to explore socialist alternatives for the management and development of the economy (Boddy, 1984b). The Urban Left have seen in local government an opportunity to use the resources and moral authority of one arm of the state to challenge established interests. As Benington (1986, pp. 16–17) puts it, local authorities can 'mobilise the weight of the state':

> A local authority, when it uses its authority as a body elected to represent the interests of the whole community, has a capacity to redefine problems, to move certain issues into the centre of political attention and to begin to shift the balance of power in favour of new interests.

The Urban Left's vision, then, is of a local socialism that is, on the one hand, more responsive and open to a wider range of interests and, on the other, is more active and more strongly interventionist in challenging the power of vested interests.

This vision is seen as likely to appeal to a broad coalition of the public, combining traditional elements of the industrial working class with the 'new constituency' of women's groups, environmentalists, ethnic minority organisations and so on, which informed the development of the Urban Left. Such a coalition was viewed as essential given that the manual working class, the core of traditional socialist parties, was rapidly contracting as a result of economic changes (Hobsbawm, 1981; Massey, 1983). According to Livingstone (1984, p. 271):

> The Labour Party, whether it likes it or not, has become a party that can only win power if it actually maintains its skilled working-class role, but also attracts the votes of the really poor and of those without work experience.

There are, as we shall see, some differences of emphasis in the components of and the significance accorded to the building of the 'rainbow' coalition. Nevertheless it can be regarded as an important factor in the Urban Left's approach.

Some of the key themes in the philosophy and style of Urban Left have been outlined. The remainder of the chapter discusses the practice of this loose political grouping. In doing so it draws on the experience of the GLC, ILEA, most of the Labour-controlled London boroughs, some of the pre-1986 metropolitan county authorities, and many Labour local authorities in the towns and cities of Britain. In these authorities the Urban Left have found themselves in positions of control or at least influence in local policy-making.

Specifically excluded from this discussion, however, is the practice of the militant-influenced controlling group of Liverpool City Council (1983–7). Labour's political practice in Liverpool during this period is out of tune with the general style and philosophy of the Urban Left (Blunkett and Jackson, 1987; Widdicombe, 1986e, p. 129). In particular its emphasis, noted in Chapter 5, was on class politics to which race and women's issues were seen as subordinate. Its commitment was to controlling local authority decision-making through the party organisation rather than opening up the council to the influence of a wider range of external interests. Thus although the achievements of Liverpool, for example, in building public housing and its determination to challenge Thatcher's Government have stimulated admiration from the Urban Left neither they, nor the Liverpool councillors, regarded themselves as engaged in the same project.

The next two sections describe the practice of the Urban Left local authorities. The emphasis is on providing a broad sketch of the range of activity rather than a detailed account of particular initiatives. In the light of the two themes identified previously the first section examines policies whose rationale rests on using the power and authority of local government. The second section concentrates on efforts to reform and democratise local authority administration and politics.

**Using the power and authority of local government**

In considering the Urban Left's attempts at using the power and authority of local government to challenge vested interests it is useful to introduce a further distinction between initiatives based on direct provision and in-house action and those that rest on efforts at influencing the behaviour of other major organisations and institutions.

*Direct provision and in-house action*

A number of initiatives can be considered under this heading including those relating to public transport, job creation, low pay, equal opportunities and leisure and arts. In 1981 the GLC's 'Fares Fair' public transport policy which was based on a commitment to cut fares on London Transport's buses and tubes by an average of 25 per cent was launched. The reduced fares depended on subsidy from the rates. A similar programme emerged at the same time in the other metropolitan counties which came under Labour control, including the West Midlands, Merseyside and Greater Manchester. The GLC's policy was soon undermined by a House of Lords ruling following legal action by Conservative-controlled Bromley (Loughlin, 1986, pp. 68–78). This decision had a knock-on effect on the other schemes and, as a consequence, they were all short-lived.

In contrast, South Yorkshire's cheap fares policy was maintained for over a decade. Blunkett and Jackson (1987, Ch. 4) describe the South Yorkshire scheme as 'a practical contribution to the social and economic life of the community which held the support of the people of the area because they could see that it worked for their benefit'. It reflected a commitment to planning and collective provision to meet need. As well as freezing fares at 1975 levels the county council took a number of measures to provide a comprehensive, regular and reliable public transport service. A number of innovative approaches were developed including the famous 'bendibuses', articulated single deckers that operated in Sheffield City Centre.

The policy was particularly beneficial to the half of South Yorkshire's households without access to a car; the other members of one-car families, often women; pensioners, young people and the unemployed. To these people the policy brought mobility, freedom and choice. It also brought economic advantages; getting people to work, less road congestion and fuel savings. On the other hand, the burden on the public purse was considerable and transport workers always suspected that the low fares policy was underpinned by low wage rates for them (Blunkett and Jackson, 1987, pp. 81–2).

The combined effect of abolition of the County Council, and the rate-capping of the joint board which took over responsibility for South Yorkshire's transport, eventually killed the policy. On 1 April 1986 a 250 per cent fare increase was put into effect. De-regulation which followed the 1985 Transport Act made an integrated public transport network based on low fares not only impossible but illegal.

Direct action over job creation has also been a feature of Urban Left authorities. We noted in Chapter 1 the importance of local authorities as major employers in many towns and cities. Urban Left councils have recognised that one way to meet the crisis of unemployment is for local authorities directly to provide more jobs. Manchester City Council, employed an additional 3500 people between 1984 and 1987 to provide better community care, education, housing and other services. Several authorities have produced employment plans which if given the support of a sympathetic government, would create thousands of jobs by expanding local authority services to meet needs. Sheffield City Council estimated in 1987 that it would create over 7000 new jobs in two years through employing more home helps and care workers, and undertaking more construction work (Sheffield City Council, 1987, Ch. 3). In a direct challenge to Thatcherite attacks the Urban Left councils have reasserted the value of public sector employment in meeting needs and improving the quality of life.

Low pay is another area where Urban Left local authorities have taken direct action. As Chapter 1 noted some local authority manual and clerical workers are amongst the most poorly paid of all employees. Camden, Greenwich and Lambeth are among those authorities who have launched minimum earning guarantees. Haringey, Sheffield and other Labour councils have developed low-pay supplements. By the Autumn of 1986 Sheffield's low-pay supplement went up to a maximum of £8 a week, with some 14 000 council employees receiving the supplement, the majority of whom were women working in part-time jobs.

A number of local authorities have sought to harmonise the conditions of service – hours of work, sick pay, holidays, and so on – among all council employees. There can be little doubt that the manual and craft sector of local authority workforces have been employed on less favourable conditions than most of the white collar staff. Wrekin District Council (1985) has a well-developed strategy for achieving what is termed 'single status'. Hackney, Greenwich and Sheffield have all agreed in principle to the harmonisation of terms of conditions between blue and white collar workers. It is recognised that this process in likely to take a number of years but already action has been taken on holiday and leave entitlements, sickness pay, car allowances, and probationary periods.

Positive action on training and development has also been taken. Rather than concentrating resources solely on top managers attempts have been made to increase the access of low-paid employees to further training and education. Some of the courses on offer are directly vocational. Others aim to increase people's confidence and create opportunities to go on to courses in further education. These initiatives form part of a broader equal opportunities strategy.

Equal opportunities is a key area for in-house activity by Urban Left local authorities. There is a concern about the impact of both local authority employment practices and service delivery on women, ethnic minorities, disabled people and other disadvantaged groups. On the jobs front there are signs that more effective monitoring and a determination to open up recruitment within local authorities has begun to make some inroads (Labour Research, 1986). Discrimination and disadvantage in the delivery of housing and education services, for example, have been addressed and policies aimed at overcoming them have been devised (Jenkins and Solomos, 1987). Yet officers and councillors pushing on the equal opportunities front have faced considerable resistance from existing local authority structures (Ouseley, 1984, pp. 136–7; Ben Tovim *et al.*, 1986; Profitt, 1986). Women's, race relations and equal opportunity committees, their units and advisers, can find themselves isolated and marginalised.

Finally in this survey of in-house action by local authorities mention can be made of the development of arts and leisure strategies. Benington and White (1986, para. 7) comment that 'leisure services have been one of the important frontiers of new development by local government over the past decade'. Local authorities 'have been among the leading sponsors of imaginative leisure and arts provision'. The emphasis has been on the collective enjoyment of leisure and cultural activities and the opening-up of access to leisure facilities regardless of personal means and in response to a range of different groups and interests. The GLC's festivals celebrating the cultural diversity of London have been matched in other cities and towns with local festivals, theatre workshops, local histories and community studies. Leisure facilities have been improved and 'passport to leisure' schemes have provided free or cheap access to the unemployed and others with low incomes. All of this is seen by Benington and White and others (Blunkett and Jackson, 1987, Ch. 5) as a conscious challenge by the Urban Left authorities to the commercialisation of leisure by major private conglomerates. Through beginning to put their own house in order over low pay, conditions of service, and equal opportunities the Urban Left aim to present local government as a model which others can follow. By using the resources of local government to take direct action to provide employment, an effective public transport system or leisure and arts facilities open to all the Urban Left is indicating what can be achieved by mobilising the power of local government. It has also more directly attempted to influence its environment and the behaviour of major private sector institutions.

*The exercise of influence*

In addition to direct job creation local authorities have sought to target public sector investment in order to intervene in their local economies. The enterprise boards of the GLC, West Midlands, Lancashire, Merseyside and West Yorkshire together with the employment department of Sheffield, have established advance warning systems, identified key sectors where expansion might be possible and sought to generate and use investment funds to save or create employment. There is a considerable debate relating to the scope and limitations of, and lessons to be learnt from, these interventions (Wainwright, 1987; Blunkett and Jackson, 1987, Ch. 6; Centre for Local Economic Strategies, 1987). As of the end of 1986 the five enterprise boards alone claimed to have created or saved 14 000 jobs. A valuable but modest contribution in the context of mass unemployment. As Marples (1986, p. 26) comments 'much of the local economics is hypothetical, an account of what could be done with more resources, powers and time for local authorities'.

Local authorities have also attempted to use their purchasing power to strengthen linkages with their local economy. Several have set up exhibitions or other procedures to identify those products currently imported from overseas and to substitute or develop locally manufactured alternatives. In the case of the construction industry local authority capital programmes can provide a planned and certain demand. In return, local authorities have made demands over the local content and quality of employment.

The purchasing power of the local authority has also been used to produce benefits for its customers. In Glasgow, the Housing Department successfully negotiated, on behalf of its tenants, tariff and other concessions from the Electricity Board through a Heating with Rent Scheme. Sheffield supported the development of a dehumidifier to tackle the pervasive problems of dampness and condensation in older housing and then used its purchasing power to make the product available to council tenants. At the same time it provided a stable market for the producers.

Local authorities have begun to explore the potential of contract compliance. Carr (1987) describes the experience of the GLC and ILEA in this subject and identifies modest progress. The commitment is to using local authority purchasing power to encourage good employment practices (trade union recognition, equal opportunities) in firms carrying out work for, or supplying goods to the council. The GLC concluded written agreements with some 134 companies and set in motion a monitoring process. The UK experience, as Carr notes, is limited but evidence from the USA suggests that a concerted effort by a range of public sector agencies including local authorities could achieve significant success in promoting greater equality for ethnic minorities and women. The contract compliance initiative shows that local authorities have not only considerable latent economic power but also a range of levers of influence providing they are prepared to use them.

This belief is also reflected in Glasgow's housing strategy aimed at private sector volume builders and developers. Between 1980 and 1986 the policy created some £100 million of additional investment often in areas that had been starved of such resources for years. The key to this activity was the local authority's move from a passive role to that of a positive promoter or public entrepreneur. The tools it has used include its ownership of land, provision of grants, powers of planning, powers of compulsory purchase and of land assembly. Control has been exercised over housing design and quality: who the houses are built for, and where investment is directed. In short 'the Council has attempted to use its powers and its muscle to intervene positively and creatively in the development sector of the economy, in the interests of Glasgow's people and its communities' (Glasgow District Council, 1985, p. 7).

These various initiatives reflect a commitment by the Urban Left to using the authority and power of local government in what they can see as imaginative and innovative ways. Their concern has been to intervene and to challenge established interests and to support those whom they perceive as disadvantaged. In the finance, purchasing policies and organisational resources of local government they have seen a reservoir of power capable of being mobilised. Through the legitimacy of elected government they have perceived an opportunity to exercise authority and influence.

More generally the Urban Left have seen local government as a platform from which to raise issues of concern such as nuclear defence, health care and law and order. They have then sought to exercise influence through the nuclear free zones policy (Gyford, 1985, p. 16), through the establishment of health committees (Moran, 1986) or through initiatives such as Islington's crime survey and other crime prevention measures (Jones *et al.*, 1986). Welfare rights and social security benefit take-up have also been key areas for not only investigative work (Manchester City Council, 1986) but campaigning activity (Fimister, 1986).

## Reforming and democratising the local state

Our examination of the Urban Left's practice now moves on to focus on efforts at improving service delivery and open up the local political process. They can be considered under separate headings.

### *Responsiveness in service delivery*

As we have seen the Urban Left has criticised traditional welfare provision for its elements of inefficiency, paternalism and authoritarianism. It is possible to distinguish three related strategies which have been used by local authorities to improve responsiveness in service delivery. First as noted in Chapter 5, there have been attempts to develop a 'public service orientation' which stresses that services are only of real value if they are of value to those for

whom they are provided. Second Chapter 5 also identified the
growth of local authority support for voluntary sector and self-
help groups. By funding such organisations local authorities hope
to achieve a degree of flexibility and closeness to the consumer
which cannot always be achieved through direct provision. Finally
the establishment of decentralised neighbourhood or area offices
has also been noted. They constitute the most visible face of efforts
at improving responsiveness in service delivery and some brief
comments on the scope and limitations of decentralisation are
provided below.

Many decentralisation schemes have been developed within
traditional service departments at a district or neighbourhood level.
Schemes based on housing have been established by Basildon,
Norwich, Hackney, Lambeth, Southampton and Sheffield, among
many others. Social services have also proved prime candidates
for delivery through sub-authority outlets. Some more radical
initiatives have taken place across service delivery boundaries in
Islington, Walsall and Birmingham. Islington for example, provides
a network of 24 neighbourhood offices, each covering about 7000
residents. The services on offer include most social services,
housing matters (repairs, lettings, rent collection and improvement
grants), environmental health and welfare rights. Glasgow District
Council has combined with Strathclyde Regional Council to
provide a range of housing, social services, welfare rights and
employment creation centres in a number of the city's most
deprived estates. These joint initiatives cross both service delivery
and local authority boundaries.

A number of advantages are claimed for decentralisation in
improving service delivery. First ease of access: Islington's aim is
that residents will not have to walk for more than ten minutes to
reach their neighbourhood office. Second a welcoming environment: offices are designed in an 'open-plan' way and staff are
chosen and trained on the basis of their willingness to deal
sympathetically with members of the public.

There is a need, it is argued, to break from the historic
demarcation lines around which local authorities have organised.
This is reflected in a commitment to a 'one stop' service outlet for
the public. Dispersed and separate departmental offices are
brought together under one roof. Even where a service is not
provided in the neighbourhood office the staff have responsibility

for pursuing the public's enquiries. There is also a recognition of the need for a team approach so that officers relate less to their departments and more to working with their local community, although there are tensions and difficulties in developing such an approach (Hoggett, 1987). Professional loyalties and traditional departmental management structures do not easily give way to the team approach.

A fourth advantage claimed for decentralisation is that it can lead to increased efficiency in service delivery. Through computers and visual display units, with terminals in neighbourhood offices linked to a central data bank, information about rent rebates, the waiting list, repairs, welfare benefits and other services can be quickly provided to the public. Also associated with decentralisation are streamlined procedures and new work practices. They have particularly emerged for direct labour repair services, leading, it is claimed, to substantial increases in productivity and efficiency. In Islington the backlog of housing repairs was a frustrating 13 weeks. With the introduction of 16 multi-trade area teams the average waiting time for repairs was by December 1986 down to three weeks. In addition twice the volume of repairs was being dealt with (Islington, 1986, p. 21).

As indicated already, there have been considerable difficulties in moving to this new form of service provision. First there can be substantial costs involved in setting up such projects. Islington's capital costs for the establishment of its neighbourhood offices have been estimated at £10 million at 1986 prices. There are also additional staff to be employed. Furthermore, once a scheme has been established its very success can increase demand on local authority services which, in an era of public expenditure cuts and rate-capping, can be highly problematic. There can be little doubt that the financial implications have contributed to the reluctance of a number of Labour authorities to move from policy statements to full implementation of decentralisation. Moreover, many activists have concluded that decentralisation, if not backed by sufficient resources, could simply be another 'con trick'.

Decentralisation initiatives have also met substantial internal resistance from various established interests within local authorities, including senior officers and trade unions. There are difficulties about the relationship between centre and neighbourhood. Giving neighbourhood offices substantial autonomy requires the centre to become less directive and more enabling, a transformation which in the light of the tradition of hierarchical political and administrative structures in local government may prove problematic (Hoggett, 1987). Senior officers have in some instances seen decentralisation as a threat to their authority and control and have resisted it, as in Manchester between 1982–4.

Opposition has emerged from middle and junior ranking white collar staff and their union NALGO. Union action over decentralisation has taken place in Sheffield, Islington and Walsall and effectively dashed the radical plans of Hackney. (For contrasting interpretations of Hackney's experience see Hoggett *et al.*, 1984 and Tomlinson, 1986.) The underlying basis of union doubts about decentralisation appears to rest on fears about its impact on members' conditions of employment. This has been combined with claims for recognition of the additional responsibilities taken on by their members. Worries have been expressed about the physical amenities of the new neighbourhood offices, personal security, longer opening hours and the stress of sustained contact with the public. These concerns are not in principle insurmountable, but in a climate of financial constraint many union leaders have been suspicious. Manual workers appear more willing to accept and develop decentralisation initiatives, seeing them as a way of improving their direct relations with the public by providing a better service and upgrading skills. Some have worked with tenants in proposing decentralised area repair projects; and in Islington after the establishment of a successful area repairs system, the convenor of the DLO received, much to his delight, 'his first ever round of applause at a public meeting'.

There are plainly a great number of difficulties to be faced and obstacles to be overcome in the course of implementation. Progress has not been as rapid as some advocates of decentralisation would have liked. (For a more detailed assessment see Hoggett and Hambleton, 1987 and Beuret and Stoker, 1986.)

### Opening up the political process

This issue has been dealt with at several points so far. In Chapter 3 we noted the rise of direct user-control over the management of services. In Chapter 5 we argued that many local authorities had in recent years opened out, providing more information and open access to local authority policy debates, as well as committing themselves to increased consultation with various interest groups or through area or neighbourhood forums. Urban Left local authorities have been to the fore in these developments, a reflection of their desire to work with a range of community-based organisations including tenants' groups, ethnic minorities, women's groups, environmental organisations and various other action groups. Indeed their support has extended to resourcing trade union and community employment initiatives. Thus centres against unemployment, women's employment projects, industry-wide campaigns against closures, trade union and community resource centres, welfare rights and training projects for young people have all mushroomed. A whole number of grass-roots community organisations and rank-and-file trade union initiatives have as a result been able 'to move beyond hand-to-mouth survival, and to use local authority grants to come in out of the cold, to employ staff, develop campaigns and make a visible mark' (Benington, 1986, p. 16).

Urban Left local authorities in pursuing the strategy of support for and consultation with their external groups have had to face a number of dilemmas. First there are questions relating to who is being consulted. For local authorities there are difficulties in knowing who to consult and fears about the representativeness of those being consulted. Sheer lack of information can make decisions about who to consult problematic. Some local authorities have relied on the local Council for Racial Equality to organise ethnic minority consultation. Others have found the CRE local network insufficient and alternative mechanisms have been developed (Prashar and Nicholas, 1986). Given evidence (see, for example, Boaden *et al.*, 1982) about the past dominance of public participation by particular groups there is a recognition that inequalities in resources and willingness to become involved have to be tackled. As suggested in Chapter 5 community development and other resources can provide some support for disadvantaged groups. In some instances more direct steps have been taken. Thus, in the case of the neighbourhood forums established alongside Islington's 24 neighbourhood offices certain minimum conditions have been laid down. In particular forums have to guarantee the right to representation of young people, people with disabilities, women with caring responsibilities and elderly people.

There is some uncertainty about whether consultation with, for example, women and ethnic minorities can get beyond a narrow range of activists. Goss (1984, p. 127) notes the tendency for professional and middle-class women to dominate many initiatives and argues that 'there is a danger of missing out entirely the majority of local women'. Several women's committees, recognising this problem, have actively sought the involvement of local working women. However, this task is by no means easy. As Goss (1984, pp. 127–8) goes on to argue:

> There are very real reasons why women have not been drawn into organised politics – baby-sitting difficulties, the lack of public transport and the dangers of walking anywhere at night mean that many women are virtually imprisoned in their homes in the evening – and the stresses of full-time child-care or the double shift leave women precious little time for theoretical debate.

Another issue is the substance of consultation. According to Gyford (1985, p. 94) a basic uncertainty within local socialism is whether it is concerned with dispersing power in a variety of directions or mobilising a range of forces to concentrate them in a single direction. Some accept that the diversity and autonomy of local politics is its strength. Its value to socialists is long-term in that it creates an active political culture in which people expect to be able to work collectively to control social and economic conditions. Their concern is that heavy-handed attempts at intervention by party activists or local authority officials will simply undermine community and grass-root activity, creating 'sham' organisations without any real strength and capability for autonomous action (Wainwright, 1985; Benington, 1986, pp. 20–1).

Others insist on the need to 'inject socialist values at every stage and in all aspects' of community politics (Labour Co-ordinating Committee, 1984, p. 34). As Gyford (1985, 86–94) notes many of the Urban Left fear that popular politics can, at worst, degenerate into racism or scrounger-bashing and at best, can take the form of a fragmented, short-sighted pluralism. It requires the injection of socialist ideology to give it a sense of direction. Yet this vision of participation can collapse all too easily into little more than a process of controlled and circumscribed political education. 'Indeed one of the very real problems of some left activists is their difficulty in conceiving that there can be legitimately different opinions to their own once everything has been explained' (p. 105).

The result of the Urban Left's uncertainty about dispersing power has been a certain paralysis when it comes to the process of opening out politics. Thus decentralisation initiatives have concentrated on service delivery goals and associated democratisation has been limited. Islington's neighbourhood forums have control over very small budgets and have powers only to request changes in policy from the authority's main committees. Other authorities have not even gone as far as this. Assessments of consultation procedures with interest groups, such as the ethnic minorities come to similar conclusions: Left local authorities have opened up but significant limitations remain (Saggar, 1987; Ouseley, 1987).

**Difficulties and dilemmas**

The review presented above makes clear the depth and range of the activity of the Urban Left and shows the two strands of mobilising power and developing control in operation. It has also emerged that the Urban Left's programmes have met with a number of difficulties and dilemmas. This section briefly explores these further.

First the Urban Left's policies have met a hostile reaction from a number of quarters. The opposition of the Thatcher Governments has been constant and has taken its toll. The abolition of the GLC and the metropolitan counties and the rate-capping of others, such as Sheffield and the Urban Left London boroughs, has been seen as a response to the challenge posed by the Urban Left (Blunkett and Jackson, 1987). Particular initiatives have been made more difficult or impossible, as in the case of transport, because of Government moves. More generally the financial climate within local government has limited and constrained Urban Left authorities, despite their being to the fore in the 'creative accounting' developments of the period.

A further obstacle has been the opposition of interests within local government. The challenges posed by Urban Left strategies have met resistance, at times, from senior officers and public sector trade unions. The experiences of decentralisation, race relations, and women's equality units illustrate this point. Advocates have often found themselves engaged in a complex and sometimes frustrating struggle against entrenched interests within local authorities. Relationships with, in particular, the white-collar union NALGO have in a number of authorities been strained (Weinstein, 1986; Wolmar, 1984; Darke and Gouly, 1985).

The desire to see their policies implemented has led councillors in some instances to a degree of zealotry. Some claim that Left Labour councillors have made unacceptable demands on professional senior officers and have appointed political sympathisers to key posts who lack appropriate expertise or, worse, behave in a way that creates a climate of fear among less politically committed colleagues. The appropriate relationship between officers and councillors was in part as a consequence a key area for investigation by the Widdicombe Committee (1986a). Alexander (1986) has set down guidelines which provide some protection for officers. But others argue that the new demanding atmosphere has on the whole been healthy, with good officers recognising the need to support the development and implementation of new political policies (Blunkett, 1986).

The local political environment has not always been friendly. The hostility and near hysteria of some national and local media has also created problems for the Urban Left (Jenkins, 1987). While in many cases firms and businesses have not only complained about rates increases in Urban Left areas, but with respect to contract compliance and economic development activity have displayed a degree of resistance, and even hostility. The opposition of Rowntree Mackintosh to the GLC's contract compliance policy illustrates this point (see Carr, 1987, p. 15).

In addition to the understandable opposition from a range of forces 'threatened' by Urban Left policies these Labour authorities have had to face a number of daunting, and perhaps less expected, implementation dilemmas. It has proved a hard task to turn the vision of the Urban Left into an effective reality. Achieving the changes in the culture and operation of local government demanded, for example, by decentralisation has proved too great a challenge for some, and for others has led to the adoption of a form of élitist power politics which contradicts the Urban Left's commitment to developing non-hierarchical and participative forms of administration (Beuret and Stoker, 1986, pp. 16–17). The Arden Report (1987) on Hackney argues that sloppy 'anti-hierarchy' and 'anti-bureaucratic' thinking among its Urban Left councillors had led to a dismantling of basic organisational procedures and systems of control which are essential if change is going to be achieved.

In the case of economic development there has been considerable debate about what is the best approach (Duncan and Goodwin, 1985; Mawson and Miller, 1987; Gough, 1986) and what are appropriate strategies for particular sectors (GLC, 1985). Discussion has also developed around the best organisational forms for achieving implementation. The enterprise boards have some attractions but there are questions about their accountability and management (McKean and Coulson, 1987).

The turning of ideas into an effective practice has proved a demanding task. The GLC's contract compliance initiative required the establishment of a contracts compliance unit, the restructuring of the authority's purchasing operation, the establishment of a complex information and monitoring system about firms working for the GLC, and the negotiation of a legal minefield (Carr, 1987, pp. 10–16). The implementation of new initiatives has often been constrained by a series of complex organisational issues and technical uncertainties.

A third general element which has limited the ability of the Urban Left to put its policies into effect is a degree of ambiguity, conflict or uncertainty over objectives. We have already discussed the confusion in Urban Left circles between those seeking to disperse power and those seeking to mobilise a range of forces behind a single socialist direction. Jewson and Mason (1986) argue that the race relations field is particularly prone to confusion with liberal language becoming entangled with radical objectives leading to policy failure (see also Young, 1987). Policies may be presented in liberal terms to maximise support. Thus there will be calls for fair procedures in job advertising and interviews. But in reality councillors and others have expectations premised on a more radical commitment to achieving greater equality of outcomes (i.e. more jobs for ethnic minorities). The adoption of fair procedures on their own, however, cannot guarantee the achievement of these radical goals.

More generally at the heart of local socialism there is a potential conflict of objectives between the desire to mobilise the power of the local government to support disadvantaged groups and a concern to devolve control and deepen the political process. These two elements are possible to reconcile. Concepts such as 'popular planning' embody a commitment both to public intervention and support for an active community base. The GLC's support for the struggle of Coin Street residents to determine the development of their area against the demands of property developers shows both strands in operation. The GLC used its legal and financial powers to defeat the private sector's plans and purchased the land for the community group. At the same time through grant-aid it supported local opposition and the production of an alternative plan (see Brindley *et al.*, 1988). In this instance the two elements combined successfully. But what if too many competing demands emerge from the community? Which does local government support and how is the decision made? These dilemmas are of course the essence of much politics and are not the sole prerogative of the Urban Left. Yet they are particularly sharply felt since the Urban Left rejects market democracy (allocation according to ability to pay) and presents instead a vision of collective decision-making as the means of resolving such issues (see especially Blunkett and Jackson, 1987). But are existing mechanisms of collective decision-making at the local level widely perceived to be adequate to the task? The relationship between representative democracy and more participative forms has not been fully thought through.

Hard questions have also been raised about the alliances that the Urban Left has attempted to build. The rainbow coalition of traditional working-class and various minority issues has not been easily established. As one of its advocates argued in 1984: 'To try and appeal to both wings is really very difficult and the Party hasn't really given it any thought' (Livingstone, 1984, p. 271). Since then two further camps seem to have emerged. One suggests that because of the 'reactionary' nature of the white working-class male organisations the key is to concentrate on work with the minority groups. Others, to the right and centre of the party, want to see the prominence given to 'minority' issues downgraded because of their fears about losing traditional white working-class support. Indeed, Birmingham's right-wing leadership reacted to a poor local election result in 1987 by immediately announcing the scrapping of the council's race relations and women's committees!

Another alliance that has not always proved easy to assemble is that between councillors, producers and consumers of services. During the anti-rate-capping campaign and in particular initiatives – such as Hackney tenants' and direct labour workers' plan for an area repairs system or Haringey's school meal project (Haringey Women's Employment Project, 1986) – new relationships have been forged but in general unity has proved problematic. We have already noted the tension between NALGO and some Left Labour councils and in the discussion of decentralisation initiatives. We suggested that its roots relate to union anxiety about the changes demanded by Urban Left authorities in the context of a hostile climate and financial constraints. At a more fundamental level there is a long-standing uncertainty about the relationship between socialism as a political objective and the role of trade unionism. Strategies for transforming society and developing a new social and economic order do not always sit happily alongside the traditional trade union concern of getting the best deal out of the existing system. Nor is it easy to reconcile the unity required in a political campaign with the understandably sectional concerns of a range of trade unions representing professional white-collar staff, clerical and administrative grades, manual workers, teachers and fire-fighters.

A final unpleasant lesson of the 1980s is that contrary to the hopes of many there is no easy and automatic alliance between the users of local authority services and the producers even in the context of threatened cuts. Users are often highly critical of local authority service provision and providers. The Urban Left in response has encouraged new forms of service delivery. These make demands on service providers which may lead to fears of longer working hours and more stressful working environments. For service providers being more accountable to local people is not automatically an attractive prospect. For the council house tenant the immediate concern is to obtain an efficient and fast repair service and only on a secondary basis, if at all, is there likely to be a recognition of the need for service providers to be reasonably rewarded and have health and safety measures observed.

**Conclusions**

This chapter has examined the challenge posed by Urban Left Labour authorities during the 1980s. It is a political movement that has been subject to attack from Conservative and Alliance quarters as 'looney', divisive and extreme. Within its own party it has been criticised from the Left as a diversion from class politics and from the Right as a threat to party's electoral base.

Yet few would disagree with Gyford's (1985, p. 42) view that local socialism's 'immediate impact on the day-to-day workings of local government has been quite striking'. Our discussion has shown the considerable range and depth of initiatives that have emerged. Beyond this wealth of practical measures and experience local socialism can point to its contribution to a battle of ideas about how to react to the major social and economic changes affecting Britain. According to Blunkett and Jackson (1987, p. 5) local politics has 'set an agenda for what should be done and how it can be achieved'.

Local socialists, however, are likely to find their contribution to the debate about future directions increasingly marginalised. The national leadership of the Labour party remains nervous and uncertain about drawing any positive lessons from Urban Left experiments. It may be that new MPs closely associated with the Urban Left such as Bernie Grant, David Blunkett and Ken Livingstone will challenge this. With the election of the Thatcher government for a third term, the future for local socialism as a practice within local government is bleak. In a paper on post-election strategy Margaret Hodge (1987), Labour leader of Islington, comments that outright defiance of the Government is no longer an option. Labour groups should stay in power but will be faced by hard choices which may mean cutting back on services and jobs. If a choice is available then preserving services should take precedence over saving jobs. 'We . . . have to accept that the "agenda" will be dominated by the Government . . . [and] work within a tight and worsening legal framework with necessarily limited resources'.

# IV  THEORIES OF LOCAL POLITICS

# 10 Theories of Local Government and Politics

This chapter reviews and assesses some of the diverse perspectives that have dominated recent discussion of local government and politics. Various theories have already been drawn upon, sometimes explicitly and on other occasions implicitly, throughout this book. This chapter provides an opportunity to consider in more depth a number of those theoretical positions. Some readers may regard this as an unnecessary chore yet we would argue that to consider theories in a more systematic manner aids understanding and debate. An examination of different theoretical perspectives forces us to ask new questions; to consider the views of a diverse range of thinkers; and provides access to competing explanations of the world of local politics. By examining the language and arguments of different schools of thought we may be able to, at least conduct debates in a more sophisticated manner.

There are a substantial number of theoretical traditions and perspectives that could justify inclusion in a review of theories of local politics and government. Contributions to the debate about our political system have come from a diverse range of schools and approaches (Dunleavy and O'Leary, 1987; Held, 1987). A comprehensive review is not possible. We have to be more selective and concentrate on those perspectives with the most developed understanding of local politics and government.

We focus on four approaches which we label: localist, public choice, dual state and social relations. Each of these approaches will be examined in turn below. The main criteria for choosing to examine these four categories in detail is because much contemporary academic, practitioner and political argument about local government has been expressed in the language of these different approaches. They represent a cross-section of opinion, draw on a range of theoretical perspectives and can be related to different points on the political spectrum.

The localist position draws largely on the pluralist tradition and can be regarded as the new 'official' ideology of local government. The public choice literature constitutes part of the New Right approach and can be used to provide a justification for the Conservatives' attack on local government. The dual state thesis is the most widely promoted of the academic perspectives on local politics during the 1980s. It explicitly draws on a range of theoretical approaches, in particular combining elements of a corporatist and pluralist analysis. The social relations school has neo-marxist roots and echoes some of the thinking that has informed the Urban Left in its approach to local government during the Thatcher years. These four approaches give a flavour of the different directions the debate has taken in the 1980s.

The four schools of thought are each briefly outlined and then some of their key propositions are criticised. The emphasis throughout is less on the methodology of each and more on its substantive arguments about the nature of local politics. The chapter concludes with an overall assessment of the debate which provides some tentative signposts for the direction it might take in the future.

In the discussion below we use, more or less interchangeably, the terms 'local government' and 'the local state'. The localist and public choice theorists are more prone to use the former; while dual state and social relations schools are more likely to use the latter. The term local state was coined by Cockburn in a book of that name in 1977. She intended the term to cover all state institutions operating at the local level. Local authorities, local offices of the DHSS, health authorities and other quasi-governmental agencies were to be embraced by the term. But her own empirical work focused on elected local government (in particular the London Borough of Lambeth) and that is where the focus has remained in subsequent discussions. This makes it relatively unproblematic to interchange the terms local state and local government since in practice they have come to mean the same thing.

The popularity of the term local state rests to a substantial degree on its association with an opening out of the theoretical debate about the role of local government and the nature of local politics in the mid-1970s. Local government came to be viewed as an integral part of a larger political system. The phrase encouraged the making of connections with broader theories of government and politics (see Saunders, 1979, Ch. 4). The debate was launched by a sustained attack on the traditional public administration approach to studying local government (Dearlove, 1979, Ch. 2; Dunleavy, 1980, pp. 6–10). This traditional approach was criticised for narrowly focussing on local government institutions and ignoring the wider context in which they operated. The broader political, economic and social constraints on local politics were hardly considered. The public administration emphasis on formal and legal relations led all too easily to the assumption that things were as they should be: that power lies where it is supposed to lie. The role of informal influences and politics were thereby underplayed. Local government was assumed to be accountable by virtue of the fact that it was elected. Yet as we have seen in Chapter 2 there are limits to the accountability achieved through local elections. Notwithstanding its glaring weaknesses this public administration approach was seen as highly influential, finding reflection in official reports, textbooks (Redcliffe-Maud and Wood, 1974; Richards, 1973) and the assumptions of the majority of councillors and officers.

The most striking alternative to the orthodoxy of public administration was provided by Cockburn's book. She argues that we need to step outside the conventional frame of reference and see 'local government, our old red-brick town hall, for what it really is: a key part of the state in capitalist society' (p. 41). The capitalist state 'looks after the bourgeoise's interests as a whole and sets up and maintains the cultural and political domination of the working class that capitalism as a whole needs if it is to continue' (p. 47). The particular role of the local state is to ensure the reproduction of the labour force and the relations of production. Education, housing and other welfare services were delivered to provide a healthy, cooperative and appropriately located working force for capitalist production. The local state also promoted an ideology which institutionalised class conflict and encouraged people to accept dominant values and norms.

Such views were in turn criticised by marxists and non-marxists alike (Saunders, 1979, pp. 180–9; Duncan and Goodwin, 1982b).

First it is claimed that no adequate explanation is provided of why the state is constrained to act in the long-term interests of capital. The mode of explanation is crudely functionalist, namely that the state acts for capital because this is the role of the state in a capitalist society. This argument is hardly convincing. Second the model seems to allow little space for class struggle or political opposition to have an impact. In short there is a hopelessness and nihilism in the analysis which is contradicted by Cockburn's own empirical evidence, drawn from Lambeth, where she depicts people struggling and creating new terrains of conflict. Finally the model contains a rather crass view of central–local relations, with centre and localities united in their task of promoting capital's interests and local government willingly subordinate to the centre. This view not only belies the institutional complexity of the state but seems bizarre given the central–local conflicts that have characterised the 1980s and earlier periods.

If the only products of the debate over the local government and politics had been the demolition of traditional public administration's orthodoxy and the erection in its place of a crude and inadequate functionalist marxism then its contribution to our understanding would have been very limited. However, the debate has grown in breadth and sophistication. In the analysis of local politics we have available a wide range of theoretical perspectives.

## The localist view

The localist view starts from a position associated with the orthodox public administration model. Like that model it values local government. But unlike that model it explicitly argues the merits of local democracy, avoids complacency, recognises the need for local authorities to change, and moves beyond a formal/legalistic perspective. It is particularly associated with the broad-ranging defence of local government provided by Jones and Stewart (1983), the case for local government presented by the Widdicombe Committee (1986a) and the future vision of local government promoted by the three local authority associations and others (Davis, 1986; Solace, 1986). It has been widely accepted among local authority officers and councillors as a bulwark and shield against the centre's attacks and in this respect deserves the title of the 'new official' ideology of local government.

*Outline*

Traditional public administration tended to assume the case for local government (Dearlove, 1979, pp. 27–8). The localist perspective of the last decade or so has developed a forceful case for autonomous, elected local authorities. Jones and Stewart (1983) in particular have set out to establish a strong defence of local government in opposition to the strident centralisation which they argue has become part of Whitehall and Conservative ideology. Jones and Stewart's argument for local government is four-fold. First local government is grounded in the belief that there is value in the spread of power and the involvement of many decision-makers in many different localities. Diffusion of power is a fundamental value and local authorities as elected bodies 'can represent the dispersion of legitimate political power in our society' (p. 5).

A second argument rests on the view that there is strength in diversity of response. Needs vary from locality to locality, as do wishes and concerns; local government allows these differences to be accommodated. Diversity is also important because it provides scope for learning. Local authorities can learn from each other's different patterns of provisions, experimenting and pioneering. In response to the complex challenges of our time such a capacity for innovation and learning is vital.

Third local government is local. This aspect facilitates accessibility and responsiveness because councillors and officers 'live close to the decisions they have to make, to the people whose lives they affect, and to the areas whose environment they shape' (p. 6). Its smaller scale makes it more vulnerable to challenge than central government. Its visibility makes it open to pressure when it fails to meet the needs of those who live and work in its area: 'The local authority has the potential by reason of this localness to be accessible and exposed to influence by its citizens' (p. 6).

Finally local government has the capacity to win public loyalty. It can better meet local needs and win support for public service provision because it allows choice. It facilitates a matching of local resources and local needs. 'Local government, by making government less remote and more manageable, makes it more comprehensible, enabling a clear and balanced choice to be made over the extent to which people wish to promote community values' (p. 7).

These arguments in favour of autonomous, elected local authorities have won some support within the world of local government. They have been endorsed by the Society of Local Authority Chief Executives who go on to claim that each local authority has 'acted as a focus for local opinion and for a collective identity and has had an important part to play in the development of the social character of its area' (Solace, 1986, p. 7). The Widdicombe Committee support the case for local government set out by their research director, Ken Young. He stresses the ability of local government to generate innovation, maximise public choice, and promote pluralism and participation (see Young, 1986). Young's arguments, plainly, complement and develop those of Jones and Stewart.

These localist arguments rest on a pluralist approach to understanding the state and politics. As Dunleavy and O'Leary (1987) argue: 'political pluralism recognises the existence of diversity in social, institutional and ideological practices, and values that diversity' (p. 13). Pluralists are generally hostile to centralised states. 'All pluralists are firm advocates of elected local governments' (p. 57).

Localists do not necessarily share the assumptions of the simplistic pluralist model of interest group politics outlined in Chapter 5. They recognise that local authorities do not grant equal access to all. Stewart (1983, p. 135) comments:

> A local authority is in part an open organisation. There are many relations with the publics opening up the local authority. Yet the local authority is not equally open to all its publics nor does it give equal weight to all demands made.

He regards this situation as inevitable and legitimate providing that choices about access are made consciously and openly by elected representatives. This argument parallels that of most pluralists who likewise accept the reality of inequalities in different groups' influence, providing that it reflects the varying degree of intensity with which preferences are held and providing that the potential remains for new interests to mobilise and be granted access (Dunleavy and O'Leary, 1987, pp. 32–7).

Indeed the localist case has explicitly recognised that existing local authorities do not always act in a way that facilitates responsiveness to changing local needs. The organisational arrangements associated with the delivery of services can constrain the capacity for local choice (Stewart, 1983; Greenwood and Stewart, 1986). The dominance of service committees in decision-making can encourage a narrow functional focus rather than a wider understanding of community needs. Bureaucratic modes of organisation can discourage risk-taking and innovation. Professional influence, because it operates through national bodies and debates, can lead to the exclusion of local factors and interests in decision-making.

The localist case is premised on the need for a major reform of local government. Among the changes suggested by Jones and Stewart (1983) are proposals for: the enactment of a charter specifying the respective roles of central and local government; the introduction of a local income tax; a move to proportional representation in local elections; and a shift to unitary local authorities.

The agenda moves beyond institutional and structural reforms to an argument for a new management style within local government (Stewart, 1986a). The characteristics of the new management involve a commitment to openness, learning and innovation. The key task of the new management is to ensure that local government is open and responsive. What is required is a public service orientation (Clarke and Stewart, 1987): a willingness to examine services from the perspective of the public and a commitment to meeting the needs of the public as customers and citizens. A new organisational culture is required which breaks out of routinism and provides scope for innovation and choice. Staff morale and development become key issues. A new management is required if the challenge of socio-economic change is to be met.

The localist case, then, is as much about the potential of local government as its current practice. It has had a considerable impact on the thinking of officers and councillors in the local government world. There appears to be a widespread acceptance among the local government community that major reforms in institutional form and management style are required if the benefits of elected local government identified by the localist case are to be fully achieved in practice (Rhodes, 1987; Solace, 1986; Davis, 1986).


*Criticism*

Criticism of the localist case can take a variety of forms. Below we examine three common lines of attack. First while accepting the value of local democracy other commentators would not give it the absolute status which localists seem to assign to it. For them there may be a 'trade-off' between local accountability and issues of territorial and social justice. Indeed, such considerations underlie the long-standing uncertainty within the Labour party and other quarters about the value of autonomous and powerful local government (Sharpe, 1982; Gyford and James, 1983). The idea that central power is necessary to force through new policies and service improvement is well-entrenched. To put it crudely: is it realistic to expect any centre to allow localities to act persistently and brazenly against its wishes?

A second line of attack relates to the faith placed by localists in the operation of local political mechanisms. Along with other pluralists these advocates of elected local government assume that local authorities can effectively reflect the wishes of local citizens. These arguments are challenged by the New Right, as we shall see. They regard political mechanisms as inherently inferior to the market and prone to distortion and inadequacies. Theorists from the left also cast doubt on the localist faith in potential for pluralism. Thus Boddy (1987, p. 96) claims that the perspective 'entails . . . a naive though possibly conscious disregard for the realities of political power – the realities of class politics, of sexism and patriarchy, and of racism. It is these which give political direction to local government and which structure the inputs which the local authority is exhorted to seek'. It is not intensity of preference which determines access and mobilisation. Rather a structure of inequality produces biases which systematically exclude particular groups. More generally, Cochrane (1985) accuses localists of painting too rosy a picture of existing local democratic practice.

Localists might react to this last claim by referring to their commitment to major reforms and changes in the orientation of local government. But this in turn leads to a third line of criticism, namely, that localists overestimate the capacity and ease with which the local government system can be reformed. Stewart (1983, p. 136) argues that biases in the system 'can be corrected but that requires conscious choice'. He seeks to persuade top managers and politicians to make that choice. But can change simply be introduced by the conscious choice of local government's leaders? Can the very organisational structures of professionalism, bureaucracy and majority party politics, which localists recognise, constrain the existing system be swept aside by a change of mind? Moreover is it realistic to expect existing councillors and officers to step outside the context of inequalities, material interests and biases in which they currently operate?

**The New Right and public choice theory**

The label 'New Right' covers 'a diverse set of intellectuals, ranging from libertarian philosophers to defenders of reactionary values' (Dunleavy and O'Leary, 1987, p. 72). In the discussion below we concentrate on the public choice theory which is associated with the work of Buchanan and Tullock (1962), Tullock (1976) and Niskanen (1971 and 1973). Their work is strongly informed by New Right values and is among the most rigorous of contributions to that tradition. Public choice theorists have won the attention of right-wing governments in Britain, the USA and Germany. Their writings have been promoted by the Adam Smith Institute and the Institute for Economic Affairs. Nicholas Ridley, Secretary of State for the Environment, has described Niskanen's work as of 'devastating importance' (Niskanen, 1973, p. 87). The correspondence between the public choice theory and the Thatcher government's policies towards local authorities is considered in more detail in Chapter 11. Below we set out some of the main propositions and policy prescriptions of the public choice school, before moving on to a brief critical assessment.

*Outline*

For public choice theorists the optimal mechanism for allocating goods and making decisions is the market. Public bureaucracies and representative democracy are both seen as seriously flawed in comparison. In particular public sector expenditure is seen as inherently prone to excessive growth. There is an in-built tendency to over-supply on the part of public bureaucracies. According to Niskanen (1973) over-supply can be as great as twice the optimum over what a private market would provide.

This in-built tendency to over-supply reflects weaknesses in representative democracy and the operation of public bureaucracies. Party competition builds up public expectations about what the state can provide as self-interested politicians seek to maximise their vote. Once in office it is possible for them to disguise the consequences of decisions, with the true economic and fiscal situation being hidden from voters. There is a tendency to slip into deficit funding to spread the costs of current state expenditure over future years and possibly future generations of citizens.

The consequences of party competition are reinforced by the impact of the major influence exerted by sectional interest groups. Politicians and bureaucrats may seek to establish constituencies to support existing and increased levels of spending. Vocal and highly organised interest groups are formed which constantly push for more and better provision to meet their special interests. The losers are the disorganised and silent majority who finance this expenditure. Pirie (1981, p. 11) claims that local government, in particular, suffers from 'the disproportionate influence of pressure groups':

> Each service provided creates its class of beneficiaries which sees itself as a distinct interest group and will campaign for its privileges. The taxpayer and ratepayer, by contrast, are a more amorphous mass, not acting as a self-conscious interest group.

More generally, public choice theorists regard existing democratic arrangements as very poor predictors of citizens' preferences and demands. Elections every few years force people to decide on a whole range of issues simultaneously and are inadequate compared to the range of choices and options provided by the market mechanism. Public choice theorists are 'convinced that the structure of political markets, and the arrangements for citizen participation and decision-making are extremely crude in contemporary democracies. They profess to be mystified that liberal democracies have experimented so little with alternative arrangements' (Dunleavy and O'Leary, 1987, p. 98).

The tendency to over-supply is reinforced by key features of public bureaucracies. The distortions produced by an inadequate representative system are reinforced by the inherent weaknesses of public organisations. All organisations, it is argued, tend in the long-run towards the abandonment of collective goals and in their place the pursuit of self-interested goals by those holding official positions. In particular, a characteristic goal of bureaucrats is budget maximisation through the expansion of their departmental programmes.

Public choice theorists argue that bureaucrats best serve their own welfare by pushing continuously for budgetary growth, which increases their numbers, improves promotion prospects, creates discretionary patronage and generally builds up organisational slack and improves job security.

For Niskanen (1971, 1973) budget maximisation is a fairly open-ended process, only constrained by the ability of public agencies to raise the necessary level of taxation. Other checks on the process are weak. Politicians 'in charge' of the bureaucracies are often sympathetic to the process of budget expansion. In part this reflects the inadequacies of the representative system outlined earlier. It also reflects the ability of bureaucrats to 'capture' politicians, given that they control much access to information about the need for services and the costs involved in providing existing services. Specialist committee-based systems of control, such as those dominant in local authorities, are seen as particularly prone to laxity in checking bureaucratic behaviour given that councillors over time come to share vested interests or associations with particular staff or clientele.

The failings of representative democracy and public bureaucracies create in-built tendencies for local government to be wasteful and inefficient and to overspend. Henney (1984), drawing in part on the public choice theory, paints a disparaging picture of local authorities and concludes that local government has 'become too big, too distant, too politicised, too subject to pressure from vested interests, and too complicated for ordinary people to understand, let alone control'. Self-interested professionals and trade unionists are dominant, with managerial and political controls weak and ineffective. Consumer preferences are rarely taken into account, resulting in the over-supply of inadequate services 'which are widely perceived as being of low quality, unresponsive to any need or demand and yet more expensive than their private sector equivalents' (Pirie, 1981, p. 13).

Public choice theorists advocate two institutional reforms to mitigate these features of local government. Contracting-out is a central prescriptive maxim (Pirie, 1981; Forsyth, 1980). It is attractive because open competition with private contractors forces bureaucrats to reveal more information about the costs of the services they provide and makes possible comparisons of cost-effectiveness and efficiency. Public choice theorists would assume that the profit orientation of private contractors and the narrower focus of their operations would make them flexible and efficient organisations. Contracting-out also challenges the monopoly position of in-house service providers and as a consequence the restrictive practices of trade unions and professionals can be challenged (Dunleavy, 1986, p. 16).

The second institutional reform advocated by public choice theorists is the fragmentation of existing bureaucracies. Niskanen (1973) argues that all bureaus are too large, efficiency incentives are lacking and sweeping reforms are required. Local government is considered desirable but it is argued that the form of 'streamlined' system in Britain has significantly eroded citizen control of local officials by creating very large authorities (Dunleavy and O'Leary, p. 121). What is required is a large number of smaller local authorities so that the diverse preferences of many different citizens can be satisfactorily provided for (Tiebout, 1956). Smaller units may encapsulate more homogeneous social groups making it easier for citizen preferences to be met. The disaggregation of large bureaucracies with a monopoly supply of goods and services also creates 'exit options' for customers, providing opportunities for comparison and choice. Fragmentation will also discourage the tendency to over-supply, since citizens will be able to move to those public bureaucracies providing good value for money. The crucial thing is for monopoly control to be broken, leading to an increase in intra-bureaucratic competition. 'By privatizing many services and reconstituting the remaining state bureaucracies on a fragmented, mutually competitive basis, new right theorists claim that it will be practicable greatly to relieve bureaucratic stagnation and increase both citizen control and citizen choice' (Pollitt, 1986, p. 158).

Public choice theorists would support other reforms of local government practice. For example, Niskanen (1973) suggests that the self-interest of bureaucrats could be manipulated by relating their salaries and other rewards proportionately to their ability to make savings or hit budgetary targets. Such a system of perform-ance-related pay for top managers operates in Conservative-controlled Westminster City Council and has been advocated as generally desirable within local government.

Pirie (1981, p. 13) suggests that councillors looking to exert control over their authorities should bring in 'objective' outside consultants who can challenge the monopoly of information and advice held by local state bureaucrats. The use of such consultants to point to 'cost and efficiency' savings has become increasing commonplace in local authorities during the 1980s, creating boom conditions for some accountancy firms and management consult-ants (Kline and Malabar, 1986). More generally, the revamped Audit Commission can be seen as an attempt to provide a countervailing force to the budget maximising tendencies of local authority bureaucrats. Its preparation of league tables comparing the value for money achieved by different local authorities, its constant assertion of the potential for efficiency savings and its attacks on certain authorities as overspenders (see for example the assault on London's inner boroughs, Audit Commission, 1987) would win support and praise from public choice theorists.

Finally, public choice theorists in the light of their views about the tendency of public bureaucracies to over-supply would expect to see some cuts in local authority spending and manpower. Yet it is not clear that they would necessarily support the reduction of local authorities to the minimalist role envisaged by other elements of the New Right. Niskanen (1973, p. 59) for example, argues that if reconstituted along more fragmented lines and with greater scope for customer choice 'a large part of the bureaucracy would probably survive . . . by improving its performance'.

*Criticism*

Public choice theorists have faced a sustained attack on many of their core ideas. First, and most generally, their view that there is a tendency for local authorities and other public agencies to over-supply 'overlooks the fact that public provision is intended to meet a criterion of need as much as ability to pay, and that in any case state programmes have historically had to be supplemented by the market as a result of their inadequacy, rather than their surplus of provision over need' (Beetham, 1987, p. 50).

Second their attack on the inadequacies of political representa-tive processes in allocating resources and expressing citizen prefer-ences is developed against the backcloth of an uncritical view of their preferred alternative, the market. As Lindblom (1977) argues both political systems and market mechanisms have their 'incompetences'. Market defects in expressing consumer choice include the inherently limited knowledge of persons (not only about their preferences but about the qualities of the goods or services they are buying) and the costs of establishing transaction mechanisms (for example, the collecting of fees, charges or insurance-based payments creates a considerable administrative burden). Markets can create insecurity and instability among both producers and consumers. Moreover, they operate only when cooperation can be induced but in other circumstances fail. 'A market system is a limited-use institution' (Lindblom, 1977, p. 89).

Third the argument that bureaucrats always engage in budget maximisation has been questioned. Blore (1987) drawing on local government evidence suggests that the tendency is rather to staff maximisation. Others find the assumption that bureaucrats are simply self-interested and self-serving untenable. Goodin (1982) argues that bureaucrats are mission-orientated, motivated by the content of their policies and a desire to serve the public.

Dunleavy (1985, 1986) provides a sustained attack on the budget maximisation thesis but stays within the assumption of public choice theorists that bureaucrats act in a self-interested way. In particular, self-interested bureaucrats might concentrate on their individual career advancement or workload reduction rather than engage in the effort and competitive struggle required to increase their budgets. More generally public choice theorists hold simplistic assumptions about the degree to which senior officials can direct their departments and underestimate the extent of cross-cutting conflicts within bureaucracies. As we showed in Chapter 4 the reality of intra-organisational politics in local authorities is of a range of diverse and conflicting interests.

Further, public choice theorists incorrectly assume that all bureaucracies and budgets are the same. Dunleavy, for example, draws a distinction between core budgets spent on administration and other spending which is directed at service delivery. Only delivery agencies, who are directly responsible for producing goods or services, see a close correlation between their core budgets and the general level of public spending. Local authorities are predominantly delivery agencies. But their behaviour is checked by control and regulatory agency bureaucrats, such as those in central government, whose interest in budget maximisation is limited and whose resistance to cuts is likely to be minimal. Their core budgets are not necessarily threatened by cuts in programme or service delivery spending.

Dunleavy moves on to promote an alternative to the budget maximisation thesis. He argues that the self-interested bureaucrat is more likely to pursue 'bureau-shaping' strategies. Top public bureaucrats are typically interested in work-related utilities rather the income-maximisation (which is constrained by limitations on public sector wages and 'perks' compared to that of the private sector). Senior managers will want to avoid routine, troublesome and conflict-prone subordinates and work in a small, élitist and collegiate atmosphere. Indeed Dunleavy (1986) suggests such bureaucrats are likely happily to embrace the contracting-out and other solutions proposed by public choice theorists.

> Why should a Director of Technical Services in a local authority care if refuse collection is privatized, thereby removing the need for her to manage some of the best organized and most militant public service workers as well as listening to endless debates amongst councillors on the timing of refuse collection runs?

The boom in privatisation and the easy embrace of contracting-out predicted by Dunleavy has not occurred, as Chapter 8 showed. The decision-making processes of local authorities are more complex than Dunleavy's model allows. Yet he is right to claim that his vision of the self-interest of bureaucrats is just as plausible as that of public choice theorists. Both his model and that of the public choice theorists tend to over-simplify a complex system of organisational and political relations.

Three further critical points can be made. Niskanen's vision of competing bureaucracies and/or private contractors seems to ignore that in line with his own model it might be in the interests of some agencies to collude and limit their competition. This, of course, is exactly the accusation levelled at private sector firms contracting for local authority business. Public choice theorists tend to under-play the problems of coordination and duplication created within a fragmented system (Pollitt, 1986, p. 185). Finally, their emphasis on consumer choice and exit options fails to address issues of income and resource inequality. For those on low income or welfare benefits, and to whom public services are especially important, public choice theorists might provide opportunities to manage their housing, or have a say in running their school, but the other choices of these people remain severely constrained.

### The dual state thesis

The dual state thesis has attracted considerable academic interest. Its two main proponents Cawson and Saunders have developed the thesis over time, reformulating and modifying various elements and arguments. Indeed they have even changed its name to the 'dual politics' thesis. The thesis has also been subject to criticism from a range of sources. This in turn has stimulated some re-assessment by Cawson and Saunders. If nothing else the dual state/politics thesis has stimulated an extensive academic debate. We cannot hope to do full justice to this debate. Below we outline some of the key arguments of the thesis and identify what are seen by critics as the main weaknesses.

### *Outline*

A discussion of the origins of the thesis is provided by Saunders (1986) and early formulations are provided in Cawson (1978) and Saunders (1979, pp. 178–9, 1981a, Ch. 8). We take Cawson and Saunders (1983) as the initial, comprehensive and 'worked-up' version of the thesis.

The dual state thesis rests initially on a distinction between the social investment and social consumption functions of the state. Social investment policies are aimed at maintaining the production of goods and services in the economy by supporting the profitability of private sector firms. They include the provision by the state of raw materials and services, such as coal, steel, gas and electricity, which are required by private sector producers; the provison of physical infrastructure such as roads, railways and ports which service the private sector; and direct financial support in the form of loans, equity shareholdings, grants and tax concessions, all designed to bolster profit margins in various firms or industries. Social consumption policies, in contrast, are aimed primarily at supporting the consumption needs of diverse groups in the population who, for various reasons, cannot fulfil all their requirements through market purchases. This category of services includes direct income support such as pensions, social security benefits and family allowances, and provision in kind of education, health care, and housing.

Cawson and Saunders suggest that distinct types of politics have developed around production-oriented and consumption-oriented state provision. The former is characterised as a relative closed corporate sector; the latter as a more open democratic or competitive sector. In social investment policy-making, a corporate bias has developed so that traditional representational pressures are filtered out. Rather the crucial decisions are made by state officials in close consultation with a select group of capitalist producer groups, professional associations and trade unions. These groups are given direct and privileged access to the state because their cooperation is essential if policies in social investment are to be effective. The corporatist bias ensures that the state is sensitive to their interests and concerns. Social consumption politics, on the other hand, involves a much wider range of competing and diverse interests. Here the influence of elections, pressure group lobbying and public opinion remains real and effective. Access to the state is more open and democratic.

The next stage of the 'dual state' argument is that in Britain, at least, the state has found it convenient to manage social investment policies at a national level, as central government and various quasi-governmental organisations can be insulated relatively easily from broader representational pressures. Social consumption policies, however, are run primarily by local authorities whose relative visibility and accessibility make them more susceptible to a wider range of influences (Saunders, 1981a, p. 265).

The implications of this analysis for the study of the local state have particularly been considered by Saunders. First, and most obviously, local politics is viewed as having its own specifity (Saunders, 1981b). That specificity is seen as a prime concern with welfare or social consumption issues. For Saunders, unlike Cockburn, this feature marks out the local state from other elements of the capitalist state. The consumption focus of the local state leads to a distinctive form of politics which is more open and competitive and not based on class divisions, but rather shifting alliances of consumption sectors. Indeed, Saunders suggests that some form of pluralist analysis is generally most appropriate to local politics in which a diverse and shifting pattern of consumption groups compete for influence. Finally the consumption focus of local politics ensures that it is organised around an ideology of need. 'Local government has become associated with provision for need and a concern with the quality of life, and its performance tends to be evaluated accordingly' (Saunders, 1984b, p. 29).

Having specified 'the peculiarity of the local political process', Saunders (1981b, p. 33) goes on to claim that the dual state thesis provides an effective understanding of the constraints within which the local state operates.

Local authorities are seen as fundamentally constrained by the dominance of corporatist politics at the centre. Saunders (1981b, p. 34) comments:

First, social consumption functions are necessarily subordinate to social investment functions since the latter are crucial in maintaining the conditions in which production may continue. Secondly, democratic accountability to a local population is necessarily curtailed by corporatist strategies at the centre. Thirdly, ideologies of social need take second place in a capitalist society to ideologies of private property.

Saunders (1982, 1984b) applies and develops this analysis in the context of the struggle between the Conservative Governments of the 1980s and left-wing Labour authorities. Broadly the centre is seen as destined to win and local opposition as weakened by the inherently fragmented nature of consumption interests and the localised nature of their struggles. For a summary of the main propositions of the dual state thesis see Table 10.1.

**TABLE 10.1   The specificity of the local state**

|  | LEVEL | | TENSION |
|---|---|---|---|
|  | CENTRAL/ REGIONAL | LOCAL | central control versus local autonomy |
| ECONOMIC FUNCTION | social investment | social consumption | economic versus social policy priorities |
| MODE OF INTEREST MEDIATION | corporate bias | competitive struggles | rational direction versus democratic accountability |
| IDEOLOGICAL PRINCIPLE | private property | citizenship rights | profit versus need |

Source: Saunders (1981b, p. 32, Table 1).

*Criticism*

The range of attacks on the dual state thesis has been considerable (for a review and a defence see Saunders, 1986). Below we list some points which Cawson and Saunders themselves accept have some validity.

First a number of criticisms have been made of the split between consumption and production functions which is central to the thesis. The list of social consumption policies includes cash provision which is in Britain largely administered through centrally-controlled agencies rather than local authorities. Economic initiatives, with a clear social investment function, have increasingly been undertaken by local authorities. Moreover, corporatist style politics, it is claimed, have developed around these initiatives. (The patchy evidence of local corporatism was considered in Chapter 5). In short, the split between consumption and production politics is not as neat as the dual state thesis implies.

The reply to this criticism by Saunders, however, contains considerable strength. The crucial question is what style of politics is most typical at which level. The dual state thesis does not deny the possibility that elements of the politics of production may appear in the politics of consumption and vice-versa. What it argues is that local politics is most often concerned with consumption issues and usually competitive. Nevertheless Saunders (1981a, p. 271) admits that in some localities 'one particular section of the population may achieve a virtual stranglehold over the local political process, thereby reducing any effective political competition to a minimum'. In these circumstances it would appear to follow that a departure from a solely pluralist analysis of local politics would be required.

A more problematic issue for the dual state thesis is that it is very difficult to distinguish empirically between primarily production-oriented and primarily consumption-oriented interventions. For example, state housing not only meets consumer needs but creates demand for private builders. Education can be classified as a means of legitimation, as social investment in human capital or as a type of collective consumption. There appear to be intractable classification problems (Dunleavy, 1984, pp. 71–2; Rhodes, 1988). As Flynn (1983, p. 103) concludes:

> The thesis of bifurcation of functions, interests and politics is problematic because types of policy cannot be unambiguously assigned to either production or consumption.

A further problem is the assumption that the function of a policy determines the level and type of politics associated with it. But why should function be given causal primacy? As Dunleavy (1984, p. 72) comments:

> What tier of government handles an issue, and the type of decision mode adopted, help to determine the character of state expenditures, rather than governments simply responding to a predetermined set of functional requirements or imperatives.

In particular, social investment policies might be capable of being managed in a more open and competitive way if decision-makers have a commitment to that style of politics. We have seen in Chapter 9 how Urban Left authorities, such as the GLC and

Sheffield in the early 1980s, sought to develop their local economic strategies by working with trade unions, shop floor workers, tenants and residents rather than by developing a local corporation premised on a special relationship with business interests.

The dual state thesis has also been criticised for failing to deal effectively with the internal politics of the state. Its focus is on the environment of local government not the officials who manage it. In particular Dunleavy (1984, p. 77) complains that the thesis underplays the influence of professionals in policy-making and concludes that 'acknowledging the importance of professionalism in local government suggests that to see it as a differentially pluralist level of government is mistaken'.

The points about causality and internal organisation have been conceded to a large degree by Saunders. Indeed in work on the 'regional state' he has made an attempt to respond in a positive way to these criticisms (1983, 1984a, 1985b). The politics of health authorities are examined as entirely a product of the internal dynamics of various state or quasi-governmental agencies. Water authorities are seen as influenced by a combination of internal and external influences. In developing this work Saunders has made major concessions and modified the thesis considerably. Rather than function determining politics Saunders (1986, p. 35) tentatively suggests 'that it is the saliency of a given policy area for producer interests which above all else explains the level at which it is resolved, the form of interest mediation adopted, and the prevailing ideological dispositions of those involved'. The irony here is that this approach appears to lead to a crude instrumentalism and determinism – of the form that capitalist interests 'get the state and the politics they want' – which the dual state thesis was initially and consciously designed to avoid. Moreover, the general depiction of the regional state provided by Saunders has been criticised as focussed on too narrow a range of institutions and as a consequence misleading (Gray, 1985).

We would not agree with Saunders (1986, p. 37) that the dual state thesis 'appears now to be in its stride'. Rather under pressure from a number of telling criticisms it appears to be in the process of disintegration.

**The local state and social relations**

According to Cockburn, as noted earlier, the local state performs two functions: the physical reproduction of the labour force and an ideological role aimed at ensuring social harmony. This second role has attracted the attention of a number of writers and activists. But unlike Cockburn they see the process as contradictory and conflict-laden. In Chapter 9 we noted how many Urban Left authorities saw themselves as contributing to a battle of ideas, setting out an alternative agenda to that of Thatcherism. Theoretical support for this vision of the local state as arena of ideological struggle has come from a number of sources.

A group of writers, within the marxist tradition, stress that to understand the state it is necessary not to consider what the state does but how it does things. It is important to consider state form: the social relations embodied in the organisation of the state (Holloway and Picciotto, 1978; London–Edinburgh Group, 1979; CSE State Group, 1979). The capitalist state presents class conflicts as relations between individuals based on formal legal equality and freedoms. It obscures and mystifies. But at the same time oppositional space can be found and forms of state activity undertaken which empower and encourage collective consciousness. Below we examine Duncan and Goodwin's particular application and development of this argument to the local state.

*Outline*

According to Duncan and Goodwin (1982a and b, 1985) local state activities contribute to the interpretation of how society works and why. For example, it is a class society? Are markets efficient? Are women naturally subordinate to men? The local state also has a dual representational role. It represents local interests at the same time as having a responsibility to nationally-determined policies. It speaks and acts for dominant local interests (they vary from locality to locality) but is constrained by its role as a local implementer of decisions reached in central government. At national level it is large financial and industrial interests that pull most weight. The local state can be pushed into presenting national policies as fair and appropriate. Equally though the local state may seek to present issues in a way that meets the expectations of dominant local interests. This tension underlies central–local conflict.

The 'interpretational' and 'representational' roles of the local state vary in their operation in different localities. In some areas local landowner interests are dominant, in others working-class groups may run the local state. This diversity reflects the uneven social and economic development of capitalist society. Some areas industrialised, others did not. Some areas have seen continued economic growth, others have experienced de-industrialisation. Diversity also reflects different traditions of political struggle and class consciousness. It is not just that rural Suffolk is different from Manchester. It is a matter of Sheffield's radical tradition in contrast to its absence in nearby and equally industrial Doncaster. Local states develop different characters in response to their local social relations and their balance of class, ethnic or cultural forces (see also Dickens *et al.*, 1985).

In periods of major and rapid change the local state's role in managing and interpreting social relations becomes more problematic. Policies have to be adapted to meet shifts in the local social base. Thus the shift in Sheffield's local economic strategy away from interventions in the private sector to supporting public sector and local authority employment is explained by the fact that as the city de-industrialised public sector unions and workers came to be dominant in the local environment as private sector employment drained away (Goodwin, 1986).

As the pace of change increases so also the local state is thrown into the heart of an ideological battle. Sheffield and other Urban Left authorities promote their economic and social strategies as alternatives to Thatcherism. The Thatcher governments through enterprise zones and Urban Development Corporations seek to promote a business and entrepreneurial culture. The crucial role of the local state in interpreting social relations ensures there is 'a lot of fuss' about these alternative strategies (Duncan and Goodwin, 1985).

## Criticism

A critical look at Duncan and Goodwin's model reveals a number of issues. The analysis of the interpretational role of the local state appears to be inadequate and simplistic. In discussing the controversy over local economic policy in the 1980s evidence is provided that the ideological battle is seen as crucial by political activists, but there is no demonstration of any impact on public opinion or consciousness. There are grounds for suspecting that such evidence would not be forthcoming. As Taylor-Gooby (1985) has indicated in a survey of attitudes to welfare state provision, public opinion rarely shifts dramatically and is not subject to simple manipulation by political forces. Moreover, as Husbands and Dunleavy (1985) suggest the model over-emphasises the local determination of people's perceptions. It assumes that local experiences of the state are dominant in the processes of political alignment. This view is difficult to sustain in the light of substantial evidence on the influence of non-local factors in local elections (see Chapter 2) and the existence of powerful national political parties and a nationally-orientated mass media.

Second the discussion of the representational role of the local state is uncritical and determinist in its assumption that local authorities speak for local interest and that the centre always pursues the concerns of financial and industrial capital. Have not some major social welfare reforms (which could reasonably be viewed as in the interests of non-capitalist groups) been promoted and led by central government? The social relations school appears to have a rosy view of local political processes, reminiscent of simplistic pluralism. The model does not explain how particular local interests come to dominate particular local authorities. Some correlation with economic processes is suggested but what other factors condition the responsiveness of a local authority?

Finally reflected in the theory are several of the dilemmas of the political practice of Urban Left authorities, with which it is associated (see Chapter 9). Local politics is seen largely as an ideological battle and the assembly of new social and political alliances. Yet the emphasis on ideology can mean that the practical job of turning ideas into practice is neglected or not thought through. Moreover, the assembly of alliances can be seen as giving people a new consciousness which neglects real conflicts between consumers of different services and between producers and users of services. Would it be too unfair to suggest that Duncan and Goodwin provide a rationale for 'gesture' politics?

**Summing up the debate**

Each of the theories examined in this chapter can be seen to have contributed to our understanding of local politics, but as the criticism has indicated each has its limitations and weaknesses. In this concluding section we sum up the debate by reviewing the overall image of local government and politics that it provides. We also identify some gaps or omissions. Our discussion is presented in terms of input politics (who makes demands on the state and how are these demands made); local state organisation and policy-making (the internal dynamics of state decision processes); and the crises or dilemmas faced by the local state (*cf.* Dunleavy and O'Leary, 1987, p. 11).

*Input politics*

Most writers in the local state debate characterise local politics as relatively open, plural and competitive. All four perspectives see local authorities as responsive to some local interests, though each recognises that the competition is not perfect and that access to local authority officials and councillors is not open to all equally. The sharpest criticisms of input politics come from the public choice theorists who emphasise the exclusion of disorganised groups such as ratepayers or those on fixed incomes. Even they recognise the possibility of these groups becoming mobilised and organised, a fertile base for a populist politics such as Thatcherism. With the exception of public choice theorists the broad image is of relatively modest imperfections in the range and scope of demands coming from local politics and the extent of the access provided by local authorities to different local interests. In as far as imperfections exist there is a tendency to assume that they can be overcome through a shift in the focus of local parties, councillors and officials or that they will respond to changes in the social and economic composition of the locality.

There is a strong case for some harder questions to be asked about who gets mobilised and how access is granted. Localist, dual state and the social relations schools have perhaps reinforced each others assumptions to too great a degree. Plainly there are good grounds for arguing that the localness of local government carries with it the potential for a relatively responsive political system. Less resources are required to form an organisation for local campaigning compared to national levels of politics. Local government officials are physically more accessible and their activities more visible. Yet we need to address more systematically the structures of inequality and the history of powerlessness which can lead to the exclusion and non-mobilisation of the working class, women, ethnic minorities and other deprived groups within local politics. This proposition does not deny the argument of Chapter 5 that since the mid-1970s a wide range of local authorities have attempted to open out their decision-making processes and support new groups. It is to suggest that this process has made limited strides and that systematic inequalities in resources and cultural biases cannot be easily overcome.

A further consideration which the debate tends to underplay is the ability of some interests to make demands and exercise influence without necessarily having to mobilise and organise. In concluding Chapter 5 we supported the argument of Lindblom (1977), among others, that certain interests – especially major business interests – have such a crucial role in a market-oriented society that no local authority could afford to ignore their demands in the long term. Their investment and cooperation is so vital that local authorities – regardless of their political colour – are likely to recognise the need to win their support and involvement in certain key areas of local policy-making, such as economic and industrial development, land-use, property, and shopping schemes. This special business influence is best seen as restricted to such policy areas where their cooperation is essential but this additional factor in the input politics of local government should not be neglected.

### State organisation and policy-making

The dual state and social relations models underplay the significance of state organisation and internal policy-making processes within their analyses. This much we have established earlier in the chapter and in particular we noted that dual state theorists concede this weakness and have attempted to take corrective measures. Public choice and localist approaches give much more prominence to the internal dynamics of local authorities, but both treat it in rather abstract and simplified ways. The former stresses budget maximising bureaucrats, the latter general management principles. In short, it is in the area of the internal organisation and policy-making of local authorities that the debate has been most disappointing. In many ways we do not have theories of the local state but rather theories about its relationship with its environment or civil society.

If we are to develop a better understanding of the internal organisation and policy-making of the local state we need to develop our analysis of the internal dynamics of local state politics. Chapter 4 makes a start in this direction but is limited. Moreover its policy orientation fails to capture the way in which diverse class, gender and other social interests operate within local authorities, and the way that the material structure of rewards and costs creates divisions of power between and within councillors, managers, white-collar staff, blue-collar workers, part-time and full-time employees.

To understand politics within our Town Halls we need not only consider the dynamics of councillors, party groups, various professional groupings and conflicting bureaucratic interests, we need also to focus on local authorities as social structures cross-cut with competing material interests. This need is particularly urgent given the introduction of enforced competitive tendering which brings up a whole host of issues of this nature. We will return to this point in the final chapter.

The other major area for work, if we are to develop our understanding of the internal organisation of the local state, is to recognise the significance of the growth of non-elected local government. The local state debate, despite Cockburn's original intention, has focussed narrowly on elected local government. We need to broaden that focus and bring in many of the forms of non-elected local government identified in Chapter 3. These forms require to be understood in terms of their own specificity and mode of operation. Also an important issue is how the elected and non-elected elements of the local state interrelate and interact. Again a start was made on this in Chapter 3 but much more remains to be done.

*Crises*

For three out of four of the theories reviewed the main dilemma for the local state is the pressure it faces from a central government responsive to other interests. Localist, social relation and dual state models can all be read as seeing local government in imminent danger of being crushed by a centralised state. Localists provide the 'official' defence for local government, many academics rely on the dual state thesis and radicals can rest their support for local government on the social relations model.

For the public choice theorists local government's problem is not so much with central government as with itself. Indeed New Right thinkers suggest that a strong central state is needed in order to force local government to reform. Local government, they argue, is not responsive, provides little choice, lacks customer sensitivity and is too dominated by trade union and employee interests.

The bind for local government is that both the above arguments carry considerable validity. Local government's dilemma is that it is being squeezed and pressured from above and at the same time cannot automatically expect the support and commitment of its customers and electors. To survive local government needs to change – improving service delivery, opening access and providing choice – but such change in a hostile environment is extremely problematic. This point has already been illustrated in Chapter 9.

Perhaps the local state debate needs to turn its attention more towards the pace and extent of the social and economic changes that local authorities have and are likely to be coping with. These changes extend beyond the fiscal constraints and restructuring stimulated by central government. Local authorities are facing major shifts in their demographic structures, rapid changes in their economic and industrial base, new demands stemming from the impact of information technology, the rise of new social groups and cleavages and an overall increase in assertiveness and expectations about the standard and quality of service delivery. The localist literature recognises this challenge facing local government (Stewart, 1986a, Ch. 3; Local Government Training Board, 1985; Spencer, 1985) but the other perspectives do not. In particular it seems unnecessarily restrictive to continue to see local politics as social consumption issues (as the dual state thesis does) in the light of this challenge. Changes in society are pushing local politics beyond the boundaries of a competitive consumption politics.

# 11 The Future of Local Government

This chapter outlines the programme of reforms with which the third Thatcher government elected in 1987 intends to restructure local government. It discusses the nature of the Conservatives' attack and suggests that it has a certain, if limited, ideological coherence. A third section in the chapter examines the implications of the reform package for the future role and organisation of local government. The final section provides a vision of what elected local government's role should be, which stands in stark contrast to that promoted by the Conservatives. By drawing on the experience of some, predominantly Labour authorities during the 1980s, we argue the case for local authorities to take on a role as basic units of community government.

## The Conservatives' programme

There are at least five major areas where the Conservatives' programme threatens the traditional role and organisation of elected local government:

### Competitive tendering

First there is the provision to ensure competitive tendering. The new areas in which councils will be required to put services out to tender are: refuse collection; street cleaning; ground maintenance; building cleaning; vehicle repair and maintenance; and catering (including school meals). A consultation paper proposed adding the management of leisure services to the list.

This measure builds on previous legislation in the 1980 Local Government, Planning and Land Act which introduced competitive tendering for building works and maintenance DLOs. It follows, as noted in Chapter 8, the relatively weak voluntary take-up of contracting-out by local authorities in the early and mid-1980s. Having failed to choose the option local authorities are going to be pushed into competitive tendering. They will retain their statutory responsibility to provide the services outlined above but they will be required to make 'in-house' staff compete with private contractors to offer the cheapest price for the job.

If an 'in-house' workforce wishes to compete for their work they must do so on the same basis as private contractors and cannot be given preferential treatment. The Secretary of State has taken considerable discretionary powers to lay down conditions relating to the tendering process, the length of contract period, and the mode of accounting that can be adopted by an 'in-house' workforce. These powers to intervene apply at the level of individual authorities. In this way the Secretary of State aims to challenge those authorities which are felt to be protecting their 'in-house' staff and not 'playing' the competitive tendering game.

The Government has also acted to stop local authorities from attaching any 'non-commercial' criteria to their contracts. In effect this undermines to a large extent the policies of contract compliance developed by several local authorities during the 1980s. It is also seen as ensuring that future competitive tendering arrangements cannot be influenced by considerations such as terms and conditions of employment offered by contractors to their workers. Local authorities will, however, have powers to withhold contracts from private firms as part of their duty to promote equality of opportunity between races.

*Reform of the rating system*

The Government also proposes new arrangements for the financing of local government. Its aim is to extend the new system, already legislated for in Scotland, to the rest of Britain. It draws on the arguments and concerns of the Green Paper *Paying for Local*

*Government.* Three principal reforms are involved. First domestic rates are to be abolished to be replaced by a community charge or local poll tax to be levied on all adults. Some people will be exempt from the tax including medical students, nuns and monks and the Queen! Otherwise virtually everyone over 18 – about 37 million people – will be liable to pay the tax to the council(s) in whose area their main or only home is located. Everybody will have to pay a minimum of 20 per cent of their charge but for the less well-off a system of rebates will be available to cover some or all of the remainder of the charge. The new system will be introduced in Scotland in 1989 and in the rest of Britain in 1990, although in certain inner London boroughs the change will be phased in over a four year period.

The second reform takes non-domestic (or business) rates out of the control of local authorities. A uniform business rate is to be introduced with its amount fixed by central government. It will be collected into a national pool and then redistributed to local authorities in the form of a grant from central government. Any increases in the business rate will be fixed at, or below, the inflation rate so industry will contribute less to local spending in the long term. Alongside the change to a uniform business rate will be a revaluation of all industrial and commercial property. Revaluation and the switch to a uniform business rate will in some areas lead to a rapid increase in the rates that particular businesses will have to pay. In such cases there will be a phasing-in period to help the businesses to cope.

Finally a revised system of central government financial support is part of the reform package. A new grant system will be introduced which, the Government claim, will be fairer and more comprehensible in operation. The existing system of general financial support will be replaced by a new lump-sum revenue support grant distributed according to central government's assessment of local need.

## Education

The Government also proposes several education measures with major implications for local authorities. One of the most dramatic changes is the proposal to allow schools to opt out of local authority control. If a governing body decides it wants its school to opt out of local authority control it must hold a secret ballot of all parents. If there is a majority vote in favour of opting out a plan for running the school must be prepared which will either be approved, modified or rejected by the Education Secretary after a period of consultation. Opted-out schools will have funds channelled to them through central government. Their governing bodies will contain a mixture of elected parents, the headteacher, one or two elected teacher governors, and enough co-opted governors from business and the community to outnumber the rest.

Schools that stay within local education authorities will have greater powers over their budgets and their governors will have the power to appoint all staff including heads and deputies. The governing bodies of colleges of further education will also assume greater powers over budgets and the recruitment and dismissal of staff. No more than 20 per cent of the governing bodies will be local authority nominees and over half the governing body of a college will be composed of businessmen.

No local education authority or governing body will be allowed to set a limit on admissions which is lower than its physical capacity. This could well have the effect of increasing the disparity between 'popular' and 'unpopular' schools leading to further under-utilisation of facilities and the prospect of more pressure on education officers to look for school closures.

The bill initially proposed the break-up of the Inner London Education Authority (ILEA) by giving individual London boroughs the right to opt out of ILEA and set up their own education service. Under pressure from its backbenchers this provision was changed by the Government to the outright abolition of ILEA. Responsibility for education services will pass to individual London boroughs in 1990.

Schools will operate in the context of a national curriculum of specified subjects for primary and secondary schools. There will be three core subjects – Mathematics, English and Science (and Welsh in Welsh-speaking areas). In total between 70 and 80 per cent of lesson time will be taken with those core subjects plus additional subjects as laid down in the national curriculum. There will also be a system of learning targets involving a test for every child at the ages of 7, 11, 14 and 16.

The bill removes polytechnics and colleges of higher education from local authority control. They will become 'independent' bodies run by businessmen and academics. The bill also gives central government power to make long-term agreements with business sponsors for joint funding of city technology colleges. These colleges will concentrate on providing vocational and technical training.

## Housing

The Conservatives seek to substantially reduce the role of local authorities in housing provision. Council tenants are to be given the right to 'pick a landlord'. It is proposed that all council tenants will have a chance to transfer the ownership of their homes to another landlord – a housing association, a housing trust, a cooperative or a private landlord – and continue as an 'assured' tenant with that new landlord. As an assured tenant the house-holder is likely to face a higher rent level. At the same time, however, council rents will be forced up by ending the ability of councils to subsidise rents from their rate revenue funds. Tenants who make the change from council tenancy will not be allowed to opt back.

The bill also enables the Government to set up Housing Action Trusts (HATs) to take over and sell off council estates. HATs will be run by a group of people 'with direct experience of the area' chosen by the Environment Secretary. The HAT will have the task of modernising the estate and producing a greater diversity of tenure. If a local authority resists the HAT's schemes then its planning and environmental health powers may be transferred to the HAT. Finance for HATs will come from rents, borrowing, central government grants and private sector sources. It is expected that initially four HATs will be operational by 1989.

The Government's plans involve a wider role for housing associations, which as well as taking over council estates, are to be encouraged to meet the housing needs of younger, middle-class, professional groups by providing higher rent homes for their occupation. The associations are to be encouraged to seek a much greater degree of private finance to support their building programmes. The Government is also concerned to give incentives to private landlords to provide new short-term tenancies at market-level rents. Generally the changes involve substantial increases in rent levels for council, housing association and other tenants.

*Inner cities*

The changes in the rating system, housing and education will, the Government claim, benefit the inner cities by forcing their local authorities to be more responsible and by creating new opportunities for their residents. A number of other initiatives are to be directed at inner city areas, including the establishment of a range of 'mini' Urban Development Corporations. These UDCs, like their larger counterparts, will take over control of planning and development from local authorities. Their aim will be to attract private sector investment and revitalise economic and business activity in their areas. The Government's *Action for Cities* programme, launched in the spring of 1988 included a proposal for a national, private sector-led urban renewal agency and a number of job creation initiatives.

*Other proposals*

In addition to the five main areas of change the Government's programme is likely to include other initiatives which will substantially affect the operations of local authorities. Changes in the management of community care policies may lead to a shift in the responsibilities held by local authorities and health authorities. In Scotland a new housing agency – Scottish Homes – directly responsible to the Scottish Office is to be created and will seek to challenge local authorities in the management of the council stock. Legislation, drawing on the Widdicombe Committee's findings, is promised in the Conservatives' manifesto.

**The nature of the Conservatives' attack**

*Building on past conflicts*

The Government's programme reflects several features of the Thatcherite approach to central–local relations identified earlier in the book. First the programme is driven to some extent by 'gut' reactions to events or past policy initiatives. The proposals relating to the rating system can to a large extent be seen as the outcome of a policy panic following rate revaluation in Scotland in 1985/6; and a growing realisation that the constantly changing system of grant reductions, targets, penalties, and rate-capping was not achieving the local financial discipline that the Government desired. The introduction of the reforms of the rating system is a last ditch attempt to control local authority expenditure. Equally, the attack on ILEA seems to have been motivated to a large extent by the annoyance its policies have caused to the Government and some of its key supporters.

Second the Government seems as keen as in the past to maximise the electoral benefit it reaps from changes in local government. The opting-out provisions for schools and council tenants it is hoped will prove as popular as 'Right-to-Buy' council house sales. Generally the Government appears to be committed to undermining the still substantial political and electoral base held by the Labour party in local government by imposing a strict financial regime and removing the powers and influence of local authorities in education, housing, planning and economic development.

Third the Conservatives have retained their clear determination to by-pass opposition and overcome resistance to their policies. Local authorities are offered the choice of cooperating or being 'removed from the frame'. Urban Development Corporations, Housing Trusts, the strict rules surrounding competitive tendering, and the extraordinary discretionary powers that the Secretary of State has available to interfere in the detailed operation of local authority 'in-house' workforces, suggest that the Government intends to brook no opposition.

Finally the proposals, particularly those relating to the inner cities, reflect the Government's continuing belief in private enterprise and private sector solutions to problems.

### A new vision of local government?

The Government's programme, however, is more than a mixture of *ad hoc* measures, electoral ambition, power politics and a belief in the enterprise spirit. There is an ideological coherence which holds together the various initiatives and pieces of legislation.

Central elements of New Right thinking are reflected in a concern for financial constraint, competition, citizen choice and new forms of accountability. Within the Conservative programme there is new vision of what local government should be.

As we noted in Chapter 10 New Right thinking, particularly that within the public choice mainstream, argues that there is an inbuilt tendency for government organisations to spend too much because electoral checks on their behaviour are weak and because producer interests within such organisations have too much power. The reform of the rating system can be seen as an attempt to counter this tendency to over-supply and establish effective mechanisms for financial constraint. It increases the numbers of electors contributing towards local authority finances through a highly visible tax. In effect it increases the numbers of electors with a direct material interest in levels of expenditure. The reform also removes the 'soft' option of relying on business rates to cushion the impact of local spending and it forces even those on the lowest income to make a contribution. Local spending which is 'excessive' will have to be paid for, in part, by those least able to afford it. Local decision-makers will therefore be forced to consider to a greater extent the electoral and social consequences of their expenditure plans. Financial constraint should be the result.

New Right thinking also emphasises the need for efficiency to be achieved through competition. As Green (1987, p. 211) comments:

> As far as possible competition should prevail, or at least every supplier should be open to competition. Neither private nor government contrivances should be allowed to obliterate or blur the crucial signalling role of the free market.

The introduction of competitive tendering undermines the 'monopoly power' of local authority workforces and opens their operations to competition. Schools are to be made more subject to the laws of supply and demand through parental choice. Housing supply is to be restructured by allowing higher rents, closer to 'pure' market levels, to be charged.

A related theme is the commitment to citizen choice. This is to be achieved by the fragmenting of existing governmental bureaucracies. By breaking up the monopoly control of schools and housing estates and creating 'exit options' for customers new opportunities for comparison and choice are provided. The crucial thing is to establish intra-bureaucratic competition as this provides the basis for increased consumer choice.

A final theme moves beyond choice to the issue of citizen control. New Right thinkers, as noted in Chapter 10, regard representative democracy as a crude mechanism for determining citizen preferences and are keen to encourage other experimental forms of citizen participation in decision-making. Participation, it is argued, is most likely to occur on the basis of a particular interest in a specific function. Representatives in centralised, multi-purpose authorities tend to become part of the bureaucratic system and divorced from the desires and wishes of everyday consumers. A more effective mechanism for control is achieved where those making decisions have a direct material interest in that particular service because they are everyday consumers. Hence Conservative lip-service to parents having a say in schools and tenants running housing. The Secretary of State for the Environment during the 1987 election campaign even managed to extend this logic to industrial and business domination of Urban Development Corporations. He argued that many parents know more about education than local authorities, that tenants know more about housing than many councils, and that industrialists and developers know more about economic regeneration than local authority bureaucrats and councillors.

Embedded with the Conservative attack is a challenge to the legitimacy of local authorities as representative bodies. Low turn-out and the limited number of electors who are direct ratepayers are identified as flaws. But beyond this the principle of representative democracy is itself questioned. It is viewed as providing an inadequate mechanism for citizen control and other forms of citizen participation are required to supplement it.

## The gap between rhetoric and reality

The above account of an ideological coherence to the Conservatives' attacks should not be pushed too far. As we noted earlier, *ad hoc* measures, gut politics and electoral considerations still influence Government thinking to a substantial degree. Moreover, there is a considerable gap between rhetoric and reality in many of the Government's plans. More effective local electoral checks are seen as the mechanism to ensure financial restraint. But in practice central government's control of grants and the new uniform business rate take much of the responsibility away from local decision-makers. The Government's reserve powers to 'cap' the community charge that a local authority can levy also suggests that it has less than total confidence that its new mechanism of local accountability will deliver financial restraint.

The commitment to competition is real enough. However, in the case of competitive tendering it seems that the Government has been concerned to ensure that local authorities carry several disadvantages into the tendering process. It might be suggested that the Government is as much concerned with creating new profit-making opportunities for private contractors as it is in stimulating competition.

The citizen choice offered in housing and education proposals has been widely criticised as offering a choice for a few at the expense of choice for the many. Better-off schools in better-off areas are those most likely to opt out, it is argued, leaving local authorities to manage schools with the worst buildings, the most disadvantaged pupils, in the context of shrinking financial resources. The HAT proposals and the plans to widen the role of housing associations may create new opportunities for owner-occupation and renting for some higher-income households but they do not help to solve the housing problems of many lower-income families. In particular as the controller of the Audit Commission notes the Government's proposals will do nothing to 'resolve the principal crisis issue in housing today, the poor quality of large amounts of our national housing stock' (Davies, 1987, p. 5). Doubts too have been raised about the voting procedures associated with the opting out of parents or tenants from the local authority system. The Government's approach appears to embody the odd principle that those who do not vote are not supporters of the status quo but can be counted as on the side of those wishing to opt out.

Finally the Government's commitment to greater citizen control appears in practice lukewarm and half-hearted. In both opted-out and local authority-managed schools parent governors are to be outnumbered by other interests, and subject to a great deal of central government direction over the curriculum and other matters. Moreover, tenants may find their attempts to form housing management cooperatives blocked because they will not meet the Government's criteria of having a track record in financial and housing management. In general the Government pays little attention to the support, training and time involved in giving tenants (or parents) the confidence, know-how and skills necessary for them to take over effectively the running of facilities they use.

## Implications for local government

The previous discussion suggests that a debate will rage into the 1990s over the interests to benefit or suffer from the Conservative Government's package of reforms. There are good grounds for believing that the Conservatives' plans will further disadvantage already disadvantaged groups. For the present, however, we focus our attention on the implications of the Conservatives' plan for the future role and organisation of local government.

### A threat to jobs and services

First several of the reforms involve a substantial threat to local authority jobs and services. Indeed one dire production from the controller of the Audit Commission suggests that by 1992 local authority expenditure might be reduced by about a third, with a similar reduction in the number of local authority employees. As the controller notes his calculations may well be way off the mark. The calculations assume, for example, that local authorities will lose control of half of the school service and half of the existing council housing stock. The controller's predictions do, however, 'give some idea of the scale of the change which *could* occur' (Davies, 1987, p. 7). Another way of illustrating the scope of the threat involved is to note that competitive tendering on its own implies that in non-metropolitan district authorities half of all local authority jobs will have to be competed for if they are to be retained.

It would also seem that the financial pressures on many local authorities are going to increase as the deferred payments associated with earlier 'creative accounting' measures have to be met, rate-capping continues and a new financial system is introduced. Several Labour-controlled London boroughs and inner city authorities have already shown signs of considerable financial stress in the immediate post-election period. Indeed the pressure has been so great that Margaret Hodge, Leader of Islington Council, has suggested to other Labour London boroughs that the option of protecting jobs *and* services may in some circumstances be closed, and that if a choice has to be made the emphasis should be on preserving the quality of service delivery. 'Where a conflict of interest arises, the services must take precedence over trade union interests, or even jobs. Without the support of the people for whom we provide services, we shall not be able to protect any jobs' (Hodge, 1987, p. 2). More generally other local authority leaders expect to face difficult choices as we move into the 1990s. It seems unlikely that local authorities will have as much success as in the past in protecting local authority jobs and services. As Newcastle's Jeremy Beecham (1987, p. 23) argues 'Neil Kinnock's famous dented shield will not be enough to protect services and people from injury'.

### A limited role for local authorities and local choice

The Conservatives' reform package implies a considerable reduction in the role of local authority activities and the scope for local choice. In particular the role of local authorities as direct service providers is challenged by the education, housing and contracting-out provisions. Local authorities will retain some of their responsibilities in these areas but the Government's vision is of a more 'hands-off' style where control over the direct delivery of services rests in other agencies. As Beecham (1987, p. 21) rather gloomily puts it:

> From being a major provider of services, local authorities seem destined to be confined to the role of monitoring and inspecting – in short a glorified town hall version of community health councils.

Another commonly expressed vision of the future is one where a local council meets just once a year to set its community charge rate and let contracts for the provision of its services! Plainly there is a considerable degree of exaggeration associated with such predictions but it is clear that the role of local authorities as direct service providers is under challenge.

The scope of local authority activities is also under threat. The Government seems committed to taking responsibilitiy for inner city policy and economic regeneration out of local authority hands. It has outlawed most contract compliance measures in local authority dealings with the private sector. Generally it is keen to discourage any activity which places local authorities in a wider governmental role.

The Government's proposals seem likely to reduce the ability of local authorities to develop alternative policies and practices. Central government is going to have still further control over the extent and scope of resources available to local authorities through its control of grants, the new uniform business rate and its ability to 'cap' rates in the short term and community charge levels in the long run. Legislation in contracting-out, housing and education constrains the room for manœuvre held by local authorities. It seems particularly unlikely that the radical initiatives of local socialism will continue with the same pace or scope. As Islington's Margaret Hodge (1987, p. 1) comments: 'We . . . have to accept that the "agenda" will be dominated by the Government'.

As a consequence of the Government's attack on elected local authorities we are likely to see an increasing role for the assorted non-elected agencies identified in Chapter 3. Further UDCs and Housing Trusts as well as various *ad hoc* and user organisations in housing and education will take on a range of activities. Powerful agencies such as the Manpower Services Commission will continue their activities, while others such as the Scottish Development Agency will have their role restructured to suit Thatcherite policy objectives better.

The role of local authorities as the dominant governmental agencies of their localities is threatened by the Government's proposals. Powerful multi-purpose and elected local authorities will be further challenged by the rise of single-purpose and non-elected governmental bodies.

*New management structures and processes*

The Government's plans involve considerable changes in the

organisation, structures and management approaches of local authorities. Contracting-out on its own 'implies fundamental changes in the way that authorities are managed' (Flynn and Walsh, 1987, p. 41). There will be a need to separate client departments from those adopting a contracting role. Separate committees within a service area might be appropriate. One to lay down contract conditions and to decide which tender to accept, and another to oversee the operation of any 'in-house' workforce winning a contract. Service departments which have to compete for work will demand a different relationship with central departments providing financial, personnel and other functions. They will not want to carry unnecessary central overheads as they enter the competitive tendering battle. In short, competitive tendering is likely to have a direct or 'knock-on' effect throughout an authority.

More generally the Conservatives' programme implies a considerable shift in the management style of local authorities. The new management style would build on and reinforce several of the trends which can be observed from the mid-1970s onwards. Table 11.1 outlines some of the key differences between 'traditional' local government management and organisation and the 'new' approach implied by the Government's challenge. Local authorities will be smaller and local government generally will be populated by a fragmented range of organisations. Local authorities will no longer be as self-sufficient. They will have to learn to operate alongside or through other agencies. Resource constraint implies a sustained and continuing concern for value-for-money and efficiency savings. The dominance of professionals, which was to a large extent premised on growth and service development,

**TABLE 11.1   Changes in local authority management and organisation**

| Traditional organisation and management characteristics | New organisation and management characteristics |
|---|---|
| Large | Small |
| Self-sufficient | Linked with other organisations |
| Growth-oriented | Resource-constrained |
| Professionally controlled | Managerially controlled |
| Concerned with structure | Concerned with process |

Source: Adapted from Flynn and Walsh (1987), Figure 1, p. 50.

has increasingly given way to an emphasis on management in a period of financial constraint. This trend is likely to continue as the ability to manage resources, personnel and relationships with external organisations take precedence over the technical knowledge and expertise of traditional professionals. Finally in the past local authorities have focussed their organisational concern on department and committee structures. Structures will remain important but an increasing emphasis on processes will be developed. As Flynn and Walsh (1987, p. 52) argue:

> There will be a need to make the organisation work as a 'network' rather than a command structure, both with internal employees and external contractors. Skills of linking and working across boundaries will be required and the ability to work through influence rather than power.

The implications for local government of the Government's proposals are that local authority jobs and services are substantially threatened, as is the role of the local authority as a direct service provider. The scope of local authority activity is also challenged and the opportunities for developing alternative policies based on local choice are reduced. Local authorities will operate in a world in which other governmental and quasi-governmental organisations take an increasing role. New organisational structures and management processes, as a result of these changes, will be required if local authorities are to operate effectively in their new environment.

**An alternative debate**

The Conservatives' programme contains within it the potential seeds of its own destruction. Community charge seems as likely to lose public support as win it. Its impact on people's income and the intrusions into people's lives that its collection will involve may bring more discredit than credit to the Government. Uniform business rates, combined with revaluation, are unlikely to be universally popular with business interests.

Having the opportunity to be 'under new management' may appear to be a hollow gain for council tenants if more resources are not provided to maintain and repair their houses. Parents may see their choice over the quality and nature of their children's education as restricted rather than enhanced by the Government's proposals. The inner cities will not be revived by private investment and enterprise. Physical renewal may take place in some locations but the disadvantages of lower income groups within our inner cities will remain. In short, there are grounds for believing that contradictions and failures will bedevil the Government's programme as we move into the 1990s.

Yet to challenge the Thatcherite agenda for local government it is not sufficient to point to the shortcomings and failings of the Government's policies in practice. It is important to develop an alternative vision of what the future role of local government should be.

Various alternatives do exist but it is not intended here to develop a systematic analysis of their form and content (Davey, 1986). Our purpose is more limited. In particular we seek to build on the experience of primarily those Labour local authorities which during the 1980s have experimented with new roles and ways of working. We examined the activities of many of those local socialists in Chapter 9. Below we aim to selectively and critically draw on their policies and practices to offer a vision of local government which stands as a radical alternative to that offered by Thatcherism. (These arguments are developed further in Stewart and Stoker, 1988.)

The starting point for this alternative vision is a set of values which stand in contrast to those promoted by Thatcherism. First there is a commitment to collective service provision to meet people's social and economic needs. Second there is a belief that collective action led by government can challenge powerful vested interests and lend support to disadvantaged groups. Elected public bodies have the moral authority to redefine problems, identify certain issues and shift the balance of power in favour of new interests (*cf.* Benington, 1986). Third there is a belief in cooperative values, that in the long run partnership and sharing benefit society more than competition and the pursuit of self-interest. Fourth there is a commitment to extending the democratic process, empowering people to have greater control over their lives and their environment.

Our view of the proper role of elected local authorities is that they should be the basic unit of community government concerned to meet the needs of their area. This means a role which extends beyond running existing services. It involves developing new initiatives and services in response to changing needs. Many Labour and some non-Labour local authorities have during the 1980s begun to see themselves in that role. New economic development policies, women's committees, the work of race relations units, a concern for health issues, policies relating to diet and food production, anti-poverty campaigns, energy-saving initiatives, campaigns against deportation orders, policies to tackle law and order issues and improve the chances of crime prevention all testify to the concern to develop a wider role. Local authorities have rejected the definition of their purpose as simply the administration of services and have responded to the problems and issues faced by their communities. In developing these new activities they have faced problems and obstacles, often laid down by the Thatcher governments. We argue, in contrast, that local authorities should be encouraged and supported in a broadening of their role. Local authorities should have the equivalent of a 'power of general competence' to encourage within them a wider vision and give them the ability to act as basic units of community government.

This wider role for local government will involve new strategic ways of working. Local authorities should use their considerable powers as employers, purchasers and investors to influence events in the community. Contract compliance, the use of purchasing power and attempts at directing pension fund investment towards the benefit of local people provide signposts of what might be achieved. Local authorities would seek to work in partnership with the major institutions of the private corporate sector. But it would not be a passive or reactive form of partnership which could end up in simply subsidising private sector activity. Rather the aim would be to direct and steer the private sector to move in line with local authority policies. A further strategic role would involve the attempt to influence the policies and practices of non-elected agencies operating in the local area.

New forms of service delivery would also be encouraged. It is not necessary for local authorities to always deliver services themselves. Local authorities should be encouraged to experiment with schemes which pass on direct responsibility for service delivery to other organisations. Various models are available. In Sunderland women got together in a cooperative and offered their services to the local authority as home helps. Many authorities provide grants to voluntary and self-help groups. Others have experimented with user control of housing, leisure centres and other facilities. In some instances contracting out a service to the private sector might be appropriate. So like the Conservatives we agree that local authorities should not always find it necessary to be a direct service provider. Unlike the Conservatives we argue that these initiatives should be the product of local choice and developed within a strategic framework laid down by local authorities as the principal elected bodies responsible for their area.

For those services that local authorities continue to provide in house we argue for greater responsiveness in service delivery. This may involve decentralisation but more generally it involves developing a public service orientation, a concern to provide services in an accessible, flexible and responsive manner.

For these changes to be effective adequate resources will be required but so too will a new relationship between service producers and consumers. As Beecham (1987, p. 22) comments Labour councils 'must avoid the trap of being thought primarily to represent town hall workers – white collar, blue collar or teachers – rather than the people who need the services'. Producers and consumers both have legitimate rights and needs. However, as Margaret Hodge argues, local authorities as elected bodies must ultimately put the interests of their electors and consumers first (Hodge, 1987). Moreover, 'trade unions and professional associations must assume the political responsibility for devising ways to defend their members' interests while at the same time promoting the most committed and effective service to the customer' (Blunkett and Jackson, 1987, p. 213). What is required is a new relationship between local authority councillors, the workforce and its customers. One which avoids collapsing into the formula of 'the management's right to manage' and, which recognises the positive contribution to service delivery and development that grass-roots local authority workers can make. It is crucial however to focus on the quality of the service provided to the customer.

If the local authority is to act as an effective agent of local government then a greater degree of public involvement in decision-making is essential. Community government demands that local authorities become learning, changing and involving organisations. Reliance on the principle of representative democracy is not sufficient. We need to encourage more direct forms of democracy in local government. Again local authorities in the 1980s have experimented with community forums, neighbourhood councils and area committees. There is a strong case for developing these initiatives and giving such bodies real decision-making authority. A local authority might also consider the use of public opinion research and customer panels as mechanisms for allowing a voice to the wider public.

Local representative democracy we have suggested is not sufficient. We would also argue that it is inadequate in its current form. Low turn-out is one problem. Another is the permanent domination of one party in many areas. As Blunkett and Jackson (1987, p. 212) comment:

> Long-guaranteed party majorities – whether of the Right or Left – have often led to the emergence of party cliques or bosses who take little account of the needs of the community. Such cliques and their associated pressure groups – whether in business, the professions or unions – can become the predominant channel for influencing policy or distributing resources.

In order to encourage higher turn-out and avoid the problem of the 'one-party state' we would support the introduction of some system of proportional representation in local elections. The legitimacy of local authorities rests ultimately on their electoral base. At a basic level the local electoral system must provide some opportunity for an effective challenge to be mounted to the ruling party, and a move to proportional representation would facilitate such a development.

Our vision of what the future role of local government should be stands in stark contrast to the agenda for local government set by the Conservatives. We see elected local authorities at the heart of a system constituted for local choice. We recognise that we would disagree with some of those local choices. On the other hand we recognise that the central government will continue to have a crucial role in guiding and encouraging good practice within local government. Local authorities should have clear duties and operate within a statutory framework laid down by Parliament. We are not arguing against constraints but for a strict limit to their scope. Our vision of local government as a basic unit of community government would extend the scope for collective action in and deepen the political process of our society. On both counts it provides a more worthy role for local government than that being promoted and advocated by the 'New Right' and the Conservatives.

# Guide to Further Reading

Each chapter within this book contains references to other works which the reader may find it helpful to follow up. Below a more *selective* guide to further reading is provided.

## 1 Local government in context

We lack a good historical account of local government which places its development in the context of the changing social and economic structures of society. One of the most readable historical accounts we have is Ken Young's essay on the growth of party politics in Widdicombe (1986e). There are several books which provide a good understanding of the impact of local government on particular social and economic interests including Dunleavy (1980), Newton and Karran (1984) and Saunders (1980).

## 2 Elected local government

One of the best detailed accounts is Bryne (1986). The research produced for the Widdicombe Committee is very important and useful in providing an up-to-date picture (see especially Widdicombe 1986b, c and d). For a detailed understanding of the structures and ways of working of individual local authorities their annual reports are a good source of basic information. Some authorities are more willing to part with such reports than others but a letter to the Chief Executive usually achieves success. On the post-abolition position in metropolitan area see Leach *et al.* (1987).

## 3 Non-elected local government

It is not easy to recommend a particular text in this area. Again the collection of annual reports and statements of account can provide useful insights into the operation of some non-elected agencies.

## 4 The internal politics of local authorities

The Widdicombe material (1986b) is vital reading in this area. One of the best books for giving a feel for departmental politics is Young and Mills (1983), and still very useful is Malpass (1975). Good, relatively current case studies are provided, for example, in Blowers (1987), Stoker and Brindley (1985), Barrett and Fudge (1981), Short *et al.* (1986), Tomlinson (1986) and Parkinson's essay in Widdicombe (1986e).

## 5 Local interest group politics

Gyford's essay in Widdicombe (1986e) is very interesting and useful. Some of the 'classics' such as Newton (1976) and Dearlove (1973) provide valuable insights but it is important to remember as this chapter argues, that the world of local interest group politics has changed to a substantial degree. Something of the flavour of this changed world is provided in Ben-Tovim *et al.* (1986), Lowe (1986) and Smith (1985).

## 6 Central–local relations and policy networks

Dunleavy (1986), Dunleavy and Rhodes (1986), and Rhodes (1988) are very useful in developing an understanding of this area. Much of ESRC-sponsored research is brought together under Michael Goldsmith's editorship in *New Research in Central Local Relations* (1986). Loughlin (1986) is also very helpful in looking at the change in central–local relations from a legal viewpoint.

## 7–9 Key issues for local government

Lots of pamphlets, articles and journal pieces provide the basis for understanding these critical issues faced by local government. On the struggle over local spending see Travers (1986) and Blunkett and Jackson (1987). The issues raised by privatisation can be considered further by looking at Young (1986), Forrest and Murie (1985), and Ascher (1987). Those interested in local socialism should look at Gyford (1985) and Wainwright (1987).

## 10  Theories of local government and politics

The localist case finds its clearest expression in Jones and Stewart (1983). New Right thinking can be considered further by looking at Green (1987). Duncan and Goodwin (1988) express in detail the social relations perspective of the New Left and provide an assessment of theories of the local state. For those wishing to look at the dual politics thesis in more detail Cawson and Saunders (1983) and Saunders (1986) provide good starting points.

## 11  The future of local government

Davis (1986) provides a useful account of the issues facing local government. The unfolding of the Conservatives' programme is best followed through newspaper and journal articles. The reader may find it useful to consult a special issue of *Local Government Policy Making* Vol. 14, No. 4, 1988.

## Journals

There are a number of very good journals which can provide valuable sources of information and analysis. They include: *Local Government Studies*, *Local Government Policy Making*, *Critical Social Policy*, *Policy and Politics*, *Local Economy*, *International Journal of Urban and Regional Research*, *Social Policy and Administration*, *Public Administration*, *Political Studies* and *British Journal of Political Science*. Magazines which cover local government include *New Society*, *New Statesman*, *Local Government Chronicle*, *Municipal Journal*, *Public Services and Local Government* and *Public Money* (now defunct).

# Bibliography

Alexander, A. (1982a) *The Politics of Local Government in the United Kingdom* (London: Longman).

Alexander, A. (1982b) *Local Government in Britain since Reorganisation* (London: Allen & Unwin).

Alexander, A. (1985) *Borough government and politics: Reading 1835–1985* (London: Allen & Unwin).

Alford, R. and Friedland, R. (1985) *The Powers of Theory: Capitalism, the State and Democracy* (Cambridge: Cambridge University Press).

Ambrose, P. and Colenutt, B. (1975) *The Property Machine* (Harmondsworth: Penguin).

Arden Report. Final Report by Andrew Arden (London: Hackney Borough Council).

Ascher, K. (1983) 'The politics of administrative opposition – council house sales and the right to buy' *Local Government Studies* vol. 9, no. 2.

Ascher, K. (1987) *The Politics of Privatisation* (London: Mamillan).

Association of County Councils (1986) *Rate Support Grant England, 1986/87* (London: ACC).

Association of County Councils (1987) *Making an Equal Opportunities Policy Work: The County Experience* (London: ACC).

Audit Commission (1984) *The Impact on Local Authorities' Economy, Efficiency and Effectiveness of the Block Grant Distribution System* (London: HMSO).

Audit Commission (1987) *The management of London's authorities: preventing the breakdown of services*, OP no. 2 (London: The Audit Commission for Local Authorities in England and Wales).

Bacon, R. and Eltis, W. (1976) *Britain's Economic Problem: Too Few Producers* (London: Macmillan).

Bains, M., Chairman (1972) *The New Local Authorities: Management and Structure* (London: HMSO).

Barker, A. (1982) *Quangos in Britain* (London: Macmillan).

Barker, B. (1983) *The Operation of the Bristol Labour Party: a view from the edge*, WP 27 (University of Bristol: School for Advanced Urban Studies).

Barlow, Montague, Chairman (1940) *Royal Commission on the Distribution of Industrial Population, Report*, Cmd. 6153 (London: HMSO).

Barr, A. (1977) *The Practice of Neighbourhood Community Work*. Paper in Community Studies no. 12 (University of York: Department of Social Administration and Social Work).

Barrett, S. and Fudge, C. (1981) *Policy and Action* (London: Methuen).

Bassett, K. (1980) 'The Sale of Council Houses as a Political Issue' *Policy and Politics* vol. 8, no. 3, pp. 290–307.

Bassett, K. (1981) 'Political Responses to the Restructuring of the Local State' in M. Boddy and C. Fudge (eds) *The Local State: Theory and Practice* WP 20 (University of Bristol; School for Advanced Urban Studies).

Beecham, J. (1987) *Local Government: the challenge ahead* in *Tract* 521 (London: Fabian Society).

Beetham, D. (1987) *Bureaucracy* (Milton Keynes: Open University Press).

Benington, J. (1975) *Local Government Becomes Big Business* (London: CDP).

Benington, J. (1986) 'Local Economic Strategies: Paradigms for a Planned Economy' *Local Economy*, vol. 1, no. 1, pp. 7–33.

Benington, J. and White, J. (1986) *Leisure*, The Future Role and Organisation of Local Government Study Paper no. 4 (Birmingham: Institute of Local Government Studies).

Ben-Tovim, G., Gabriel, J., Law, I., and Stredder, K. (1986) *The Local Politics of Race* (London: Macmillan).

Beresford, P. (1987) *Good Council Guide: Wandsworth 1978–1987* (London: Centre for Policy Studies).

Beuret, K. and Stoker, G. (1984) *The Attack on Labour's Centralist Faith: Local Paths to Socialism?* Paper presented to Political Studies Association Annual Conference, 3–5 May.

Beuret, K. and Stoker, G. (1986) 'The Labour Party and Neighbourhood Decentralisation: Flirtation or Commitment?' *Critical Social Policy*, no. 17, p. 4–22.

Bidwell, L. and Edgar, B. (1981) 'Promoting Participation in Planning: A Case Study of Planning Aid', in L. Smith and D. Jones (eds) *Deprivation, Participation and Community Action* (London: Routledge & Kegan Paul).

Birdseye, P. and Webb, T. (1984) 'Why the Rate Burden on Business is a Cause for Concern' *National Westminster Bank Quarterly Review*, February.

Bishop, J. and Hoggett, P. (1986) *Organizing Around Enthusiasms: Mutual Aid in Leisure* (London: Comedia).

Blore, I. (1987) 'Are Local Bureaucrats Budget or Staff Maximizers?' *Local Government Studies*, vol. 13, no. 3, pp. 75–85.

Blowers, A. (1977) 'Checks and Balances – The Politics of Minority Government' *Public Administration*, Autumn, pp. 306–16.

Blowers, A. (1980) *The Limits of Power* (Oxford: Pergamon).

Blowers, A. (1987) 'The Consequences of Minority Rule in an English County' *Local Government Studies*, vol. 13, no. 5, pp. 31–51.

Blunkett, D. and Green, G. (1983) *Building from the Bottom: The Sheffield Experience*, *Tract* 491 (London: Fabian Society).

Blunkett, D. and Jackson, K. (1987) *Democracy in Crisis: The Town Halls Respond* (London: Hogarth).

Boaden, N., Goldsmith, M., Hampton, W. and Stringer, P. (no date) *Public Participation in Local Services* (London: Longman).

Boddy, M. (1982) *Local Government and Industrial Development*, OP7 (University of Bristol: School for Advanced Urban Studies).

Boddy, M. (1984a) 'Local Councils and the Financial Squeeze', in M. Boddy and C. Fudge (eds) *Local Socialism?* (London: Macmillan).

Boddy, M. (1984b) 'Local Economic and Employment Strategies', in M. Boddy and C. Fudge (eds) *Local Socialism?* (London: Macmillan).

Boddy, M. (1987) 'Review of the New Management of Local Government by John Stewart' *Local Government Studies*, vol. 13, no. 4, pp. 95–7.

Boddy, M., Lovering, J. and Bassett, K. (1986) *Sunbelt City? A Study of Economic Change in Britain's M4 Growth Corridor* (Oxford: Clarendon).

Brindley, T., Rydin, Y., Stoker, G. (1988) *Re-Making Planning* (London: Unwin Hyman).

Brindley, T. and Stoker, G. (1987a) *Partnership in Urban Renewal: A Critical Analysis* Paper presented at the International Housing Conference 'City Renewal Through Partnership', Glasgow, 6–10 July.

Brindley, T. and Stoker, G. (1987b) 'The Privatisation of Housing Renewal Dilemmas and Contradictions in British Urban Policy' in W. van Vliet (ed.) *Housing Markets and Policies under Fiscal Authority* (New York: Greenwood).

Brindley, T. and Stoker, G. (1988) 'The scope and limitations of the privatisation of housing renewal', *Local Government Studies*, forthcoming.

Bristow, S. (1982) 'Rates and Votes – the 1980 District Council Elections', *Policy and Politics*, vol. 10, pp. 163–80.

Bristow, S. and Stratton, J. (1983) 'Professional Values and the Policy Implementation Process in Local Government', *London Review of Public Administration*, no. 15, pp. 35–60.

Bryne, T. (1986) (Fourth Edition) *Local Government in Britain* (Harmondsworth: Penguin).

Buchanan, J. and Tullock, G. (1962) *The Calculus of Consent* (Ann Arbor: University of Michigan Press).

Bulpitt, J. (1967) *Party Politics in English Local Governments* (London: Longmans).

Bulpitt, J. (1983) *Territory and Power in the United Kingdom* (Manchester: Manchester University Press).

Burch, M. and Wood, B. (1983) *Public Policy in Britain* (Oxford: Martin Robertson).

Business in the Community (1987) *Directory: Enterprise Agencies, Trusts and Community Action Programmes* (London: BiC).

Butcher, H., Collis, P., Glen, A. and Sills, P. *Community Groups in Action* (London: Routledge & Kegan Paul).

Butler, E. (1985) 'Contracting Out Municipal Services: Fading Official Interest, Growing Public Concern' *Local Government Studies*, vol. 11, no. 6, pp. 5–11.

Campey, L. (1987) 'A Tale of Three Cities: The Far Left in Control at Leicester, Peterborough and Southampton' *Politics Today*, no. 12 (London: Conservative Central Office).

Carr, J. (1987) *New Roads to Equality*, Tract 517 (London: Fabian Society).

Carter, N. (1986) *Hung Councils in the South West* Paper presented at the Annual Conference of the Political Studies Association, Nottingham, 8–10 April.

Castells, M. (1977) *The Urban Question* (London: Edward Arnold).

Castells, M. (1978) *City, Class and Power* (London: Macmillan).

Cawson, A. (1978) 'Pluralism, Corporatism and the Role of the State' *Government and Opposition*, vol. 13, pp. 178–98.

Cawson, A. (1985) 'Corporatism and Local Politics' in W. Grant (ed.) *The Political Economy of Corporation* (London: Macmillan).

Cawson, A. and Saunders, P. (1983) 'Corporatism, Competitive Politics and Class Struggle', in R. King (ed.) *Capital and Politics* (London: RKP).

Centre for Policy Studies (1985) *Qualgos Just Grow* (London: CPS).

Clapham, D. (1985a) 'An alternative route to local control' *Going Local?* no. 3, July.

Clapham, D. (1985b) 'Management of the Local State: The Example of Corporate Planning' *Critical Social Policy*, no. 14, pp. 27–43.

Clapham, D. and English, J. (1987) *Public Housing: Current Trends and Future Developments* (London: Croom Helm).

Clarke, M. and Stewart, J. (1985) *Local Government and the Public Service Orientation* (Luton: LGTB).

CLES (1987) *Enterprise Boards* (Manchester: Centre for Local Economic Strategies).

Cochrane, A. (1985) 'The attack on local government: what it is and what it isn't', *Critical Social Policy*, no. 12, pp. 46–62.

Cockburn, C. (1977) *The Local State* (London: Pluto).

Collingridge, J. (1986) 'The Appeal of Decentralization', *Local Government Studies*, vol. 12, no. 3.

Conservative Manifesto (1987) *Our First Eight Years. The Next Moves Ahead* (London: Conservative Central Office).

Corkey, D. and Craig, G. (1978) 'CDP; Community Work or Class Politics' in P. Curno (ed.) *Political Issues and Community Work* (London: Routledge & Kegan Paul).

Councils for Voluntary Service (1983) *Voluntary Action in Shire Districts* A Conference Report (Nottingham 26–7 July) (London: CVS National Association/National Council for Voluntary Organisations).

Cousins, P. (1973) 'Voluntary organisations as local pressure groups' *London Review of Public Administration*, no. 3, pp. 22–30 and no. 4, pp. 17–26.

Cousins, P. (1976) 'Voluntary organisations and local government in three South London boroughs', *Public Administration*, vol. 54, 63–81.

Crawford, P., Fothergill, S. and Monk, S. (1985) *The Effect of Rates on the Location of Employment: Final Report* (University of Cambridge: Department of Land Economy).

CSE State Group (1979) *Struggle Over the State* (London: Conference of Socialist Economists).

Darke, R. and Walker, R. (1977) *Local Government and the Public* (London: Leonard Hill).

Darke, J. and Gouly, K. (1985) 'United We Stand' *New Socialist*, February, p. 48.

Davies, H. (1987) 'Local Government Under Seige', Text of a speech to the Annual Conference of the Society of Local Authority Chief Executives, Nottingham, 8 July.

Davies, J. (1972) *The Evangelistic Bureaucrat* (London: Tavistock).

Davies, T. (1979) 'Employment Policy in One London Borough' in G. Craig *et al.* (eds) *Jobs and Community Action* (London: Routledge & Kegan Paul).

Davies, T. (1981) 'Implementing Employment Policies in One London Borough' in G. Craig *et al.* (eds) *Jobs and Community Action* (London: Routledge & Kegan Paul).

Davies, T., Mason, C., with Davies, L. (1984) *Government and Local Labour Market Policy Implementation* (Aldershot: Gower).

Davis, H. (ed.) (1986) *Reports on the Future Role and Organisation of Local Government* (University of Birmingham: Institute of Local Government Studies).

Davey, K. (1986) 'A Future for Local Government: An Overview' in H. Davis (ed.) *Reports on the Future Role and Organisation of Local Government* (University of Birmingham: Institute of Local Government Studies).

Dearlove, J. (1973) *The Politics of Policy in Local Government* (Cambridge: Cambridge University Press).

Dearlove, J. (1979) *The Reorganisation of British Local Government* (Cambridge: Cambridge University Press).

Dennis, N. (1972) *Public Participation and Planners' Blight* (London: Faber).

Dennis, N. (1975) 'Community Action, Quasi-Community Action and Anti-Community Action' in P. Leonard (ed.) *The Sociology of Community Action*, Sociology Review Monograph no. 21 (University of Keele).

Department of the Environment (1981) *Local Government Financial Statistics: England and Wales 1979/80* (London: HMSO).

Department of the Environment (1983) *Local Government Financial Statistics: England and Wales 1981/82* (London: HMSO).

Department of the Environment (1985a) *Home Improvement: A New Approach* Cmnd 9513 (London: HMSO).

Department of the Environment (1985b) *New Homes for Old*, Urban Housing Renewal Unit (London: DoE).

Department of the Environment (1985c) *Competition in the Provision of Local Authority Services* (London: HMSO).

Department of the Environment (1986) *Local Government Financial Statistics: England and Wales 1984/85* (London: HMSO).

Dickens, P., Duncan, S., Goodwin, M. and Gray, F. (1985) *Housing, States and localities* (London: Methuen).

Docklands Consultative Committee (1985) *Four Year Review of the LDDC* (London: Greater London Council).

Doorly, M. (1983) 'Involving the People' *New Statesman* 14 October, pp. 11–2.

Douglas, I. and Lord, S. (1986) *Local Government Finance. A Practical Guide* (London: Local Government Information Unit).

Downey, P., Mathews, A. and Mason, S. (1982) Management Co-operatives: *Tenant Responsibility in Practice* (London: HMSO).

Duke, V. and Edgell, S. (1984) 'Public expenditure cuts in Britain and Consumption Sectoral Cleavages' *International Journal of Urban and Regional Research*, vol. 8, pp. 177–201.

Dumbleton, B. (1976) *The Second Blitz. The Demolition and Rebuilding of Town Centres in South Wales* (Cardiff: Bob Dumbleton).

Duncan, S. and Goodwin, M. (1982a) 'The Local State and Restructuring Social Relations: Theory and Practice' *International Journal of Urban and Regional Research*, vol. 6, pp. 157–86.

Duncan, S. and Goodwin, M. (1982b) 'The Local State: Functionalism, Autonomy and Class Relations in Cockburn and Saunders' *Political Geography Quarterly*, vol. 1.

Duncan, S. and Goodwin, M. (1985) 'The local state and local economic policy: why the fuss?' *Policy and Politics*, vol. 3, no. 3, pp. 227–53.

Duncan, S. and Goodwin, M. (1988) *The Local state and uneven development* (Cambridge: Polity).

Dunleavy, P. (1977) 'Protest and quiescence in urban politics: a critique of some pluralist and structuralist myths' *International Journal of Urban and Regional Research*, 1, 193–218.

Dunleavy, P. (1979) 'The urban bases of political alignment', *British Journal of Political Science*, vol. 9, pp. 409–43.

Dunleavy, P. (1980) *Urban Political Analysis* (London: Macmillan).

Dunleavy, P. (1984) 'The Limits to Local Government' in M. Boddy and C. Fudge (eds) *Local Socialism?* (London: Macmillan).

Dunleavy, P. (1985) 'Bureaucrats, budgets, and the growth of the state' *British Journal of Political Science*, vol. 15, pp. 229–328.

Dunleavy, P. (1986) 'Explaining the Privatisation Boom' *Public Administration*, vol. 61, pp. 13–34.

Dunleavy, P. and Husbands, C. (1985) *British Democracy at the Crossroads* (London: Allen & Unwin).

Dunleavy, P. and O'Leary, B. (1987) *Theories of the State* (London: Macmillan).

Dunleavy, P. and Rhodes, R. (1986) 'Government Beyond Whitehall' in H. Drucker *et al.* (eds) *Developments in British Politics* (London: Macmillan).

Elkin, S. (1974) *Politics and Land Use Planning* (Cambridge: Cambridge University Press).

Elliot, J. (1975) 'Political Leadership in Local Government: T. Dan Smith in Newcastle-upon-Tyne' *Local Government Studies*, vol. 1, pp. 33–45.

Evans, A. and Hoyes, L. (1984) *Bus Services in the Hereford Trial Area*, WP 44 (University of Bristol: School for Advanced Urban Studies).

Evans, C. (1985) 'The Privatisation of Local Services', *Local Government Studies*, vol. 11, no. 6, pp. 97–111.

Fimister, G. (1986) *Welfare Rights Work in Social Services* (London: Macmillan).

Flynn, N. and Leach, S. (1984) *Joint Boards and Joint Committees: An Evaluation* (University of Birmingham: Institute of Local Government Studies).

Flynn, N., Leach, S. and Vielba, C. (1985) *Abolition or Reform? The GLC and the Metropolitan County Councils* (London: Allen & Unwin).

Flynn, N. and Walsh, K. (1987) *Competitive Tendering* (University of Birmingham: Institute of Local Government Studies).

Flynn, R. (1983) 'Co-optation and Strategic Planning in the Local State' in R. King (ed.) *Capital and Politics* (London: Routledge & Kegan Paul).

Flynn, R. (1986) 'Urban politics, the local state and consumption' in M. Goldsmith and S. Villadsen (eds) *Urban Political Theory and the Management of Fiscal Stress* (Aldershot: Gower).

Foot, M. (1975) *Aneurin Bevan: Vol. II 1945–1980* (St. Albans: Paladin).

Forrest, R. (1987) 'Privatisation, Marginality and Council Housing', in D. Clapham and J. English (ed.) *Public Housing: Current Trends and Future Developments* (London: Croom Helm).

Forrest, R. and Murie, A. (1984) *Right to Buy? Issues of need, equity, and polarisation*, WP 3a (University of Bristol: School for Advanced Urban Studies).

Forrest, R. and Murie, A. (1985) *An Unreasonable Act? Central-local government conflict and the Housing Act 1980*, Study no. 1 (University of Bristol: School for Advanced Urban Studies).

Forrester, A., Lansley, S. and Pauley, R. (1985) *Beyond our Ken* (London: Fourth Estate).

Forsyth, M. (1980) *Re-servicing Britain* (London: Adam Smith Institute).

Forsyth, M. (1982) 'Winners in the Contracting Game', *Local Government Chronicle*, 10 September.

Foster, C., Jackman, R. and Perlman, M. (1980) *Local Government Finance in a Unitary State* (London: Allen & Unwin).

Frankin, M. and Page, E. (1984) 'A Critique of the consumption approach in British Voting Studies', *Political Studies*, vol. 32, pp. 531–36.

Friedland, R. (1982) *Power and Crisis in the City* (London: Macmillan).

Fudge, C. (1981) 'Winning an Election and Gaining Control' in S. Barrett and C. Fudge (eds) *Policy and Action* (London: Methuen).

Game, C. (1984) 'Axeman or Taxman – who is now the more unpopular' *Local Government Studies*, vol. 10, January/February.

George, V. and Wilding P. (1984) *The impact of social policy* (London: Routledge & Kegan Paul).

Gibson, J. (1983) 'Local "overspending": why the Government have only themselves to blame' *Public Money*, vol. 3, no. 2, pp. 19–21.

Gibson, J. (1987) 'Where's the U-Turn?' *Public Services and Local Government*, March, pp. 21–2.

Gibson, J. and Travers, T. (1986) 'The Financing of Local Government' in H. Davis (ed.) *Reports on the Future Role and Organisation of Local Government* (University of Birmingham: Institute of Local Government Studies).

Glasgow District Council (1985) 'Housing Policy and Private Sector' (Glasgow: GDC).

Golding, P. and Middleton, S. (1983) *Images of Welfare* (Oxford: Martin Robertson).

Goldsmith, M. (1986) 'Managing the Periphery in a Period of Fiscal Stress' in M. Goldsmith (ed.) *New Research in Central Local Relations* (Aldershot: Gower).

Goodin, R. (1982) 'Rational bureaucrats and rational politicians in Washington and Whitehall', *Public Administration*, vol. 62, pp. 23–41.

Goodwin, M. (1986) 'Locality and local state: Sheffield's economic policy', Working paper in Urban and Regional Studies no. 52 (Brighton: University of Sussex).

Goss, S. (1984) 'Women's Initiatives in Local Government' in M. Boddy and C. Fudge (eds) *Local Socialism?* (London: Macmillan).

Gough, J. (1986) 'Industrial Policy and Socialist Strategy', *Capital and Class*, no. 29.

Graham, C. and Prosser, G. (1988) 'Introduction' in *Waiving the Rules: The Constitution Under Thatcher* (Milton Keynes: Open University Press).

Grant, M. (1986) 'The Role of the Courts in Central–Local Relations' in M. Goldsmith (ed.) *New Research in Central–Local Relations* (Aldershot: Gower).

Grant, W. (1983) *Chambers of Commerce in the UK System of Business Interest Representation*, WP 32 (University of Warwick: Department of Politics).

Grant, W. (1985) *The Political Economy of Corporatism* (London: Macmillan).

Gray, C. (1985) 'Analysing the Regional Level', *Public Administration Bulletin*, no. 49, pp. 45–64.

Greater London Council (1984) *Responses by GLC Committees to the Government's White Paper Streamlining the Cities* (London: GLC).

Greater London Council (1985a) *Community Areas Policy: A Record of Achievement* (London: GLC).

Greater London Council (1985b) *Strategy for the London Clothing Industry: A Debate*, Economic Policy Group Strategy Document, no. 39 (London: GLC).

Greater London Council (1985c) *Women and Housing Policy* Housing Research and Policy Report no. 3 (London: GLC).

Green, D. (1981) *Power and Party in an English City* (London: Allen & Unwin).

Green, D. (1987) *The New Right* (Brighton: Wheatsheaf).

Greenwood, R., Lomer, M., Hinings, C. and Ranson, S. (1975) *The Organisation of Local Authorities in England and Wales 1967–1975* (University of Birmingham: Institute of Local Government Studies).

Greenwood, R., Hinings, C., Ranson, S. and Walsh, K. (1976) *In Pursuit of Corporate Rationality* (University of Birmingham: Institute of Local Government Studies).

Greenwood, R. and Hinings, C. (1977) 'Local Government: Towards an Organisational Analysis', *Public Administration Bulletin*, no. 23, pp. 2–15.

Greenwood, R. and Stewart, J. (1986) 'The Institutional and Organizational Capabilities of Local Government' *Public Administration*, vol. 64, Spring, pp. 35–50.

Gyford, J. (1978) *Town Planning and the Practices of Politics*, DP 29 (London: Bartlett School of Architecture and Planning).

Gyford, J. (1984) *Local Politics in Britain*, 2nd edn (London: Croom Helm).

Gyford, J. (1985) *The Politics of Local Socialism* (London: Allen & Unwin).

Gyford, J. and James, M. (1983) *National Parties and Local Politics* (London: Allan & Unwin).

Hague, C. (1985) 'The Radical Institute Group: the First Ten Years', *The Planner* 71, 22–4.

Hain, P. (1975) *Radical Regeneration* (London: Quartet).

Hain, P. (1983) *The Democratic Alternative* (Harmondsworth: Penguin).

Hall, S. (1979) 'The Great Moving Right Show', *Marxism Today*, 23(1).

Ham, C. (1985) *Health Policy in Britain* (London: Macmillan).

Hambleton, R. and Hoggett, P. 'The democratisation of public services' in P. Hoggett and R. Hambleton (ed.) *Decentralisation and Democracy*, OP 28 (University of Bristol: School for Advanced Urban Studies).

Hampton, W. (1970) *Democracy and Community* (London: Oxford University Press).

Hampton, W. (1987) *Local Government and Urban Politics* (London: Longman).

Haringey Women's Employment Project/NUPE (1986) *School Meals in Haringey* (London: Haringey Women's Employment Project and the London Food Commission).

Heald, D. (1983) *Public Expenditure* (Oxford: Martin Robertson).

Heath, A., Jowell, R. and Curtice, J. (1985) *How Britain Votes* (Oxford: Pergamon).

Heclo, H. and Wildavsky, A. (1974) *The Private Government of Public Money* (London: Macmillan).

Heigham, D. (1984) 'Local "Overspending"', *Public Money*, vol. 4, no. 4.

Held, D. (1987) *Models of Democracy* (Cambridge: Polity).

Henderson, P., Wright, A. and Wyncoll, K. (1982) *Successes and Struggles on Council Estates* (London: Association of Community Workers).

Henney, A. (1984) *Inside Local Government: A Case for Radical Reform* (London: Sinclair Browne).

Henney, A. (1985) *Trust the Tenant*, Policy Study no. 68 London Centre for Policy Studies.

Heseltine, M. (1983) *Reviving the Inner Cities* (London: Conservative Political Centre).

Heseltine, M. (1986) *Where There's A Will* (London: Hutchinson).

HM Government (1983) *Streamlining the Cities*, Cmnd 9063 (London: HMSO).

HM Government (1986) *Paying for Local Government*, Cmnd 9714 (London: HMSO).

HM Government (1987) *Housing: The Government's Proposals*, Cmnd 214 (London: HMSO).

HM Treasury (1982) *The Government's Expenditure Plans 1982–83 to 1984–85*, vol. II, Cmnd 8494 (London: HMSO).

HM Treasury (1987) *The Government's Expenditure Plans 1987–88*, vol. II, Cmnd 56-II (London: HMSO).

Hobsbawm, E. (1981) 'The Forward March of Labour Halted?' in M. Jacques and F. Mulheran (eds) *The Forward March of Labour Halted?* (London: Verso).

Hodge, M. (1987) 'Post-Election Strategy for ALA' Paper presented to Association of London Authorities Labour Group, 26 June.

Hoggett, P. (1987) 'Going Beyond a "Rearrangement of the Deckchairs": Some Practical Hints for Councillors and Managers' in P. Hoggett and R. Hambleton (eds) *Decentralisation and Democracy*, OP 28 (University of Bristol: School for Advanced Urban Studies).

Hoggett, P., Lawrence, S. and Fudge, C. 'The politics of decentralisation in Hackney' in R. Hambleton and P. Hoggett (eds) *The Politics of Decentralisation* WP 46 (University of Bristol: School for Advanced Urban Studies).

Hoggett, P. and Hambleton, R. (eds) (1987) *Decentralisation and Democracy* OP 28 (University of Bristol: School for Advanced Urban Studies).

Holloway, J. and Picciotto, S. (1978) *State and Capital* (London: Edward Arnold).

Hood, C. (1983) *The Tools of Government* (Oxford: Martin Robertson).

Houlihan, B. (1984) 'The Regional Offices of the DoE: Policeman or Mediator' *Public Administration*, 62, 401–22.

House of Commons (1983) *The Problems of Management of Urban Renewal (Appraisal of the Recent Initiatives in Merseyside) – Report: vol. 1*, Third Report from the Environment Committee (London: HMSO).

Howard, E. (1948) 'Joint Authorities' in C. H. Wilson (ed.) *Essays on Local Government* (Oxford: Basil Blackwell).

Hoyle, S. (1987) 'Deregulation: the view from the bus stop', *Transport*, June, pp. 115–6.

Industry Department for Scotland (1987) *1986 Review of the Scottish Development Agency* (Edinburgh: IDS).

Islington (1986) *Going Local: Decentralisation in Practice* (London: Islington Borough Council).

Jacobs, S. (1982) 'The Sale of Council Houses: Does it Matter?' *Critical Social Policy*, no. 2, pp. 35–48.

Jenkins, J. (1987) 'The Green Sheep in "Colonel Gadaffi Drive"', *New Statesman*, 8 January, pp. 8–10.

Jenkins, R. and Solomos (eds) (1987) *Racism and Equal Opportunities in the 1980s* (Cambridge: Cambridge University Press).

Jewson, N. and Mason, D. (1986) 'The theory and practice of equal opportunities policies' *Social Review*, vol. 34, no. 2, pp. 307–34.

Johnson, P. (1981) *Voluntary Social Services* (Oxford: Basil Blackwell and Martin Robertson).

Jones, B. (1986) 'Welsh Local Government – A Blueprint for Regionalism?', *Local Government Studies*, vol. 12, no. 5, pp. 61–75.

Jones, G. W. (1969) *Borough Politics* (London: Macmillan).

Jones, G. and Stewart, J. (1983) *The Case for Local Government* (London: Allen & Unwin).

Jones, S. *et al.* (1981) *Working Together: Partnerships in Local Social Service* (London: Bedford Square Press).

Jones, T., Maclean, B. and Young, J. (1986) *The Islington Crime Survey* (Aldershot: Gower).

Karran, T. (1984) 'The local government workforce – public sector paragon or private sector parasite', *Local Government Studies*, vol. 10, July/August, pp. 39–58.

Keating, M. and Boyle, R. (1986) *Re-Making Urban Scotland* (Edinburgh: Edinburgh University Press).

Keating, M. and Midwinter, A. (1983) *The Government of Scotland* (Edinburgh: Mainstream).

Keith-Lucas, B. and Richards, P. (1978) *A History of Local Government in the Twentieth Century* (London: Allen & Unwin).

King, R. (1983) 'The Political Practice of Local Capitalist Associations' in R. King (ed.) *Capital and Politics* (London: Routledge and Kegan Paul).

King, R. (1985) 'Corporatism and the Local Economy' in W. Grant (ed.) *The Political Economy of Corporatism* (London: Macmillan).

King, R. and Raynor, J. (1981) *The Middle Class*, 2nd edn (London: Longman).

Kline, J. and Malabar, J. (1986) *Whose value? Whose money?* (London: Local Government Information Unit).

Klein, R. (1983) *The Politics of the NHS* (London: Longman).

Labour Co-ordinating Committee (no date) *Can Local Government Survive?* (London: LCC).

Labour Co-ordinating Committee (1984) *Go Local to Survive* (London: LCC).

Labour Party (1982) *Labour's Programme 1982* (London: Labour Party).

Labour Party (1986) *Environment A Discussion Paper* (London: The Labour Party).

Labour Research (1986) 'How well are councils tackling jobs race bias?', *Labour Research*, May, pp. 11–4.

Laffin, M. (1986) *Professionalism and Policy: The Role of the Professions in the Central–Local Relationship* (Aldershot: Gower).

Laffin, M. and Young, K. (1985) 'The Changing Roles and Responsibilities of Local Authority Chief Officers', *Public Administration*, vol. 63, pp. 41–59.

Lambert, J., Paris, C. and Blackaby, B. (1978) *Housing Policy and the State* (London: Macmillan).

Lansley, S. (1985) 'The Phoney War', *New Socialist*, July 1985, pp. 28–31.

Laurence, J. (1983) 'Is Big Business Moving into Caring', *New Society*, 10 February, pp. 211–4.

Lawless, P. (1981) *Britain's Inner Cities* (London: Harper and Row).

Lea, J. and Young, J. (1984) *What is to be done about Law and Order?* (Harmondsworth, Penguin).

Leach, B. (1987) 'Conservatism, Local Government and the Community Charge', paper presented to the Urban Politics Group of the Political Studies Association, University of Birmingham, 31 October.

Leach, S. (1985) 'Inner Cities' in S. Ranson, G. Jones and K. Walsh (eds) *Between Centre and Locality* (London: Allen & Unwin).

Leach, S. (1986) *The Politicisation of British Local Government*, The Future Role and Organisation of Local Government Study Paper No. 7 (Birmingham: Institute of Local Government Studies).

Leach, S. *et al.* (1987) *The Impact of Abolition on Metropolitan Government* (University of Birmingham: Institute of Local Government Studies).

Leach, S. and Moore, R. (1979) 'County/District Relations in Shire and Metropolitan Counties in the Field of Town and Country Planning' *Policy and Politics*, vol. 7, pp. 165–79.

Leach, S. and Stewart, J. (1986) 'The Hung County Councils', *New Society*, 4 April, pp. 7–9.

Lees, R. and Mayo, M. (1984) *Community Action for Change* (London: Routledge & Kegan Paul).

Le Grand, J. (1982) *The Strategy of Equality* (London: Allen & Unwin).

Lindblom, C. (1977) *Politics and Markets* (New York: Basic Books).

Livingstone, K. (1984) 'Local Socialism: the Way Ahead', Interview in M. Boddy and C. Fudge (eds) *Local Socialism* (London: Macmillan).

Local Government Training Board (1985) *The Management Challenge for Local Government* (Luton: LGTB).

London–Edinburgh Group (1979) *In and Against the State*, London Conference of Socialist Economists (revised edition published in 1980 by Pluto).

Loughlin, M. (1986) *Local Government in the Modern State* (London: Sweet & Maxwell).

Loughlin, M., Gelfand, M. and Young K. (1985) *Half a Century of Municipal Decline 1935–1985* (London: Allen & Unwin).

Lowe, S. (1986) *Urban Social Movements* (London: Macmillan).

Low Pay Unit (1985) *Low Pay: What Can Local Authorities Do?*, 3rd revised edition (London: Low Pay Unit).

McCulloch, D. (1987) 'The Financial Aspects of Change' in D. Clapham and J. English (eds) *Public Housing: Current Trends and Future Developments* (London: Croom Helm).

McDonnell, J. (1984) 'Decentralisation and the new social relations', *Going Local?*, no. 1, December, p. 1.

McHale, J. (1984) *The Sale of Council Houses*, Unpublished Dissertation, MA Urban Processes, Policies and Problems, Leicester Polytechnic.

McKean, B. and Coulson, A. (1987) 'Enterprise Boards and Some Issues Raised by Taking Equity and Loan Stock in Major Companies', *Regional Studies*, vol. 21, 4, pp. 373–84.

Mallaby, Sir G., Chairman (1967) *Committee on The Staffing of Local Government*, Report (London: HMSO).

Mallinson, H. (1987) 'Parternship future for local authority housing', *Local Government Chronicle*, 3 July.

Malpass, P. (1975) 'Professionalism and the Role of Architects in Local Authority Housing', *Royal Institute of British Architects Journal*, vol. 18, no. 6, June, pp. 6–29.

Malpass, P. (ed.) (1986) *The Housing Crisis* (London: Croom Helm).

Manchester City Council (1986) *A–Z Guide to Council Services* (Manchester: Manchester City Council).

Manchester City Council (1987) *City Report* (Manchester: Manchester City Council).

Marriott, O. (1967) *The Property Boom* (London: Pan).

Marsh, D. (1983) 'Introduction: Interest Groups in Britain' in D. Marsh (ed.) *Pressure Politics* (London: Junction).

Massey, D. (1983) 'The Contours of Victory . . . the Dimensions of Defeat', *Marxism Today*, July.

Materson, M. (1980) *Community Councils in Tayside and Fife Regions: 1976–79* (Edinburgh: Scottish Office).

Maud, Sir John, Chairman (1967) *Committee on the Management of Local Government, Vol. 1*, Report (London: HMSO).

May, T. (1984) 'The Business Man's Burden: Rates and the CBI', *Politics*, 4 (April), 34–8.

Mawson, J. and Miller, D. (1987) 'Interventionist Approaches to Local Employment and Economic Development: the Experience of Labour Local Authorities' in V. A. Hausner (ed.) *Critical Issues in Urban Economic Development* (Oxford: Oxford University Press).

Mellors, C. (1984) 'Political Coalitions in Britain: The Local Context', *Teaching Politics*, vol. 13, pp. 249–59.

Midwinter, A. (1984) *The Politics of Local Spending* (Edinburgh: Mainstream).

Midwinter, A. and Mair, C. (1987) *Rates Reform* (Edinburgh: Mainstream).

Moore, C., Richardson, J. and Moon, J. (1985) 'New Partnerships in Local Economic Development', *Local Government Studies*, September/October, pp. 19–33.

Moran, G. (1987) 'Radical Health Promotion: A Role for Local Authorities' Ties' in S. Rodmell and A. Watt (eds) *The Politics of Health Education* (London: Routledge & Kegan Paul).

Muchnick, D. (1970) *Urban Renewal in Liverpool* (London: Bell).

Mullan, B. (1980) *Stevenage Limited. Aspects of the Planning and Politics of Stevenage* (London: Routledge & Kegan Paul).

NAHA (1986) *Acting with Authority*, A Consultative Paper on the

Appointment, Training and Work of DHA Members (Birmingham: National Association of Health Authorities).

National Council for Voluntary Service (1985) *The voluntary sector* (A Response to the Centre for Policy Studies – Qualgos just grow) (London: NCVO).

Newby, H., Bell, C., Rose, D. and Saunders, P. (1978) *Property, Paternalism and Power* (London: Hutchinson).

Newton, K. (1976) *Second City Politics* (Oxford: Oxford University Press).

Newton, K. and Karran, T. (1985) *The Politics of Local Expenditure* (London: Macmillan).

Niskanen, W. (1971) *Bureaucracy and Representative Government* (New York: Aldine–Atherton).

Niskanen, W. (1973) *Bureaucracy: Servant or Master?* (London: Institute for Economic Affairs).

NUPE (1983) *Scottish Public Services Under Attack* (Edinburgh: National Union of Public Employees).

O'Leary, B. (1987) 'Why was the GLC abolished?' *International Journal of Urban and Regional Research*, vol. 10, pp. 193–217.

O'Mahony, N. (1984) *The State and Business Interest Organisations*, Unpublished Dissertation, MA, Urban Processes, Problems and Policies, Leicester Polytechnic.

O'Malley, J. (1977) *The Politics of Community Action* (Nottingham: Spokesman).

Ouseley, H. (1984) 'Local Authority Race Initiatives' in M. Boddy and C. Fudge (eds) *Local Socialism* (London: Macmillan).

Ouseley, H. (1986) 'Narrowing the gulf between councils and consumers?' *Local Government Chronicle*, 21 November, pp. 1342–3.

Page, E. and Midwinter, A. (1979) *Remote Bureaucracy or Administrative Efficiency: Scotland's New Local Government System* (Glasgow: University of Strathclyde).

Paris, C. and Blackaby, B. (1979) *Not Much Improvement* (London: Heinemann).

Parkinson, M. and Wilks, S. (1986) 'The Politics of Inner City Partnerships' in M. Goldsmith (ed.) *New Research in Central–Local Relations* (Aldershot: Gower).

Paterson, I., Chairman (1973) *The New Scottish Local Authorities: Organisation and Management Structures* (Edinburgh: Scottish Development Department).

Perrin, J. (1986) 'Power to the Parishes', *Going Local?*, Decentralisation Newsletter of the Polytechnic of Central London No. 5, July, pp. 15–6.

Pinkney, R. (1983) 'Nationalising Local Politics and Localising a National Party: The Liberal Role in Local Government', *Government and Opposition*, vol. 18, pp. 347–58.

Pinkney, R. (1984) 'An Alternative Political Strategy? Liberals in Power in English Local Government', *Local Government Studies*, vol. 10, pp. 69–83.

Pirie, M. (1981) 'Economy and Local Government' in E. Butler and M. Pirie (eds) *Economy and Local Government* (London: Adam Smith Institute).

Pollitt, C. (1986) 'Democracy and bureaucracy' in D. Held and C. Pollit (eds) *New Forms of Democracy* (London: Sage).

Poulton, K. (1984) 'Local authorities and the sale of public assets', *Critical Social Policy*, no. 9, pp. 88–99.

Prashar, U. and Nicholas, S. (1986) *Routes or Roadblocks? Consulting Minority Communities in London Boroughs* (London: Runnymede Trust/GLC).

Preston, E. (no date) *The Local Counter Attack* (Heaton Moor: Independent Labour Party).

Profitt, R. (1986) 'The Role of the Race Adviser' in V. Coombe and A. Little (eds) *Race and Social Work* (London: Tavistock).

Rahman, N. (1985) *Pricing Into Poverty. Council Manual Workers Pay*, Low Pay Pamphlet no. 38 (London: Low Pay Unit).

Rahman, N. (1986) *Council Non-Manual Workers and Low Pay*, Low Pay Pamphlet no. 41 (London: Low Pay Unit).

Raine, J. and Webster, B. (1984) *Strategy, Choice and Support*, A Review of Grant-Aid to Voluntary and Community Organisations from the London Borough of Camden (University of Birmingham: Institute of Local Government Studies).

Ranson, S. (1985) 'Education' in S. Ranson, G. Jones and K. Walsh (eds) *Between Centre and Locality* (London: Allen & Unwin).

Ranson, S., Hinings, B., Leach, S. and Skelcher, C. (1986) 'Nationalising the Government of Education' in M. Goldsmith (ed.) New Research in Central–Local Relations (Aldershot: Gower).

Ranson, S. and Walsh, K. (1986) *Community Education for Equal Rights and Opportunities in Haringey* (London: Haringey Council).

Ravetz, A. (1980) *Remaking Cities* (London: Croom Helm).

Redcliffe-Maud, Lord, Chairman (1969) *Royal Commission on Local Government, Vol. 1 Report*, Cmnd. 4040 (London: HMSO).

Redcliffe-Maud, Lord and Wood, B. (1974) *English Local Government Reformed* (Oxford: Oxford University Press).

Rhodes, G. (1986) 'Protecting Local Discretion: The Experience of Environmental Health and Trading Standards' in M. Goldsmith (ed.) *New Research into Central–Local Relations* (London: Gower).

Rhodes, R. (1981) *Control and Power in Central–Local Government Relations* (London: Gower).

Rhodes, R. (1985) 'Inter-governmental Relations in the Post-War Period', *Local Government Studies*, vol. 11, no. 6, pp. 35–57.

Rhodes, R. (1986) *The National World of Local Government* (London: Allen & Unwin).

Rhodes, R. (1987) 'The reform of local government: revival of an industry', *Public Administration*, vol. 65, no. 2.

Rhodes, R. (1988) *Beyond Westminster and Whitehall: The Sub-Central Government of Britain* (London: Allen & Unwin).

Richards, P. (1973) *The Reformed Local Government System* (London: Allen & Unwin).

Robinson Committee (1977) *Remuneration of Councillors: Volume 2: The Surveys of Councillors and Local Authorities* (London: HMSO).

Robson, W. (1966) *Local Government in Crisis* (London: Allen & Unwin).

Rose, H. and Rose, S. (1982) 'Moving Right Out of Welfare and the Way Back', *Critical Social Policy*, vol. 2, no. 1.

Rose, R. (1983) *Understanding the United Kingdom* (London: Longman).

Rosenberg, D. (1985) 'The Politics of Role in Local Governments: Perspectives on the Role Sets of Treasurers in their Relationships with Chief Executives', *Local Government Studies*, vol. 10, pp. 47–63.

Rowbotham, S., Segal, L. and Wainwright, H. (1979) *Beyond the Fragments* (London: Merlin Press).

Rutherford, A. *et al.* (1984) *Community Councils in Scotland after 5 years* (Glasgow: Community Council Resource Centre).

Saggar, S. (1987) 'The Rediscovery of Race in London: Developments in Local Government in the 1980s', Paper presented to the Annual Conference of the Political Studies Association, University of Aberdeen, 7–9 April.

Saunders, P. (1980) *Urban Politics: A Sociological Interpretation* (Harmondsworth: Penguin).

Saunders, P. (1981a) *Social Theory and the Urban Question* (London: Hutchinson).

Saunders, P. (1981b) 'Notes on the specificity of the Local State' in M. Boddy and C. Fudge (eds) *The Local State: Theory and Practice* WP 20 (University of Bristol: School for Advanced Urban Studies).

Saunders, P. (1982) 'Why Study Central–Local Relations?' *Local Government Studies*, vol. 8, pp. 55–66.

Saunders, P. (1983) *The Regional State: A Review of the Literature and Agenda for Research*, Urban and Regional Studies Working Paper No. 35 (Brighton: University of Sussex).

Saunders, P. (1984a) *'We Can't Afford Democracy Too Much': Findings from a Study of Regional State Institutions*, Urban and Regional Study Paper No. 43 (Brighton: University of Sussex).

Saunders, P. (1984b) 'Rethinking Local Politics' in M. Boddy and C. Fudge (eds) *Local Socialism?* (London: Macmillan).

Saunders, P. (1985a) 'Corporatism and Urban Service Provision' in W. Grant (ed.) *The Political Economy of Corporatism* (London: Macmillan).

Saunders, P. (1985b) 'The Forgotten Dimension of Central–Local Relations: Theorising the Regional State', *Government and Policy*, vol. 3, pp. 149–62.

Saunders, P. (1986) 'Reflections on the dual politics thesis: the argument, its origins and its critics' in M. Goldsmith and S. Villadsen (eds) *Urban Political Theory and the Management of Fiscal Stress* (Aldershot: Gower).

SCAT (1985) *The Public Cost of Private Contractors*, Privatisation Audit (London: Services to Community Action and Trade Unions).

Schumpter, J. (1954) *Capitalism, Socialism and Democracy* (London: Allen & Unwin).

SDA (1986) *Annual Report 1986* (Glasgow: Scottish Development Agency).

Seabrook, J. (1984) *The Idea of Neighbourhood* (London: Pluto).

Sharpe, L. J. (1970) 'Theories and Values of Local Government', *Political Studies*, vol. 18, no. 2, pp. 153–74.

Sharpe, L. J. (1982) 'The Labour Party and the Geography of Inequality' in D. Kavanagh (ed.) *The Politics of the Labour Party* (London: Allen & Unwin).

Sharples, A. (1986) 'The New Local Economics' *Local Economy*, vol. 1, no. 1, pp. 25–33.

Sheffield City Council (1985) *Sheffield Jobs Audit* (Sheffield: Sheffield City Council).

Sheffield City Council (1987) *Working it Out* (Sheffield: Sheffield City Council).

Short, J., Fleming, S. and Witt, S. (1986) *Housebuilding, Planning and Community Action* (London: Routledge & Kegan Paul).

Simmie, J. (1981) *Power, Property and Corporatism* (London: Macmillan).

Simmie, J. (1985) 'Corporatism and Planning' in W. Grant (ed.) *The Political Economy of Corporatism* (London: Macmillan).

Smith, J. (1978) 'Hard lines and soft options: a criticism of some left attitudes to community work' in P. Curno (ed.) *Political Issues and Community Work* (London: Routledge & Kegan Paul).

Smith, J. (1985) *Public Involvement in Local Government* (London: Community Projects Foundation).

Smith, J. and Wheen, F. (1985) 'Labour Turns Its Back on Knight's Last Stand' *New Statesman*, 26 July, pp. 14–5.

Smith, L. (1981) 'A model for the development of public participation in local authority decision making' in L. Smith and D. Jones (eds) *Deprivation, Participation and Community Action* (London: Routledge & Kegan Paul).

Smith, S. (1983) *From Capitalist Domination to Urban Planning: Dartford, 1841–1980*, Paper presented to the Fourth Urban Change and Conflict Conference, University of York, 4–6 January.

SOCPO (1987) *Manpower Services Commission. Impact on Local Authorities*, Society of Chief Personnel Officers.

Social Trends (1987) *Edition No. 17* (London: HMSO).

Solace (1986) *Local Government: The Future* (Northampton: The Society of Local Authority Chief Executives).

Specht, H. (1975) *Community Development in the UK* (London: Association of Community Workers).

Spencer, K. (1985) *Demographic Social and Economic Trends: An Overview*, The Future Role and Organisation of Local Government, Introductory Paper No. 2 (University of Birmingham: Institute of Local Government Studies).

Spencer, K. *et al.* (1986) *Crisis in the Industrial Heartland*. A Study of the West Midlands (Oxford: Clarendon).

Stewart, J. (1983) *Local Government: The Conditions of Local Choice* (London: Allen & Unwin).

Stewart, J. (1986a) *The New Management of Local Government* (London: Allen & Unwin).

Stewart, J. (1986b) *The Management of Influence – Implications for Management Development* (Luton: Local Government Training Board).

Stewart, J. and Clarke, M. (1987) 'The Public Service Orientation: issues and dilemmas' *Public Administration*, vol. 65, no. 2, pp. 161–77.

Stewart, J. and Stoker, G. (1988) Local Government as Community Government, Forthcoming (London: Fabian Society).

Stewart, M. *et al.* (1984) 'The Future of Local Democracy' *Local Government Studies*, vol. 10, March/April, pp. 1–8.

Stoker, G. (1985) *The Politics of Urban Renewal in Withington Village, Manchester 1962–1983*, PhD Thesis, University of Manchester.

Stoker, G. (1987) 'Decentralisation and Local Government', *Social Policy and Administration*, vol. 21, no. 2, pp. 157–71.

Stoker, G. and Brindley, T. (1985) 'Asian Politics and Housing Renewal', *Policy and Politics*, vol. 13, no. 3, pp. 281–303.

Stoten, B. (1986) 'On Being an Appointed Member' *Local Government Studies*, vol. 12, January/February, pp. 6–8.

Taylor-Gooby, P. (1984) *The Welfare State From the Second World War to the 1980s* D355, Unit 5 (Milton Keynes: Open University Press).

Taylor-Gooby, P. (1985) *Public Opinion, Ideology and State Welfare* (London: Routledge & Kegan Paul).

Teague, P. (1987) 'The Potential and Limitations of Community Businesses in Local Economic Development' *Local Government Studies*, vol. 13, no. 4, pp. 17–35.

Thane, P. (1982) *The Foundations of the Welfare State* (London: Longman).

Thomas, D. (1976) *Organising for Social Change: A Study in the Theory and Practice of Community Work* (London: Allen & Unwin).

Thomas, D. (1983) *The Making of Community Work* (London: Allen & Unwin).

Tiebout, C. (1956) 'A Pure theory of local expenditures' *Journal of Political Economy*, vol. 64, pp. 416–24.

Todd, J. and Butcher, B. (1982) *Electoral Registration in 1981* (London: Office of Population Censuses and Surveys).

Tomlinson, M. (1986) *Decentralisation: Learning the Lessons?*, Planning Studies No. 18 (Polytechnic of Central London: School of Planning).

Travers, T. (1986) *The Politics of Local Government Finance* (London: Allen & Unwin).

Underwood, J. (1980) *Town Planners in Search of a Role*, OP6 (University of Bristol: School for Advanced Urban Studies).

Ungerson, C. (1985) *Women and Social Policy* (London: Macmillan).

Waller, R. (1980) 'The 1979 local and general elections in England and Wales: is there a local/national differential?', *Political Studies*, vol. 20, pp. 443–50.

Walsh, K. (1986) 'The Relationship between Central and Local Government' in H. Davis (ed.) *Reports on the Future Role and Organisation of Local Government* (University of Birmingham: Institute of Local Government).

Wainwright, H. (1985) 'Sharing power: popular planning and the GLC' *Going Local?*, No. 2, April, pp. 6–7.

Wainwright, H. (1987) *Labour: A Tale of Two Parties* (London: Hogarth).

Webb, A., Wistow, G. and Hardy, B. (1986) *Structuring Local Policy Environments; Central–Local Relations in the Health and Personal Social Services*, Final Report (London: ESRC).

Weinstein, J. (1986) 'Angry arguments across the picket lines: left Labour Councils and white collar trade unionism', *Critical Social Policy*, no. 17, pp. 41–60.

Weir, S. (1982) 'The citizen and the town hall', *New Society*, 9 March, pp. 345–6.

Wheatley, Lord, Chairman (1969) *Royal Commission on Local Government in Scotland, Report*, Cmnd 4150 (Edinburgh: HMSO).

Widdicombe (1986a) *The Conduct of Local Authority Business*, Report of the Committee of Inquiry into the conduct of Local Authority Business (Chairman: David Widdicombe QC) Cmnd 9797 (London: HMSO).

Widdicombe (1986b) *Research Volume I: The Political Organisation of Local Authorities* (S. Leach, C. Game and J. Gyford) Cmnd 9798 (London: HMSO).

Widdicombe (1986c) *Research Volume II: The Local Government Councillor* (J. England, P. Ramsdale and S. Capon) Cmnd 9799 (London: HMSO).

Widdicombe (1986d) *Research Volume III: The Local Government Elector* (K. Young, W. Miller) Cmnd 9800 (London: HMSO).

Widdicombe (1986e) *Research Volume IV: Aspects of Local Democracy* (P. Ramsdale and S. Capon; M. Parkinson, K. Young, J. Gyford, M. Goldsmith and K. Newton) Cmnd 9801 (London: HMSO).

Wilding, P. (1982) *Professional Power and Social Welfare* (London: Routledge & Kegan Paul).

Williams, G. (1981) *The Role of the Voluntary Sector in the Implementation of Inner City Policy*, OP no. 8 (Manchester University: Department of Town and Country Planning).

Williamson, O. (1975) *Markets and Hierarchies* (New York: Free Press).

Wilson, E. (1977) *Women and the Welfare State* (London: Tavistock).

Wimpey (1987) *The Unique Partner* (London: Wimpey Homes).

Wolfenden, Lord (1978) *The Future of Voluntary Organisations* (London: Croom Helm).

Wolmar, C. (1984) 'Divided we stand', *New Socialist*, December, pp. 13–5.

Wood, B. (1976) *The Process of Local Government Reform 1966–1974* (London: Allen & Unwin).

Wrekin District Council (1984) *Towards Single Status*, Report of Personnel Manager, Wrekin District Council.

Wright, M. (1987) *Policy Community, Policy Network and Comparative Industrial Policies*, paper presented to Political Studies Association Annual Conference, University of Aberdeen, 7–9 April.

Young, K. (1977) 'Values in the Policy Process', *Policy and Politics*, vol. 5, pp. 1–22.

Young, K. (1986) 'What is local government for?' in M. Goldsmith (ed.) *Essays on the Future of Local Government* (Wakefield: West Yorkshire County Council).

Young, K. (1987) 'The space between words: local authorities and the concept of equal opportunities' in R. Jenkins and J. Solomos (eds) *Racism and Equal Opportunities in the 1980s* (Cambridge: Cambridge University Press).

Young, K. and Kramer, J. (1978) *Strategy and Conflict in Metropolitan Housing* (London: Heinemann).

Young, K. and Mason, C. (eds) (1983) *Urban Economic Development* (London: Macmillan).

Young, K. and Mills, L. (1980) *Public Policy Research* (London: SSRC).

Young, K. and Mills, L. (1983) *Managing the Post-Industrial City* (London: Heinemann).

Young, S. (1974) (with A. V. Lowe) *Intervention in the Mixed Economy* (London: Croom Helm).

Young, S. (1982) 'Regional Offices of the Department of the Environment: their roles and influence in the 1970s' in B. W. Hogwood and M. Keating (eds) *Regional Government in England* (Oxford: Clarendon Press).

Young, S. (1986) 'The Nature of Privatisation in Britain 1979–85', *West European Politics*, vol. 9, no. 2, pp. 235–52.

Young, S. (1987) 'The Implementation of Britain's National Steel Strategy at the Local Level' in Y. Meny and V. Wright (eds) *The Politics of Steel: Western Europe and the Steel Industry in Crisis Years 1974–84* (Berlin: de Gruyter) pp. 369–415.

Young, S. (1988) *Privatisation and Planning in Declining Areas* (London: Croom Helm).

# Index

This index contains references for subject, plus some major authors discussed in the text.